LITERATURE
AND LIMINALITY

LITERATURE
AND LIMINALITY

Festive Readings in the Hispanic Tradition

Gustavo Pérez Firmat

Duke University Press Durham 1986

Library of Congress Cataloging-in-Publication Data
Pérez Firmat, Gustavo, 1949–
Literature and liminality.
Bibliography: p.
Includes index.
1. Spanish literature—History and criticism.
I. Title.   II. Title: Liminality: festive readings in
the Hispanic tradition.
PQ6045.P47   1986   860'.9   85-13077
ISBN 0-8223-0658-1

For Rosa,
my margin of safety

Contents

The important thing, if you want to
find the correct idea, is to begin by
thinking off-center.
POINCARÉ

¡Palabra o muerte! ¡Liminaremos!
GUILLERMO CABRERA INFANTE

Acknowledgments

I would like to thank the American
Council of Learned Societies and
Duke University for grants during
the tenure of which most of this
book was written.

I would also like to thank Jorge
Olivares, Paul Ilie, David William
Foster, Michael Ugarte, and, especially, John Kronik for their careful
reading of the manuscript. Their
suggestions made me rethink, and
even rewrite, several sections of the
book.

Parts of several chapters appeared
originally in *Hispanic Review*
(chapter 1), *Diacritics* (chapter 4),
Notebooks in Cultural Analysis
(chapter 6), and *PMLA* (chapters 7
and 8). I am grateful to the editors
for permission to reprint.

The last person who has to be
thanked doesn't need to be thanked.
Rosa, who reads me like a book,
knows that this book of readings
would not exist without her.

Preliminaries

Of late, margins have been everywhere. As is indicated by such titles as Barbara Herrnstein Smith's *On the Margins of Discourse,* Jacques Derrida's *Marges de la philosophie,* or Aron Gurwitsch's *Marginal Consciousness,* contemporary reflection in literary studies and related disciplines (anthropology and philosophy, especially) has been powerfully drawn to diverse manifestations of the marginal, to phenomena that, in Victor Turner's words, fall "betwixt and between the positions assigned and arrayed by law, custom, convention, and ceremonial."[1] This book proposes to utilize insights derived from this ongoing discussion in order to shed new light on a sequence of important Spanish-language texts. My aim, therefore, is less to elaborate a theory of marginality (or liminality, the term I prefer) than to explore and exploit the interpretive power, the hermeneutic reach of the concept. I would like to think, nonetheless, that some of the ideas generated by my readings may have broader application.

   Modern discussion of liminality begins with Arnold van Gennep's *Les Rites de passage* (1909), where the liminal or marginal moment marks the interstitial stage in the three-step process of ritual initiation (separation, margin or limen, and reaggregation).[2] For van Gennep, then, liminality is a phase, a fleeting, ephemeral moment destined for supersession. More recently, Victor Turner has expanded van Gennep's definition by adding a synchronic dimension to the concept. According to Turner, liminality should be looked upon not only as a transition between states but as a state in itself, for there exist individuals, groups, or social categories for which the liminal "moment" turns into a permanent condition.[3] Turner, in effect, supplements van Gennep's temporal, processual view of liminality with a spatial one. While for van Gennep the limen is always a threshold, for Turner it can also be a place of habitation.

[In the chapters that follow I will be employing the concept in a sense allied to Turner's. Although I also speak of liminal moments, liminality appears in this study, initially and predominantly, not as a phase, not as a transitional state, but as a *position*. Going back to the word's topographical roots, I use the term to designate the spatial relationship between a center and its periphery. For my purposes the liminal entity, whatever its nature (an individual, a group, an event, a text), is one that in a given situation takes up a position of eccentricity, one that occupies the periphery in relation to a contextually determined center. (I say "contextually determined" to indicate the shifty, even reversible character of the center-periphery assignation; some of the texts I will discuss capitalize precisely on this shiftiness.)]

Defined in this fashion, *more geometrico,* liminality is less a concept than a conceptual archetype. Better still, it is less a concept than a *structure,* if we understand "structure" as a relation of at least two terms that is subject to multiple transformations. Indeed, in a well-known essay Jacques Derrida has pointed out that the center-periphery dichotomy delimits the very concept of structure; the intelligibility of a structure, in other words, depends on its being centered, for it is the center that "orients, balances, and organizes the structure."[4] I should then say not only that liminality is a structure, but that the idea of structure may well presuppose some form of the liminal relation.

By conceiving of liminality in this abstract way I mean to call attention to the *convertibility* of the notion. Not only is liminality an umbrella term, a kind of master trope that subsumes diverse phenomena; these phenomena imbricate to such an extent that it is difficult, if not impossible, to discuss any one of them in isolation. As Turner has remarked, liminality is "a semantic molecule with many components."[5] One reason I prefer "liminality" to "marginality" lies precisely in the former's multiple associations: etymologically, limen connects with nouns like limit, limb, limbo, limbus, slime, lintel; with verbs like limn, delimit, and eliminate;

and with adjectives like preliminary, sublime, and subliminal. The
suggestiveness of the word helps make the point that it is not
possible to investigate liminality, even in van Gennep's restricted
sense, without engaging a whole host of related ideas (the ideas
of "whole" and of "host" among them, as we will see). Thus, even
though the three sections of the book initially address only one
liminal entity—carnival (part 1), *choteo* (part 2), and disease
(part 3)—other "conversions" of the structure infiltrate each part.
In the first part I will also discuss imitation and belatedness; in the
second, dirt and exile; and in the third, doubling. Even "conversion" itself suffers several conversions in the course of my argument, for it will reappear both in a religious and in a Freudian
context.

Since the connections between all of these terms emerge from
concrete textual juxtapositions, they will, I trust, become clear as
my argument unfolds. Nonetheless, it might be useful at this point
to make explicit some of the affinities between my principal terms.
As I have just said, the three parts of the book deal respectively
with literary representations of carnival, *choteo,* and disease.[6] Although these phenomena refer to different levels of generality—the
cosmic (carnival), the social (*choteo*), and the somatic (disease)—they all occupy a position of eccentricity with respect to established patterns and norms. Carnival, an interstitial, transgressive moment in the yearly calendar, ushers in a topsy-turvy world,
a *mundus inversus* where the usual rules and restraints are temporarily suspended; *choteo* is a flank attack on society's structures
and strictures, a subversion of the social order; and disease may be
looked upon as a disruption of anatomical order, of the body's normal functioning. Like other liminal entities, these three are expressions of disorder, ragged margins, or "margins of mess," in Aldous
Huxley's phrase. If carnival is cosmos-disrupting, "cosmoclastic,"
choteo and disease are, respectively, "socioclastic" and "somato-
clastic." One disrupts the physical body, the other the body politic,
and the third the world's body. In order to establish the connections between these terms, to "convert" one into another, one need
only enlarge or narrow one's perspective. My own approach has
been to proceed from the general to the particular, from the
cosmic to the corporal: from carnival to *choteo* to disease.

I should say, however, that I did not embark upon the writing of the book with the notion of convertibility firmly in tow; rather, as I advanced in the writing and as text led to text and topic to topic, I realized that the increasingly apparent—and increasingly disconcerting—heterogeneity of my materials emerged from my subject's many disguises (and disguise is also another of the masks of liminality). Diversity then converted into principle (the principle of conversion) and the book's parts fell into place. This staged awakening to my argument's inner logic also explains why the liminal structure, which comes gradually into focus as my readings unfold, does not achieve sharp and complete visibility until the final chapters, where I address most directly the affinities between the texts in my corpus. Not until the body is fully formed does the harmony of its parts come into view.

For better or for worse, then, the reader's experience of the book will reproduce some of my own puzzles and discoveries as I proceeded in its composition. Especially in the opening chapters it may seem that the issue of marginality is itself marginal, an impression abetted perhaps by my expository style, which at times dispenses with some of the connective tissue customary in scholarly writing. The reader may well feel that he is being taken on a trip through a pleasant enough and intriguing countryside but without being told where he is headed or when he will get there. Yet I believe that, once reached, the destination will explain both the itinerary and the manner of transportation.

The liminal entities I have enumerated do not, to be sure, exhaust the transformational possibilities of the structure. They do not even exhaust the possible conversions within one domain—say, the social or the anatomical. The reason I have singled out these entities, and not others, is that they are the ones that emerge from my initial choice of texts. But the practical options are, of course, endless, and this book may itself be regarded as only one partial actualization of the many possibilities disclosed by its title.

It may be wondered, in fact, whether the alliterative dyad of my title is not also a "conversion" of the center-periphery connection. Is literature a "central" cultural fact that arises in opposition to the "liminal" genres of popular consumption (some of which—jokes and song lyrics—will figure in my readings)?[7] And if so, is it not misguided, or even contradictory, to search for the liminal in the literary? Although the answer to these questions is implicit in the pages that follow, let me say now that my effort in this book has been, in part, to "liminalize" a group of texts that are usually considered "central" to their respective traditions. Among them are José Zorrilla's *Don Juan Tenorio,* the paradigmatic example of Spanish romantic drama and perhaps the best-known Spanish play of any period; Jorge Mañach's *Indagación del choteo,* one of the authoritative explorations of the "Cuban character"; and Luis Martín-Santos's *Tiempo de silencio,* a work that laid the foundations for the renascence of the contemporary Spanish novel. Indeed, the mere act of attempting a joint study of such diverse texts may already be considered an act of liminalization, for this project wrenches these works from their usual surroundings and inserts them into an entirely different "text-milieu,"[8] one in which, for example, the wager scene in *Don Juan Tenorio* becomes a variant of a Cuban joke.

My invocation of tradition in the book's subtitle is, therefore, a polemical gesture. The question is, how is it possible for works as diverse as these to coalesce into a tradition? Tradition implies continuity, linear descent, the orderly transmission of a code of devices, motifs, or attitudes. For the most part, the works I will be analyzing do not, in these obvious senses, partake of the same tradition. But it is sometimes forgotten that there is another (semantic) tradition in "tradition," for the word's etymological doublet is "treason." To traduce tradition is to affirm tradition: nothing is more traditional, in one sense of the word, than the break or discontinuity achieved by an act of treason. By bringing together such disparate texts, I am betraying our usual notions of the Hispanic literary tradition, but only in an effort to limn the borderlines of an alternate, eccentric tradition.

This disruptive, treacherous element in tradition, moreover, points to a key link in my argument: however diverse, the works I bring together here are all alike in that they inscribe an unstable, aggressive, treacherous liminality, one that consistently threatens to collapse the center-periphery distinction. In these texts liminality is a structure that subverts structure, an "antistructural" structure, to use Victor Turner's term, since it assumes mobile, expansive forms. The most striking instance of this mobility is found in *Tiempo de silencio,* a novel pervaded by images of cancerous growth. Here the center-periphery connection is embodied in the relationship between a body and a malignancy that inhabits its margins. Yet cancer clearly embodies a marginality on the move, ever on the verge of centrality; and this centripetal impulse is rendered in the novel by the idea of the tumor as twin: underlying the oncological references is the notion that if the cancer spreads, it will constitute itself as the organism's monstrous double, as an alternate center (the corresponding geometrical figure then being not the circle but the ellipse, with its twin foci). A similar assault from the flanks appears in the other conversions: in the context of carnival, it appears as carnival's subversion of the part-whole hierarchy; in the context of belatedness, as the epigone's urge to take the place of the precursor; in the context of exile, as the expatriate's return; and in an aesthetic context, as the copy's striving after identity with the original.

This expansiveness will allow me to recover van Gennep's processual definition in a somewhat different form. The liminal structure behaves like a phase insofar as its peripheral components do not abide in the margins. They occupy the periphery only transitorily, while maintaining the center under constant siege. The impending return does not, however, as in van Gennep's conception, bring about an integrative reunification—any more than a cancer's metastasis brings about a reconciliation of the healthy and the diseased cells. On the contrary, the periphery's convergence poses a deadly threat to the central order. In this respect all of my conversions are metastatic, since they aggressively repudiate stasis or immobility. We will find, moreover, that in these works the metastatic impulse coexists with an arresting force, be it the fathers in *Don Juan,* the constraints of social convention in *Indagación del choteo,* or the sadistic fantasy of the immobilized body in *Tiempo de silencio.* These texts and the others I will be analyzing are thus constituted by a productive tension between restraint and mobility, order and disorder, tradition and treason—a tension that increases in proportion with the strength of the flank attack. Hence in *Tiempo de silencio,* where the liminal force assumes its most aggressive embodiment, the containing action surfaces as violent fantasies of immobilization.

Although I have already mentioned the principal works in my corpus, a further word on the constitution of this "body" may be in order. I begin in the first chapter with an analysis of the function of the carnival setting in *Don Juan Tenorio;* but since the role of carnival cannot be adequately understood without a consideration of the characters' imitative behavior, the second chapter undertakes a discussion of imitation; and this leads, in the third chapter, to a consideration of *Las galas del difunto,* Ramón del Valle-Inclán's playful imitation of Zorrilla's imitative play. Part 2 begins also by focusing on a limited aspect of one text, Mañach's definition of *choteo* in *Indagación del choteo* (chapter 4); once again, however, the focus broadens to encompass other texts, as I find it necessary to test the definition against two works contemporary with the essay: Carlos Loveira's novel, *Juan Criollo* (chapter 5), and Fernando Ortiz's compendium of Cuban words, *Un catauro de cubanismos* (chapter 6). In part 3 the analysis of physical disease in *Tiempo de silencio* (chapters 7 and 8) leads to a discussion of mental illness apropos of Martín-Santos's psychoanalytic treatise, *Libertad, temporalidad y transferencia en el psicoanálisis existencial* (chapter 9), a work that—in an ironic demonstration of van Gennep's idea of integrative reunification—takes us back to my point of departure, Zorrilla's play. In a very real generative sense, then, this book is itself expansive, metastatic, since what began as a reading of three unconnected texts (*Don Juan Tenorio, Indagación del choteo,* and *Tiempo de silencio*) eventually became a coordinated consideration of half a dozen works belonging to several authors, genres, and periods. As I have already said, one reason for this "growth" has to do with liminality's convertibility. But there is a second, methodological reason.

Joint or comparative studies of several authors or texts are generally delimited by well-defined but—I believe—largely conventional boundaries. In order for the comparison to be warranted, in order for it to make critical sense—*comparaison n'est pas raison*—certain kinds of common ground must exist between the texts before the exercise begins. This common ground can be generic (several novels, for instance), chronological (works from the same period), geographical (works belonging to the same region or national literature), or biographical (works belonging to the same author). This requirement of antecedent communality grows out of a belief in the inherent coherence or significance of generic, chronological, geographical, or biographical units.[9] Hence, to cite an extreme example, if one finds the same feature recurring in works written by different authors, in different genres and periods, but within the same national literature, one can posit that the recurrence of the feature reveals a characteristic trait of that literature or people. So one says, for instance, that the persistent struggle between the flesh and the spirit in many works of Spanish literature responds to a fundamental dualism in the psyche of the Spanish people. But what if one detects a shared element—an element, moreover, that sounds unfamiliar: let us say, "phonic rape"—in works that do not tread any of these kinds of common ground? What then does one make of the pattern? A first reaction, of course, is to dismiss the pattern as patter, as the result of coincidental or glib or far-fetched or "free" associations. One may also look upon the pattern, however, as a challenge to the conventional boundaries of critical sense; that is, as an illustration of a kind of coherence whose best analogue, perhaps, is the coherence of a fictional plot. Obviously this is how I would regard my associations. I admit that in putting together such an apparently disparate corpus—a polymorphous perverse corpus, to resort to the psychoanalytical language that will play a significant part in my discussion—I am deliberately fetching far for my connections; I admit, further, that I may have occasionally pursued my associations too fast or too far. I have done so in both cases to explore what happens when one elects not to observe some of the governing critical decora.

Consider, besides, the inherence of eccentricity in the work of the critic. In spite of recent pronouncements to the contrary, literary criticism continues to be regarded as secondary or derivative, and therefore of lesser stature than other, overtly fictional or poetic types of discourse. David Hirsch voices the majority view when he declares, "The argument for criticism as a primary activity is doomed to fail because it is repugnant to common sense. The critic must start by recognizing that whereas the great poet (novelist, playwright, etc.) converts energy into matter by translating undifferentiated experience into language, the critic starts with that which is already shaped into language."[10] Although I think that Hirsch ignores the extent to which "great poets," like humble critics, do *not* work on undifferentiated experience, I do not wish to take issue with his views; in fact, I want to endorse them. Since criticism typically (though not exclusively) adopts the mode of commentary, in a genetic sense it must always take second place to the "primary," the commented texts. Not coincidentally, the mark of reading is a line in the margin, for the critic is fated to limn marginal notes, eccentric jottings. The movement from literature to criticism, from "creation" to "commentary," thus appears as a displacement away from the center, from the body of the text to its limbs or limen (appropriately, "limen" is an obsolete plural of "limb"). If so, however, the critical act is by nature eccentric (ex-centric), and my unusual grouping of texts only obeys the defining tropism of the discipline. If so, also, a critical inquiry into margins cannot but reflect on the nature of criticism itself. A move to the margins places one in the center of the critic's domain.

Literature and Liminality thus joins preoccupations of two different but converging orders, substantive and methodological. Substantively I will be concerned with mapping the conversions of the liminal structure in a heterogeneous group of Spanish-language texts. Methodologically I am interested in the questions that such an exercise can pose about the limits—the limens—of critical privilege. This desire to push academic commentary toward its limits, which explains the irreverent tone and lexical license of some of what follows, is the aspect of the book I want to designate with the adjective "festive," a term that I would oppose not to "serious" (as in "serious scholarship" or "serious writing") but to "ordinary" (in the sense of customary or conventional). Mine is, therefore, a festive exploration of festivity, a book about margins written, to some extent, in a marginal mode.

LITERATURE
AND LIMINALITY

Part One

CARNIVAL

Cuando en las alas de la idea quiere volar
nuestra fantasía hasta el empíreo, una
expresión incorrecta, una voz impropia,
un sonido duro, o bien un galicismo o un
neologismo insufrible nos advierte que
estamos pegados al fango de la tierra.

(When on the wings of an idea our imagination
wants to fly to the empyrean, an incorrect
expression, an improper word, a harsh sound,
a gallicism, or an insufferable neologism
reminds us that we are mired in the mud of
the earth.)

ALBERTO LISTA, on *Don Juan Tenorio*

1

❧

The Spirit of the Letter

Everything begins with a letter. In the first act of José Zorrilla's *Don Juan Tenorio,* the curtain rises to reveal Don Juan, in a frenzy of inspiration, dashing off impassioned verses to Inés. The play begins, thus, with the portrait of an artist in the act of composition, a portrait that perhaps will remind us of Zorrilla himself, hurriedly composing the play.[1] A few steps away, out of Juan's earshot, Ciutti and Buttarelli provide a running, albeit misleading, commentary on Juan's efforts, with Buttarelli wanting to know more than Ciutti is willing to allow. From the beginning Juan's letter to Inés becomes the focus of the characters' curiosity and speculation. From the beginning, also, it is trammelled in deceit, since Ciutti tells Buttarelli that Juan, good son that he is, writes to his father. Juan's verses, of course, are not intended for Don Diego, and Ciutti knows it; but his fib does anticipate the letter's uncanny capacity for falling into the wrong hands—and in this play the wrong hands will always belong to the father, be it Juan's father or Inés's.

Once Juan has finished the letter, he signs and folds it, places it inside a book of hours, and instructs Ciutti to take it to the convent, where Brígida, Inés's *dueña* (in more ways than one), will see to it that the book reaches the right hands. In the second act Brígida reports that Inés must be reading the *papelito* at that very moment, though the actual reading does not take place until the third act when Brígida coaxes her charge into opening the gift. Soon after Juan steals Inés away from the convent, but the letter is carelessly left behind in the cell, there to be found by Gonzalo.

In the last act of part 1, the letter figures twice. Its first appearance again involves a lie, for Brígida explains their flight from the convent by telling Inés that, in the excitement of reading the letter, they did not notice the fire raging around them, a fire from which they were rescued by Don Juan. The real circumstances surrounding the elopement are brought up by Gonzalo, who confronts Juan with the "written proof" of his treachery (1.4.9). Thus the letter, though Ciutti could not possibly have foreseen it, does eventually wind up in the hands of the father. By the fourth act, Ciutti's lie has become a half-truth. And I say half-truth to indicate not only that the remark, "escribe . . . a su padre" ("he writes . . . to his father"; 1.1.1), ostensibly refers to Diego, not Gonzalo (although in retrospect these words, these four words, possess a rich ambiguity), but also that the document originally presented as a concession to paternal authority ends up precipitating the death of Inés's father.

Following a kind of Brownian movement, thus, the letter travels in an irregular circular route, eventually returning to its point of origin. But as happens with particles in a light beam, the letter that returns to Don Juan at the end of part 1 is not the same entity that had left his hands at the opening of the play. In a sense, the fate of the letter is that of any text: as it becomes detached from its author and passes from interpreter to interpreter, it begins to accrue meanings that the author did not necessarily intend. The letter means different things to the different characters who have occasion to reflect upon it. To Buttarelli it shows that Juan is a good son; to Brígida it is a trap being laid for Inés; to Inés it is a token of Juan's affection; to Gonzalo it is proof of his dishonor. Indeed, one outstanding feature of the letter is its indeterminacy of meaning. In this respect it is quite a modern text, and perhaps the meaning that it holds for us, its modern readers, is that one should not dismiss a work like the *Tenorio* with "four words," as Zorrilla did. In this instance four words cannot do justice to one letter, to the richness and complexity of one letter. Something of this richness comes across in the various metaphors that describe the letter: Brígida calls it *una red* and *un anzuelo;* Inés compares it to a burning flame, to a charmed amulet, to an irresistible magnet, and to a poisonous philter; Gonzalo reprises this last image in his reference to "the poison of those letters" (1.4.9); and in his well-known remarks on the *Tenorio*, Pérez de Ayala observes that Inés falls victim to "Don Juan's diabolical romantic contamination."[2] But the focus of contamination, the carrier of the disease, is not so much Juan as his letter, which "contaminates" not just Inés but several other characters as well. In fact, Inés does not even meet Juan until after she has been spirited away from the convent. Her decisive contaminating contact takes place only through his verses.

The letter is Don Juan's equivocal *don,* a treacherous gift that circulates from hand to hand disseminating its poison. It is also an instrument of usurpation, a gift that possesses the receiver rather than being possessed by her. And I intend "possess" here in its carnal sense, for the letter is indeed the perpetrator of Inés's seduction. As she puts it:

¡Ay! ¿Qué filtro envenenado
me dan en este papel,
que el corazón desgarrado
me estoy sintiendo con él?
¿Qué impulsos jamás sentidos?
¿Qué luz, que hasta hoy nunca vi?
¿Qué es lo que engendra en mi alma
tan nuevo y profundo afán? (1.3.3)

(Oh! What poisoned philter does this paper contain that I feel my heart rending? What impulses are these that I have never felt before? What light is this that I have never seen before? What engenders in my soul this new and deep distress?)

For Inés the reading of the document marks a moment of self-revelation, of awakening: dormant feelings quicken, novel impulses crowd into consciousness. But it marks also a moment of erotic contact or contamination, since the letter "tears" ("el corazón desgarrado") and "engenders" ("¿Qué es lo que engendra en mi alma . . . ?"). One can hardly overlook the sexual suggestiveness of the scene, especially in view of the intercession of a *trotaconventos* like Brígida. In what is perhaps a travesty of the Annunciation, Inés becomes the object of a kind of acoustic insemination or phonic rape (the reading is done out loud), with the entirely unholy Brígida filling the role of the messenger angel. Don Juan's culminating seduction therefore takes place with the seducer *in absentia.* The protagonists are a novice, a procurer, and a bit of paper that slips out. The *papelito* plays the part of Don Juan, the part of Don Juan's part, of his phallus. The really odd thing about this symbolism, however, is that by forgetting the *papelito* in the convent, Don Juan finds himself in the position of a man who completes the act, flees—but leaves his member behind; that is, in the position of a man who forgets to re-member himself. And imagine Gonzalo's astonishment when he barges into his daughter's cell only to find her seducer's phallus there on the floor. His reaction:

¡Ay! Por qué tiemblo no sé.
¡Mas qué veo, santo Dios! (1.4.8)

(Oh! I don't know why I am trembling.
But what am I seeing, Holy God!)

This interpretation may seem far-fetched; the letter may not, as it were, look the part. Let me point out, therefore, that this reading of the convent scene is consistent with the widely held view that Don Juan is one of the Western embodiments of the trickster figure common to many mythologies.[3] I say this because the motif of the detachable phallus appears in many trickster tales; in one of the best known of these, the Winnebago cycle, one even encounters an incident reminiscent of Inés's remote-control seduction. Trickster wakes up from a nap one day with an erection propping up his blanket, which he mistakes for the tribal chief's banner. Just as some people nowadays soothe their plants by talking to them, Trickster proceeds to talk to his penis, hoping to calm it down. The stratagem succeeds; and once the penis has become flaccid, Trickster coils it and puts it in a box. Some time later he sends his penis across the river where it copulates—illicitly and covertly—with the chief's daughter.[4] Both in *Don Juan Tenorio* and in the Trickster story the detachable phallus serves to overcome obstacles (the convent walls, the river) and mock the authority of the father (Gonzalo, the tribal chief). The moral of both incidents, of the two prick-tricks, seems to be: if you can't take it with you, let it come by itself.

Another important feature of the letter as it moves through the first part of the play is that it acts as the point of convergence of a number of inconsistencies in the plot, inconsistencies that generally involve a dislocation or reversal of temporal sequence. The most apparent of these dislocations has to do with Juan's motives for writing the letter. Even though it is written before Gonzalo cancels Juan and Inés's engagement, when Inés finally reads the letter the passion of Juan's feelings is interpreted as a reaction to the dissolution of the agreement. As Brígida explains it, his vehemence is born of his desolation at having lost Inés. But since Gonzalo's intervention occurs only *after* the letter has been sent, in Brígida's interpretation the letter anticipates the event that is said to have produced it. Indeed, not only does the letter precede its cause, it partly causes its cause, since Gonzalo decides to intervene only after hearing that Juan intends to seduce a novice; and the successful completion of Juan's plan in turn depends upon the letter. The problem—but is it a problem?—seems to be that Juan arranges for Inés's capture before he has any need to. When the play begins Juan is already in cahoots with Brígida, who has agreed to let him into the convent. But what is the reason for such an arrangement? How could Juan have known, first, that Luis was going to dare him to seduce a nun, and second, that Gonzalo was going to witness the challenge? The letter is both part of the background of the wager and a consequence of it; it is both an antecedent effect and an after-cause: the cause of its own cause, the effect of a cause that it itself created. In Juan's verses normal temporal and causal sequence collapses, for future events are always catching up and outstripping the present, as if time were circular and past, present, and future travelled the circle at different speeds.

A similar collapse of sequence affects Inés, who doesn't become a postulant until after Gonzalo has rescinded the promise of marriage. At the moment that Juan, thinking of Inés, commits himself to seducing a novice who is about to take vows, this is not yet her status, and it only becomes her status as a result of Juan's acceptance of the dare. These inversions are equally apparent on a more localized plane. When Juan hands the letter to Ciutti, he instructs his servant:

> Este pliego
> irá dentro del horario
> en que reza doña Inés
> a sus manos a parar. (1.1.1)

(This sheet will reach Inés's hands inside the book of hours with which she prays.)

To which Zorrilla riposts, in "Cuatro palabras sobre mi *Don Juan Tenorio*": "No, of course not! In the book of hours where she *will* pray, once you have given it to her; but not in the one with which she prays already, since you have not yet given it to her."[5] Here again the future anticipates the present. Inés begins to read even *before* she has the book. Similarly, in the second act, Brígida anticipates the reading of the *papel* when she informs Juan that Inés "leyendo estará ahora en él" ("she must be reading it now"; 1.2.9). Though of course Brígida is employing the future of probability, the use of a future tense (*estará*) alongside a deictic designating a present (*ahora*) does suggest the coupling or collapse of present and future that characterizes the narrative syntax of the play. For Brígida the future is now, literally now: *estará* is *ahora*. In *Don Juan* future occurrences are constantly encroaching upon the present; the reading of the letter, an event of central importance, is repeatedly announced and repeatedly deferred. And, let it be noted, I have not yet mentioned the most prominent instance of such a dislocation, which occurs in part 2 when Juan, apparently still alive, witnesses his own funeral. In this incident one also encounters the same proleptic use of verbal tense in Gonzalo's much discussed assertion:

El capitán te mató
a la puerta de tu casa. (2.3.2)[6]

(The captain killed you at your doorstep.)

Classical rhetoric has a name for this kind of distortion—metalepsis, the reversal of the temporal order of cause and effect, or past and present. The first thing I should like to claim about the structure of the play, particularly its first part, is that it features a pattern of metaleptic reversals. The unfolding of the action, which folds into the successive unfoldings of the letter, depends crucially on the kind of dislocation or reversal I have been detailing. Of course, one man's metalepsis is another man's muddle, and the incidents I have mentioned may be taken as evidence of the work's flawed design. Furthermore, Zorrilla himself ridiculed the pattern of temporal acceleration in the play, joking that in his *Tenorio* clock hours must have two hundred minutes.[7]

Before taking sides with Zorrilla, however, we should remember that these strange events all take place during carnival, the so-called *tiempo loco.* I want to suggest, then, that the anomalies in the play can be naturalized by being referred back to the setting in which they unfold. This is not to say that placed against the backdrop of carnival temporal reversals no longer appear as such— just the opposite. I mean to say that carnival by its nature establishes a dislocated, up-ended, reversed temporal flow. Indeed, Edmund Leach has argued that during festival celebrations time flows backward from future to present and from present to past, and Roger Caillois has maintained that festivals bring about a retrocession to the primordial *Ur-zeit,* the mythical time of creation.[8] This would indicate that metalepsis is precisely the trope of carnival, the figure of festival disarray. Metalepsis is the temporal analogue of the carnival topos of the *mundus inversus;* as the instrument for the creation of a kind of *tempus inversus,* it furnishes a chronological correlate of carnival's topographical reversals.

When one foregrounds the inconsistencies, the anomalies, the improbabilities in the *Tenorio,* one must remember that, during the brief interval of carnival, anomaly, inconsistency, and improbability reign supreme. If the *Tenorio* abided by the usual canons of tidiness and verisimilitude, then one would have reason to censure the play. At any other moment during the year two-hundred-minute hours would be anachronistic, but during carnival anachronisms become the norm. Zorrilla's anecdote that in the first performance of the play the clock in the theater belied the characters' assertions about the hour serves only to emphasize the distance between carnival time and quotidian chronology and, by extension, between narrative syntax and the succession of real events. When Juan told Ciutti that they should meet in the convent at nine o'clock it was already nine forty-five—but so what? Given the circumstances of the letter's and the play's unfolding, it could not have been otherwise.[9]

In fact, the *setting* of the letter should have alerted us to the importance of the setting of the play. Carnival represents a break in time, a hiatus in the course of the year. One might compare it to a blank page intercalated between the leaves of the calendar, or to a letter set between the pages of an *horario*. The letter, which in one respect acts as the agent of temporal distortion, in another respect reminds us of the location of such distortions. Carnival is a letter lodged in a book of hours. The letter is an emblem of carnival discontinuity. And the *Tenorio* itself may be seen as a book of hours, a theological *tour de force* that attempts to contain the carnival spirit of the letter. But as we know, the letter will slip out, fall to the floor, and be read by Brígida, Inés, and Gonzalo. My approach has been to open the book, to unbind the play, so that the letter can slip out.

We should also notice that the escape of the letter is but one instance in an intricate network of spatial transgression that also forms part of the work's carnival spirit, and whose exemplary formulation is embodied in Don Juan's account of his exploits:

Yo a las cabañas bajé,
yo a los palacios subí,
yo los claustros escalé,
y en todas partes dejé
memoria amarga de mí. (1.1.12)

(I went down to cottages; I went up to palaces; I scaled convent walls; and everywhere I left bitter memories.)

Bajar, subir, escalar: one of the striking things about *Don Juan Tenorio* is that it is full of walls that neither enclose nor exclude, of prisons that do not imprison, of doors that do not protect from intrusion, of barriers that do not bar access. The play's borders, its barriers and limits, are observed mostly in the breaches that the characters make in them. When at the end of the play Gonzalo's statue goes through the walls of Juan's dining room, it is performing a feat that others have already accomplished several times before. In part 1 alone, Juan escapes from prison, breaks into and out of Ana's residence, into and out of the convent, and flees from his own house. Luis also escapes from prison, arranges for entrance into Ana's house, and finally escapes from the custody of Juan's men. Gonzalo himself has little difficulty first entering the convent and subsequently slipping into Juan's villa. The letter thus functions as an emblem of both the spatial and the temporal transgressions, of the play's hostility toward limits. These transgressions ultimately emerge from the carnival setting, and this too is a fact signified by the letter, embedded as it is in the pages of the *horario*. There exists, in addition, a parallel between the "evil chaos" that the letter begets in Inés (1.2.9) and the disorder in Seville. Early in act 1, after sending Ciutti on his way, Don Juan leaves the tavern to fight the boisterous mob that had been disturbing him while he was writing the letter. The melee that ensues causes Buttarelli to remark, "anda ya Sevilla / toda revuelta" (1.1.3). The city is *revuelta,* or topsy-turvy, mixed-up, in a state of *revolución.* This revolution, which describes the action of carnival, also describes the action of the letter. Compare Inés's own depiction of her condition:

No sé qué tengo, ¡ay de mí!,
que en tumultuoso tropel
mil encontradas ideas
me combaten a la vez. (1.3.2)

(I don't know what's the matter with me! Like a tumultuous throng, a thousand conflicting ideas are warring inside me.)

Her mental struggle reprises the fight outside Buttarelli's tavern. Inés's mind is also a carnival site. Through the letter festival disorder filters into the convent and possesses her. When *Don Juan* begins, the chaos remains offstage, if barely: "The curtain rises and through the door in the back one sees masked men, students, and townspeople go by with torches, music, etc." Don Juan will soon go out to the street and bring the disorder back with him into the tavern, from where it will spread to the other characters, and especially to Inés. By the end of the first part an "evil chaos" has enveloped all of the protagonists.

But the *papelito* in the prayerbook is not the only instance of embedding in the play; there is another, equally significant, *mise en abîme* that also draws attention to the enveloping carnival ambience. I am referring to the wager between Juan and Luis staged in the opening act. According to Mikhail Bakhtin, carnival "belongs to the borderline between art and life. In reality, it is life itself, but shaped according to a certain pattern of play."[10] Life itself shaped according to a certain pattern of play—does this not seem a remarkably precise description of the wager, which is labelled at one point "un juego ilusorio" (1.1.16)? In the wager the two

Spanish senses of *jugar* converge: it is both a game and a gamble. The two English senses of *play* also converge: it is both a performance and a game, play and play in equal parts. Carlos Feal is quite right, therefore, to insist on the theatricality of Luis and Juan's confrontation.[11] Buttarelli's tavern is indeed a stage within a stage; and the entire scene may be seen as a drama *en abîme,* a specular reflection of the larger play that contains it. This embedding has its material and textual tokens. Materially the embedding is reflected in the table around which the characters sit, which one can regard as the recessed or secondary stage: the table, that is, becomes *las tablas.* Textually the embedding is signified by the lists of conquests and murders, which serve as the "script" of the inner play. Like the letter, the table and the lists act as indices of specularity.

What has to be added, nevertheless, is that the wager is a performance of a peculiar sort, since it does not observe the distinction between actors and spectators; here we have a play, in other words, that violates the enabling condition of dramatic form. From the beginning of Luis and Juan's encounter the boundaries between actors and spectators are not well drawn. Juan, who is fully aware that he is performing on the stage of the tavern, does not object to the presence of witnesses. People crowd around the table, partake of the same repast, kibbitz, declare their allegiance to one or the other of the rivals. Only two members of the audience, Diego and Gonzalo, maintain their distance. Even when urged by Juan to join the proceedings, they refuse. Yet, in a clear illustration of the precariousness of such detachment, it is precisely Diego and Gonzalo who at the end of the scene will occupy center stage. On first entering the tavern Gonzalo asks for a contiguous room from which to overhear the conversation. Told by Buttarelli that no such room exists, he settles instead for a less secure dividing membrane, a mask. But mask and wall are both intended for the same purpose, to separate Gonzalo from Juan, father from son, observer from protagonist. Appropriately, then, Gonzalo's irruption into the scene a bit later will be marked by his unmasking. Just as he attempts to secure his daughter behind the walls of a convent, he will first try to cloister himself in another room; unable to get one, he accepts the fragile security of the mask, though this protection too is soon stripped away. From thick wall to thin mask to naked skin: Gonzalo's staged striptease, weirdly foreshadowing the seduction of his daughter, converts him from bystander to participant. Diego's actions follow a similar course. He also hides behind a mask, is eventually discovered, and as with Gonzalo the unmasking also signals his entrance into the play.

The wager is then framed by parallel occurrences. It begins when Juan and Luis are recognized and unmasked; it ends when Diego and Gonzalo are unmasked and recognized. On either end, anagnorises and unmaskings. Structural boundaries, one might say, replace physical ones. But the whole point of the wager is that such boundaries do not actually inhibit or contain. Indeed, just as the distinction between actor and spectator is blurred, the separation between the wager and the frame is negated. The defining feature of the wager, as of the letter, is that it is not self-contained. Just as the letter does not stop at Inés's hands, the wager spills over its original confines. The original *plazo* of one year is extended for another day, and the meeting that was to have ended the competition actually inaugurates a new intensification of the rivalry. Since the first part of the play grows out of the bet, and since the second part works out the consequences of the first, the whole play, in fact, evolves from the wager. In this way the framed play, the play within the play, overwhelms the larger context in which it is inserted. Everything was to have ended with the meeting a year later in the tavern; instead, however, the reunion triggers a sequence of events that will occupy all of the subsequent acts.

The expansiveness of the wager, the invasion of the frame by the inlay, is another feature that contributes to the *Tenorio's* carnival content. Like Buttarelli's tavern, "carnival does not know footlights, in the sense that it does not acknowledge any distinction between actors and spectators."[12] Here again we see a transgression of boundaries, boundaries both physical (the proscenium that separates the stage from the seats) and social (the behavior that separates the actors from the spectators).[13] More generally, it is the very principle of embedding that carnival calls into question. Embedding depends on the discrete specularity of larger and smaller segments inside a text, and might be defined, in effect, as the mimesis of the whole by the part. It thus presupposes a stable separation of part and whole, of inlay and frame. In the *Tenorio,* however, this separation is rendered problematic, for just as the prayerbook does not contain the letter, the outer play does not contain the wager. An incident that at first sight appears to be a self-contained representation turns out in the end to monopolize all of the action.

Because carnival operates by destabilizing oppositions, by inverting hierarchies, it leads to the cancelling out of the framed-frame division. The paradox of this particular negation, of course, is that carnival is itself a "framed" spectacle, a celebration "contained" by the calendar, a "part" of the year's secular liturgy. But my discussion suggests that within the carnival setting of the play the relationship of part to whole acquires an unusual reciprocity. One might go so far as to posit a kind of rivalry of part and whole in which the larger and the smaller segments vie for supremacy, a rivalry whose model would be the competition between Juan and Luis.[14] But this competition, we should remember, unfolds *as* the wager. It is already part of the part. The wager might then be said to "thematize" its connection with the rest of the play, for it not only competes for supremacy but lays down the rules of the competition as well. This intricate, recursive connection results from carnival's torsion.

Carnival is partial to parts. Carnival is part time. During carnival every part aspires to the condition of wholeness; every part turns expansive, malignant, monstrous. And if the last epithet seems extravagant, I hasten to add that I lift it from the text of the play, where it is applied repeatedly to Don Juan, who is not only called "el monstruo de liviandad" (1.1.8) but also "un aborto del abismo" (2.1.2). Since carnival and the letter are both sources of contamination, of distortion, of violence, they too are monsters; furthermore, since carnival unfolds "between and betwixt" the normal course of events and the letter infolds "between and betwixt" the pages of the prayer book, they are both also marginal: marginal monsters (but are not monsters always marginal?).[15] Yet, precisely for these reasons, these two entities are "central" to an understanding of the play. To speak of *Don Juan Tenorio*'s flaws, of the monstrosities in its design, is to ignore that monstrosity is the very subject of the play. Accepting Zorrilla's four words at face value amounts to pretending that the letter never left Juan's hands, that the wager never took place. But the letter does circulate, and Brígida—ever the interpreter—does construe it for Inés.

If the wager embeds the generative core, the begetting nucleus of the play, the seduction scene embeds a representation of the play's decipherment. Going from one to the other we move from artistic to hermeneutic conception. Brígida, the go-between, plays the part of the interpreter; Inés, the unsuspecting victim, that of the reluctant reader. What passes between Brígida and Inés, between interpreter and reader, is nothing more substantial than a slip of paper, a few lines of verse. Since the symbolism of this scene is obvious, I will not belabor it. Let me just mention something else that my reader may already know: in this book I am Brígida and you are Inés. And a large part of my task, as we will see, is to help you read letters.

2

Fathers and Sons

> Perhaps
> the man-hero is not the exceptional monster,
> but he that of repetition is most master.
>
> WALLACE STEVENS

From the moment in the first act when Juan and Luis recognize each other, from the moment when each man confronts his double, *Don Juan Tenorio* becomes an increasingly frenzied succession of peripeties in which the two rivals alternate in achieving dominance over one another. One minute Luis has the upper hand; the next finds Juan in command. Luis has Juan arrested and we think that Juan has finally been outsmarted, only to discover immediately that Juan has also arranged for the incarceration of his competitor. At the beginning of the second act Luis, just out of jail, arranges to spend the night inside Ana's house. Again we think that he has triumphed over his rival, who is presumably still in jail; yet moments later Juan, who has also bolted from prison, is making similar arrangements. In almost every instance the competition of the two men is based on imitative action: Juan has kept a list of murders and conquests; so has Luis. Juan sends Ciutti to get the police; Luis sends Gastón. Juan has a contact inside Ana's house; Luis does also. Often even their words are identical.

The two rivals do not simply try to outdo each other. The unwritten rule of their "illusory game" is that advantages are gained by emulation. When Juan and Luis chance upon each other after escaping from jail, they are equally startled:

LUIS: ¡Sois don Juan!

JUAN: ¡Pardiez!
          Los dos ya en la calle estamos.

LUIS: ¿No os prendieron?
JUAN: Como a vos.
LUIS: ¡Vive Dios!
       ¿Y huisteis?
JUAN: Os imité.
                ¿Y qué?   (1.2.7)
(LUIS: You are Don Juan!
JUAN: By God!
       We are both out on the street.
LUIS: Weren't you arrested?
JUAN: Just like you.
LUIS: Good God!
       And you escaped?
JUAN: I imitated you.
                So what?)

Juan's last rejoinder formulates the governing principle of the
rivalry: *Os imité. ¿Y qué?* It is not enough to outwit or outdo
one's opponent; the victory must be won by copying his behavior,
by mastering repetition. As the number of murders shows, this
imitation compulsion surfaces even in small details: Juan has
killed 32 men, while Luis has murdered 23. The two numbers,
like the two rivals, are mirror images, digital doubles. One cannot
then blame Ana for failing to notice Juan's impersonation of her
fiancé. Having copied Luis throughout the preceding scenes, Juan
tops off his performance by *becoming* his double: in grafting Luis's
identity onto his own, the master of repetition becomes the monster of repetition. Because Juan and Ana's union is also the "union"
of Juan and Luis, to think of Juan in her boudoir is inevitably to
see three people. Thus, when Luis puts on his door a placard pro-
claiming, "Here is one Don Luis / who is worth at least two"
(1.1.12), he unwittingly reveals what the play makes clear
enough: Luis, like Juan, is double. Even if the two protagonists
are not twins, as they are in some earlier versions of the legend,
they could not be more identical. Luis equals two men not only
because of his valor but because Zorrilla, for all practical purposes,
has provided him with a matching twin.
    Imitative action, moreover, is not limited to the two protago-
nists. Seeming to imitate Juan and Luis's imitativeness, most of the

other characters also behave in the same fashion. In the first act, for example, both Diego and Gonzalo secretively enter the tavern, have an abrupt exchange with Buttarelli, don masks, sit across from each other, and attempt to disrupt the wager. Other pairs of characters—Ana and Inés, Ciutti and Gastón, Centellas and Avellaneda, Brígida and Lucía—also engage in specular behavior, so much so that their actions at times seem dictated not by free will but by a kind of genetic encoding that has programmed them to copy one another. And Zorrilla himself considered that the "dualismo de personajes" was one of the personal touches he added to the Don Juan legend.[1]

Os imité. ¿Y qué? Even the rhyme chimes the theme of imitation. In its coupling of *imité* and *y qué,* the rhyme also insinuates that the play will be concerned with the relations between imitation and its consequences. What happens in a world where every act—like Juan's final exploit, which consists of a dual conquest—is double? What are the consequences of character cloning? The answer seems to be that imitative action, what René Girard has dubbed "mimetic desire,"[2] is fraught with perilous results, as all of the participants in the two triangles that structure the plot—Juan/Inés/Gonzalo; Juan/Ana/Luis—suffer the consequences (death or dishonor) of their specular behavior. Here also the setting of the play is relevant, for carnival is perhaps the most appropriate situation for the unfolding of a drama of doubleness. Even if one does not accept Girard's view that festivals commemorate and reenact the scapegoating mechanism by which societies avert the dangers of mimetic desire,[3] certainly binary conflicts have always played an important part in carnival celebrations. Whether it takes the form of literary agons, or of contests between ethnic groups, guilds, and social classes, or of symbolic debates between Carnival and Lent or Summer and Winter, binary conflict suffuses the world of carnival.[4] In this light the specular wager, another double game, is a crucial element in the work's festive atmosphere.

Imitative action also helps to account for the play's two-part design, for one can speak not only of the characters' imitations but of a structural or textual doubling manifested in the many parallelisms and echoes between the first and second parts. Both sections begin with the portrait of an artist: in the first, Juan is writing his verses, and in the second, the Sculptor is putting the finishing touches on the pantheon. Both parts begin also with Juan having just returned to Seville after an extended absence; the action in both parts occurs in one night, is segmented into *plazos,* and contains several common motifs—the banquet, the *convite,* and duels. Juan's list of victims finds a correlate in the pantheon, and Buttarelli's retrospective account of the background of the wager is matched by the Sculptor's explanation of the history of the pantheon.[5] Still other parallels could easily be found, but the general tenor of the connection is clear and is summarized by Juan's initial reaction to the pantheon: "¡El palacio hecho panteón!" ("The palace turned into a pantheon!"; 2.1.2). The carnival motifs of the first part recur in the second in a religious setting. In part 2 the world is turned right side up again, as Carnival is succeeded by Lent, feast gives way to fast, and the *carpe diem* philosophy of the lists is replaced by the *memento mori* of the cemetery.

Don Juan Tenorio is Zorrilla's double-play. Zorrilla has in essence written the play twice and has set the two versions in opposition to each other. Like the two protagonists, the *Tenorio* is itself double, since its first and second parts clash and compete. The governing principle of this rivalry, like that of Juan and Luis, is that supremacy is to be achieved through emulation. Thus part 2 uses the building blocks of part 1 but rearranges them into a religious allegory. Although the basic ingredients remain the same, they are configured in part 2 into a very different whole.

We should notice, in addition, that in describing the connection between part 1 and part 2 I am also describing the connection between Zorrilla's *Don Juan* and its precursors. Indeed, if I have insisted on the importance of imitation in the *Tenorio,* it is because one can hardly overlook the fact that Zorrilla's play is itself a revisionary "imitation" of earlier versions of the Don Juan legend. In other words, the connection between parts within the play is itself a doubling or duplication of the connection between the play as a whole and its sources. Zorrilla has also kept many of the motifs, incidents, and characters of the earlier works while reworking them into a new configuration. And this means, in turn, that in rewriting the first part of the play in the second Zorrilla was performing the same gesture that the entire play performs. He was, in effect, imitating himself in the act of imitation, reviewing his own act of revision.

Zorrilla's remarkable confession that, in writing the play, he intended to "kill" *El convidado de piedra* is proof enough that he conceived of literary tradition in treacherous, competitive, agonistic terms: "I wanted, with my Don Juan Tenorio, to kill the guest of stone; and the public's bad taste gave me the idea of killing Don Juan again with a guest of stone: and this is my recasting [*mi refundición*]."[6] In light of this declaration of murderous intent, *Don Juan Tenorio*'s almost obsessive concern with imitative behavior cannot but be regarded as a symptom of Zorrilla's own worries over his place in what has been called "the Don Juan family."[7] Might one not even interpret Don Juan's regeneration as a projection of Zorrilla's own desire to create a "new" Don Juan, to extract an original morphosis from the existing type? Significantly, the conversion takes place precisely at the point where Zorrilla "swerves" (to use Harold Bloom's terminology) most noticeably from his principal precursors, Tirso and Zamora. Juan's regeneration is both a symbol of Zorrilla's efforts to create a new Don Juan and the moment in the play when those efforts become most visible. Thus, the character of Don Juan is—at least—twice double: doubled first by Luis and then again by Juan's regenerate self. There is the canonic, traditional Don Juan—faithless, rakish, diabolic; and there is the new Don Juan, Zorrilla's Don Juan, who, as his author mentioned in "Cuatro palabras," differs from his forebears principally in being won over by love to Christianity.

Having impulsively undertaken to compose still another version of the legend, Zorrilla had to confront the problem of derivativeness: how could one be original or assert his imaginative priority when handling a material that so many had worked on before? Because of his concern with this question, all of the *Tenorio* is permeated by an "originality neurosis,"[8] an obsessive worry over tardiness or epigonism. In this context the two heroes' bragging and hyperbole is nothing more than a symptom of Zorrilla's insecurity about his undertaking. The continual setting of *plazos,* with the consequent need to be on time, also reflects the same concern, as does the protagonists' insistence on being one step ahead of each other. In fact, if their behavior is dictated by the rule of imitative action, the outcome of the wager will hinge not on what Juan and Luis do (both will do the same things), but on who does it *first.* Thus, whoever sneaks first into Ana's house will win that part of the bet; and Gonzalo will be able to protect his daughter only if he reaches the convent before Juan. In *Margarita la tornera,* a poem that Zorrilla labelled the "original embryo" of the play,[9] Don Juan de Alarcón states:

Paréceme, don Gonzalo
que llegar pronto no es malo:
ya sabéis que es mi manía.
Doquier que de diversión
barrunto un ligero asomo
lo menos para ir me tomo
un mes de anticipación.[10]

(It seems to me, Don Gonzalo, that there is nothing wrong with being early: you know already that it is my habit. Wherever I antici-pate a good time, I usually get there a month early.)

Since anticipation is the opposite of belatedness, Juan's "mania" can be taken as a reflection of Zorrilla's own fears. An early arrival is precisely what Zorrilla, a latecomer to the Don Juan story, would have wished for himself. Already in his first significant treatment of the story Zorrilla betrays the preoccupations that will haunt the play. *Margarita la tornera* anticipates the *Tenorio's* con-cern with anticipation.

This concern is manifested in the play in two ways. The first takes us back to my earlier discussion of metalepsis, for as Harold Bloom has pointed out, metalepsis is a trope of anteriority.[11] Zo-rrilla wanted to kill *El convidado de piedra.* Metalepsis imaginarily and imaginatively performs this feat by placing the present before the past, effect before cause, epigone before precursor. By this rhe-torical trick the belated poet gives birth to his own father—in the same way that the letter "fathers" the circumstances that bring it into being. Since the best way to "arrive early" is to place oneself at the head of the line, metalepsis represents the absolute degree, the hyperbole of anticipation. Let us recall Luis's words to Juan shortly after Ana's seduction:

Me habéis maniatado,
y habéis la casa asaltado
usurpándome mi puesto. (1.4.6)

(You've handcuffed me and taken the house, usurping my place.)

Just as Juan conquers Ana by pretending to be her intended, the epigone metaleptically merges with the precursor, in order also to usurp his rival's place. Hence, like the sequence of imitations, the metaleptic reversals are motivated twice, first by carnival's distortional impetus, and a second time by Zorrilla's elaboration of the question of imaginative priority. As a result, the *Tenorio* is doubly double; that is to say, some of the motifs that recur in parts 1 and 2 are motivated both by the carnival frenzy and by the anticipatory mania. Thus, for example, with the *plazos,* which on the one hand augment the sense of temporal acceleration and on the other highlight the decisive importance of timeliness.

Thus also, with parricide. As a kind of supreme transgression, parricide is another manifestation of carnival chaos, perhaps even serving as carnival's crowning (or *un*crowning) spasm. It is appropriate, therefore, that the events of part 1 should culminate in Gonzalo's murder. But since the relationship between precursor and epigone is generally conceived in filial terms—the later poet being the heir or descendant of the earlier one—parricide is another way in which the play engages the question of imaginative priority. — I am not just talking about Gonzalo's murder. Besides the two triangular conflicts that structure the plot of part 1 (Juan-Ana-Luis; Juan-Inés-Gonzalo), an additional triangle also figures largely in the play. This triangle is formed by the conflict between Diego and Juan, father and son. What distinguishes this triangle from the others, however, is that one vertex seems to be missing. Although Diego and Juan are obviously at odds, their antagonism does not intersect in another character. Luis tries to protect Ana and Gonzalo tries to protect Inés, but whose interests is Diego trying to safeguard? The three triangles are congruent in that they have a common element, Don Juan; but where is the missing vertex that would make the correspondence exact? The answer, I believe, is that the object of the father and son's competition, a competition that results in the father's figurative murder, is the play itself.

I mean this in two complementary senses. First, since the conflict arises from Juan's involvement in the wager, and since the wager, as we have seen, forms the nucleus of the play, Diego's intervention in act 1 aims at truncating the action. He endeavors, in a manner of speaking, to take the play away from his son. Because the whole plot flows from the wager, by attempting to dissuade his son from participating Diego acts, in effect, to arrest the play and stop the circulation of the letter. Juan's defiance, on the contrary, signals that he intends to let letter and play unfold. To his father's authority Juan opposes his own authoring fiat. His repudiation of paternal authority, in Diego's eyes, amounts to murder:

Don Juan, en brazos del vicio
desolado te abandono:
me matas . . . , mas te perdono
de Dios en el santo juicio. (1.1.12)[12]

(Don Juan, I leave you desolate in the arms of vice: you are killing me . . . but I'll forgive you in God's holy judgment.)

Juan murders Don Diego by allowing the play to continue. For this reason the father-son confrontation, in a second, allegorical sense, embodies Zorrilla's own killer instincts toward his precursors. The issue remains control of the play. Will *Don Juan Tenorio* be Zorrilla's own play, an "original" work that will bear its author's stamp as surely as the events in part 1 bear Juan's? Or will it amount to little more than a pallid imitation of its models? Will Zorrilla, in a literary sense, turn out to be his father's son or will he strike out in unfamiliar directions? Because it addresses the question of originality and epigonism in its fundamental, artistic dimension, the triangle formed by Don Juan, Don Diego, and the wager subsumes the other two. The point is not that the third triangle is incomplete but simply that the missing vertex is, rather than another character, the text that we read or the performance that we witness.

The contrast between the letter and the lists, on one hand, and the pantheon on the other, underscores the artistic dimension of the father-son duel. As I have already mentioned, the lists and the pantheon are comparable: one contains the names, the other the remains of Juan's victims. The letter and the pantheon are also comparable: just as the letter slips out of the book of hours, Gonzalo's statue slips out of the pantheon, and if the letter penetrates the walls of the convent, the statue penetrates the walls of Juan's dining room. Ironically, the father's statue "imitates" the son's letter, with the crucial difference that Gonzalo's effigy travels not to abduct a novice but to punish her seducer. If the letter confounds and "fascinates" Inés, the statue's visit has a similar effect on Juan, who echoes Inés's description of the letter when he remarks that the statue "filters" through the wall (2.2.1). The statue's displacement seems undertaken as a reply or antidote to the letter's noxious circulation.

More generally, the pantheon itself constitutes a sort of anti-wager or counter-act with which Diego, its "founder" (2.1.1), upstages his son's performance. The letter and the lists are the documents embedded in the first part; the corresponding *mise en abîme* in the second part is the pantheon, which is also an embedded creation, but one which excludes all of the playful elements of the wager. As the Sculptor's protestations make evident, the pantheon is all work and no play. Unlike Juan's texts, which spread carnival disorder, the statues are monuments to moderation. Diego counters his son's authoring impulse by founding a memorial that will embody the opposite qualities of his son's texts. The contrasts between the father's and the son's creations are unmistakable. The pantheon is an undertaking of "giant proportions" (2.1.1), while the letter, usually referred to in the diminutive as *un papelito,* is small enough to fit inside a prayer book. The pantheon is for public viewing; the letter for Inés's eyes only. The letter unfolds; it is an "open" work, susceptible to many readings. The pantheon, on the contrary, is enclosed by a fence in order to prevent "profanation." The letter is ephemeral, fugitive, composed in a rush and designed for a special occasion; but the marmoreal statues, as the Sculptor points out, will endure forever. For this reason one would not think of calling Juan a "founder." Founding is for fathers. As a disinherited and childless son, as an offshoot truncated from the family tree, Juan creates an art that reflects his own rootlessness. Thus he chooses the temporal medium of writing and composes letters and lists—liminal, fragmentary genres that have neither the prestige nor the imposing presence of sculpture. Diego, by contrast, erects abiding icons. The pantheon is an enduring center of attention; the letter, a fleeting and fleeing margin. In its artistic dimension, the struggle between Juan and Diego boils down to the contrast between paper and stone: between a son who writes and a father who founds.

Therefore, when Ciutti states in the opening scene that Juan "writes to his father," he is naming the real target of Juan's texts.

Even when he addresses Inés, Juan is writing to his father. In order to understand the importance of imitation in the play, one must juxtapose two sets of four words: *Escribe a su padre* and *Os imité.* *¿Y qué?* The ultimate goal of imitative action is to usurp the father's place, and this is done by writing liminal letters that metaleptically invert temporal and genealogical succession.

This consideration of imitation will not be complete, however, until an additional four words are accounted for. I refer again to "Cuatro palabras sobre mi *Don Juan Tenorio,*" where the creator castigates the creation for what he sees as the flaws and inconsistencies in its construction. From the title on (note the appropriating, possessive *mi,* which recurs several times in the piece), this confessional document helps elucidate Zorrilla's complicated feelings toward the Don Juan theme. I have argued that Zorrilla saw himself as a real-life Don Juan combating his literary rivals and precursors. But this is only part 1 of the story. In part 2 we will find Zorrilla, strangely, redirecting his aggression toward his own play. When we look now at *Don Juan* as an allegory of authorship, the drama will remain the same but the actors will have exchanged roles. Although I have already cited Zorrilla's crucial declaration of murderous intent, let me quote another similar statement: "The new Don Juan will not kill the old one during my lifetime: posterity will be the one to kill him, if it doesn't kill them both, which is what is most likely, since posterity will not care for fantastic miracles."[13]

Since Zorrilla, because of the absence of copyright laws, never made much money from his best-known work, the hostility that underlies this statement is not difficult to explain. As he mentioned on one occasion, even though *Don Juan Tenorio* paid the bills for many a theater company, it yielded its author not one cent. As the years went by and the *Tenorio* grew increasingly popular, the author's disaffection only increased. This precipitated the interesting switch in sympathies to which the above quotation attests: Zorrilla no longer saw himself as the rebellious son but as the offended father, no longer as Juan but as Diego or Gonzalo. Because the play had taken on a life of its own, in which the author seemingly had no part, Zorrilla came to look upon himself as a father whose place had been usurped by an upstart son. Whatever fame the author had he owed to his creation; the chip had grown larger than the block. A strange metalepsis had turned the author into the epigone of his own work.

→ Much like Don Diego, Zorrilla developed two ways of dealing with his unruly offspring. One was simply to berate it, as Diego does when he interrupts the wager. The other was to undertake a revision of the play hoping that the "new" *Don Juan* (whose title, significantly, would echo those of Tirso's and Zamora's plays) would supersede the old one.[14] Again the model is Diego, whose pantheon rewrites (but not in words) Juan's letter. The author himself would become another guest of stone.

Zorrilla's first way of coping with the play's fame is illustrated in his many deprecatory statements, and especially in *Don Juan Tenorio ante la conciencia de su autor,* a projected book-length critique that Zorrilla mentions in correspondence with Delgado and in "Cuatro palabras," where he discloses his plans for publication:

> From what has been said it will be easily understood that a work that had been so badly thought out could not turn out well; but this is not the place to speak of this, because I plan to explain it all in a book entitled *Don Juan ante la conciencia de su autor,* to appear at the end of October so that the public, when it sees the play in November as usual, will have my opinions in mind.[15]

The fascinating thing about this passage is that it displays the same sort of metaleptic thinking that pervades the play. Although the critique will have been written and published many years after the play was composed, it is supposed to be read *before* one goes to see the yearly performance. As in the play, Zorrilla is still tampering with temporal sequence, trying to reverse the order of past and present. By having the book published in October, furthermore, he will be securing that "month of anticipation" that so obsesses Juan de Alarcón. Like Don Juan's letter, the critique will be an effect that precedes its cause.[16]

The title of the projected critique differs from that of the play only in that it alludes to the work's authorship, precisely the element that Zorrilla felt had been forgotten by the public. Since no one knows a son like his own father, the critique, by demonstrating Zorrilla's authority over his own creation (an authority that allowed him a special insight into the work's flaws) was written to restore the author to his proper place. The play goes before its author, then, like a truant before a judge or like an errant child before a censorious parent. In a fragment from the book found among Zorrilla's papers, the paternal metaphor is developed at length:

I don't say these things because I detest or scorn my Don Juan. No, I love him: he is my son, or rather, my miscarriage [*mi aborto*], since even I recognize in him so many large defects; he's a monster, yes, but he is the offspring of my worthless wit, and even with all of his handicaps, his deformities, his monstrosities, he has fought for thirty years for the reputation of his absent father, and, petulant, insolent, he still speaks Castilian and finds no rival to confront him and no woman to insult him.—For thirty years he has kept me alive in my country, bragging to my countrymen every All Souls' Day—Here's Don Juan Tenorio and there's no one like him.—My poor son! You must find your match: you cannot, you should not be eternal: someone has to take your measure, at last, and it's your misfortune that it has to be your own father.—I engendered you: you are my son and not Don Diego's. Come, then, and humble yourself before your father's verdict.[17]

The obvious rhetorical ploy of this fragment is to confound literary and biological paternity. Although Zorrilla begins by talking about Don Juan the play, he soon finds himself describing Don Juan the character. This not only puts him in Diego's shoes but leads him to describe the play in much the same teratological terms that Diego uses to describe his son: both are monsters, both are aborted fetuses. In addition, Zorrilla will require of his offspring the same kind of absolute submission that Diego tried but failed to extract from Juan.

Not enough has been made, in my view, of the way in which texts like this fragment or like "Cuatro palabras" enrich our understanding of *Don Juan Tenorio*, for in their light the play's simplifications, its "manichean antitheses,"[18] its blatant opposition of father to son and rival to rival, acquire an unsuspected resonance. If the play is inserted into the thick skein formed by its author's explanations, palinodes, and rewritings, many of its apparent dry spots become fertile ground for interpretation. *Don Juan Tenorio* can be approached from within, as in chapter 1, or it can be approached as one of the knots in a rich textual tangle that expresses Zorrilla's relationship with his play, a relationship that is no less dramatic or eventful than the work itself. In the passage just quoted, for example, mythological parallels hover just beneath the surface: while the father leaves his homeland and goes wandering, the son remains behind to defend his father's honor ("he has fought for thirty years for the reputation of his absent father"). In the drama of Zorrilla's literary career, *Don Juan* plays Telemachus to his creator's Odysseus. But this dimension of *Don Juan* will not come into view unless we look at Zorrilla's commentaries as something other than innocent, disinterested, authoritative criticisms.

Like *Don Juan ante la conciencia de su autor,* the new *Don Juan* that Zorrilla had promised to his publisher never got written. The closest Zorrilla came to this rewriting was the libretto for a *zarzuela* based on the "original" play, though he claimed that this was only a "correction" and not the full-scale revision that he had envisioned.[19] As was perhaps to be expected, the musical *Don Juan* is no match for the dramatic one. Although most of the "defects" remain, many of the memorable scenes and verses have been excised. In effect, the original has been eviscerated, and what remains is of interest only as another act in Zorrilla's autobiographical drama.

Two of the changes in the *zarzuela* are especially pertinent. The first is that the wager between Juan and Luis has been deleted. Instead of meeting in the tavern the two rivals now meet in Juan's house, and their rivalry now results from the fact that, during Juan's absence from Seville, Luis has taken his place as the foremost rogue in the city. This change is significant because it reflects the author's own dilemma. By eliminating the wager Zorrilla has extirpated the original's generative core; he has, in fact, "killed" the 1844 version and put in its place an excuse for Juan and Luis's confrontation that mirrors Zorrilla's biography. Juan explains:

El primogénito soy,
y en mi familia es notorio
que éste es el primer Tenorio:

yo cuentas a nadie doy.
Mientras anduve en destierro,
sobre mí la primacía
pretendió tomar Mejía,
y hoy le haré ver que fue yerro.[20]
(I am the first-born, and in my family this fact is well-known: I don't
account to anyone. While I was in exile, Mejía tried to take my place,
and now I will show him his mistake.)

Like Don Juan, Zorrilla came home from exile to find that the
Tenorio had achieved primacy over its author. As he acknowledges in the fragment from *Don Juan ante la conciencia de su
autor,* he saw the play much as Juan sees Luis—as a rival. But
since the author by rights should take precedence over the creation (*he* is the first-born, after all), it was necessary to cut the
usurper down to size by creating a new version that would supersede the original one. In a note to the libretto Zorrilla puts the
matter succinctly: the intent, he says, was to create "a *Don Juan
against Don Juan;* me, against myself [*yo, contra mí mismo*]."[21]
    In its own way, then, the *zarzuela* is just as recursive a construct
as the play, since Zorrilla's changes incorporate the reasons why
the revision was undertaken in the first place. In fact, Juan and
Luis seem perfectly aware that they are actors resurrecting old
roles. When Luis proposes that they recount their exploits, Juan
replies that by so doing they would be making fools of themselves.
Once upon a time such ostentation was appropriate, but no longer,

Porque lo que en cierta fecha,
y en época de capricho,
fuera cuenta muy bien hecha,
hoy la cuenta es más estrecha,
y es mal hecho y es mal dicho.
Porque nuestros dos relatos
son dos tejidos de absurdos
que nos dan por mentecatos,
asombro de pelagatos
y admiración de palurdos.
Y siendo mozos capaces
de hazañas de loa eterna,

¿por qué parecer, procaces,
dos rufianes lenguaraces
barateros de taberna?²²

(Because what might have been well done and well said at a certain
date and in an epoch of caprice, is so no longer. Because our two tales
are a web of absurdities that make us the idols of fools. And since we
are both young men capable of immortal feats, why should we act like
insolent, tavern-going loudmouths?)

Juan's self-criticism echoes Zorrilla's. The references to a "certain
date" and an "epoch of caprice" seem to allude to the author's
youth. The statement that "hoy la cuenta es más estrecha" refutes
Buttarelli's "Hoy no entra en la cuenta" (1.1.1). And in mentioning the tavern Juan singles out one of the key elements that has
been left out of the revision. Juan's reasoning throughout presupposes acquaintance with the earlier work, a familiarity that the
zarzuela's audience certainly had. The whole passage is a commentary on—one could also say, an "intertextual dialogue" with—
the earlier work, which at a distance of thirty years appears "mal
hecho y mal dicho."

The other noteworthy change in the zarzuela is the addition to
the cast of characters of a chorus of students and a gypsy singer
named Jacarilla. The festive atmosphere that in the *Tenorio* sub-
sisted just offstage is here fleshed out in these characters, who
come on stage singing and playing instruments. What is interesting about this addition is that it actually represents a borrowing
from an earlier Don Juan play, Zamora's *No hay plazo que no se
cumpla,* which begins also with a *tuna* and where a gypsy named
Pispireta sings a "jacarandaina."²³ Although in the *Tenorio* the
chorus of students blends into the general merriment and the
gypsy disappears altogether, the zarzuela resurrects them, as if to
compensate for the anteriority of the *Tenorio* with a more faithful
adherence to its sources. The procedure once more involves a metaleptic ruse, by means of which the revision attempts to situate itself before its original.²⁴ But this additional metalepsis reveals at
what cost priority over oneself is purchased, since Zorrilla can
efface the *Tenorio* only by, on the one hand, eviscerating it, and
on the other, supplementing it with borrowed characters. The
irony is that, as a result, the zarzuela is a far more derivative cre-

ation than the play. When in the *zarzuela* Juan states, "I will have no rivals, / I will be second to none,"[25] his wish is so unrealistic as to appear almost comic. The character who speaks this, after all, knows that he is a copy of a copy, an imitation of the Don Juan of the play who is himself patterned after earlier Don Juans. For such a derivative creation even a secondary status would be quite an achievement.

We are left, finally, with the melancholy paradox that *Don Juan Tenorio,* the same play that had seemed so beset by belatedness, by what might be termed genealogical marginality, eventually became for its author the precursor to be overcome. As Zorrilla himself realized, this role reversal locked him in a dilemma, for he could not wage war on this kind of marginality without fighting himself. It is one thing to kill Tirso or Zamora and quite another to murder one's younger self. When one begets his own father, parricide becomes a suicidal art.

3

Circulation

Like *Don Juan Tenorio, Las galas del difunto* also begins with a
letter. Valle-Inclán's playful imitation of Zorrilla's imitative play
begins, thus, by transcribing one of the "central" motifs in its
model. To be sure, there are important differences between the
romantic melodrama and the modern *esperpento*. Here the writing takes place in a brothel; the writer is a prostitute; and the letter
consists of a request for money addressed to her father. Nonetheless, La Daifa's missive retains several of its model's characteristics.
Much like *Don Juan*, Valle's *esperpento* opens with the writer sit-
ting at a table sealing the envelope. After she has finished she
hands the letter to a witch, who takes it to Sócrates Galindo's drugstore. Since Galindo is not there, the witch leaves the letter with
his assistant, but when Galindo arrives he wants no part of the
document and throws it into the gutter, where it is picked up by
Juanito Ventolera. Galindo then reclaims it; and when he drops
dead from a heart attack, the letter, buried in a coat pocket, goes
with him to the grave. It does not remain there for long, however,
for when Juanito steals the dead man's clothes he finds the letter,
ironically, while rummaging through the pockets looking for
money. In the last scene the letter finally returns to its point of
origin, since the *esperpento* concludes in the brothel with a reading
of La Daifa's request.

Like Don Juan's, La Daifa's letter thus travels in a circular route.
In addition, its itinerary is also a complicated and unpredictable
one: the document passes through the hands of a prostitute, an old
hag, a pharmacist's apprentice, a pharmacist, and a broken-down

soldier. It is thrown into the gutter and comes back from the dead. It comes back from the dead twice, in fact, since Juanito not only retrieves it from the grave but also saves it from the gutter. Given the vicissitudes of the journey, it is remarkable that the letter goes unread until the end of the play, and even more remarkable, perhaps, that the mere sight of it is enough to send Galindo to the grave. By delaying the reading, Valle-Inclán has made the letter coextensive with the play, which transpires entirely between writing and reading. In the *Tenorio,* we recall, the reading of the letter was also deferred, although this delay did not extend beyond the beginning of the third act. In *Las galas* the action lasts only as long as the document remains in circulation, even though this entails an inversion of the sequence of events in Valle's model. Since the reading of the letter may be patterned after the equivalent scene in Zorrilla, one would expect it to take place before the death of the Comendador character, the pharmacist; and yet the opposite is the case. In fact, the relation of cause and effect has been reversed, since it is the death of the father that provokes the reading and not the other way around, as in the *Tenorio.*

La Daifa's letter also resembles Juan's in that it raises the question of paternity, though here too Valle has recast his model. Since in a figurative sense Juan's text is indeed addressed to Don Diego, Ciutti's assertion that Juan writes to his father is not simply a white lie for Buttarelli's consumption. In *Las galas* the father's involvement is literal, for La Daifa actually writes to her father. Note how Valle has tampered with the motif of the letter: in *Don Juan Tenorio* it is written by Juan, intended for Inés, and intercepted by her father; in *Las galas* it is intended for the father, written by the Inés character, and intercepted by Juanito.[1] Valle's "literalization" of the father's role is a significant alteration. It can be regarded, on the one hand, as an interpretation of Zorrilla's plot, an interpretation that condenses my argument of the last chapter. By making Galindo the letter's destinatary, Valle restores Gonzalo and Diego to the place that properly belongs to them; Valle is, in a sense, making amends to Zorrilla's fathers for their literal omission. On the other hand, however, the literalization of the father draws attention to *Las galas*'s own filiation with its parent text— even if such attention is attracted by a deviation from the model. Like any parody, *Las galas* is a letter addressed to the father, a poisoned letter. Parody and parricide are cognate acts insofar as both share the same murderous intent. Like Don Juan, the parodist strives to usurp the father's place; and just like Don Juan, he achieves his end (that is, the father's end) by means of imitative behavior. No wonder then that Galindo drops dead from simply looking at the envelope. His collapse acts out the parodist's governing ambition.

The letter's significance goes beyond this, however. Once Juanito has finished reading it, one of the "girls" in the brothel remarks on the persuasiveness of La Daifa's plea, to which another of the prostitutes replies, "She took it out of the Manual!" [*¡La sacó del Manual!*] (p. 61).[2] This statement can be variously construed. Although the prostitute apparently means that La Daifa has been copying from a letter-writing manual, given the content of Valle's play the "manual" is simply the Don Juan legend, of which this *esperpento* represents one more incarnation. In a more specific sense, the manual is Zorrilla's text, from which not only the letter but the *esperpento* as a whole has been "taken out." The prostitute's encomium amounts to a revelation of origins, of paternity. Moreover, her words may themselves be patterned after an incident in the parent text, since Juan's letter, in a different sense of *sacar*, is also "taken out" of a manual of sorts, the book of hours. And what are we to make of the fact that this statement consists of *four* words? The coincidence is charged with meaning, especially since one of the sets of four words in the *Tenorio* also dealt with copying, "¡La sacó del Manual!" is *Las galas*'s rendition of Don Juan's insolent confession, "Os imité. ¿Y qué?" In the same way that Juan's four words describe the relationship between Zorrilla's *Don Juan* and earlier versions of the legend, the prostitute's describe the relationship between *Las galas del difunto* and Zorrilla's play.

What I find especially revealing is that Valle's paraphrase of Juan's words should be put in the mouth of a prostitute, for this shows that the connection between model and copy is disharmonious and asymmetrical. In the passage from one text to the other the features of the original have been submitted to a many-faceted process of mutilation, displacement, amplification, diminution. One character in *Las galas* will emulate—sometimes simultaneously—several characters in the original. Likewise, one scene in

Las galas will meld elements from disparate scenes in *Don Juan;* or conversely, one incident in Zorrilla will be refracted into several scenes in *Las galas.* Thus, when the unnamed prostitute speaks her four words she is miming both Inés (in the act of taking the letter out of the *horario*) and Don Juan; and Juanito's participation in this scene has points of contact both with the episode in *Don Juan* where the letter is read by Inés (in *Las galas* Juanito, momentarily playing Inés, reads it himself), and with the one where Inés is abducted (Juanito says that he has come to the brothel "to steal a girl").

Another look at the *Tenorio* will help us find a vocabulary with which to conceptualize Valle's eclectic copying. Part 2 of *Don Juan* contains two incidents that illustrate contrary conceptions of imitation. The first conception is embodied in the Sculptor's pantheon, whose statues are faithful, lifelike representations of their models; as Don Juan says,

Piezas son todas muy parecidas,
y a conciencia trabajadas. (2.1.2)

(These pieces all closely resemble their models, and they have been carefully fashioned.)

I will label this kind of imitation, after its practitioner, sculptural mimesis. Works of sculptural mimesis aim to identify as completely as possible with their models. At the limit, the original and the copy would be indistinguishable. Hence, the Sculptor employs an anthropomorphic vocabulary when addressing his creations (the apostrophe itself endows the statues with human qualities): his achievement has been to "animate" stone, to give it "being" and "form" (2.1.2). Since the Sculptor aspires to fashion living effigies, copies animated by the life and soul of the originals, he would have been pleased by the denouement of the play. The coming to life of the statues of Gonzalo and Inés furnishes living proof of his artistry, since it shows that he has indeed succeeded in "animating" lifeless stone. The improbable events of the play's conclusion reenact the old story of a statue so perfect that it obliterates the boundary between art and life. In this respect the last scenes in *Don Juan* express an aesthetic, rather than a religious, allegory. Every practitioner of sculptural mimesis, the Sculptor foremost among them, is a Pygmalion figure.

The banquet at the cemetery illustrates the second variety of imitation. The stage directions for this scene read, in part:

Don Juan knocks on the tomb of the Comendador. The tomb is transformed [*se cambia*] into a table that is a horrible parody [*que parodia horriblemente*] of the table at which Don Juan, Centellas, and Avellaneda had eaten in the previous act. Instead of [*en vez de*] the garlands that draped the tablecloths, of the flowers and luxurious place settings, snakes, bones and fire, etc. (2.3.2)

I have put in brackets the key words in this passage, and would now like to gloss them briefly. *Se cambia:* Festive mimesis (in honor of the macabre feast, this will be my term for this kind of imitation) differs from sculptural mimesis in that it changes or transforms the original. Verisimilitude is no longer a desideratum; in fact, the goal here is to alter the original as much as possible without, however, losing touch with it. The practitioner of festive mimesis must therefore achieve an even balance between reproduction and revision, for no matter how "horrible" the transformation, the original must remain *recognizable* in the copy. *En vez de:* Festive mimesis involves the artist in a complicated game of substitutions: snakes for flowers, bones for silverware, fire for food. Again, each of these substitutes must retain a vestigial resemblance to its original: snakes may be multicolored and may hang from trees; bones may be elongated; fire is used to prepare food. But none of these succedanea is, like Inés's statue, a "portrait" (2.1.2). Instead of portraits we have metaphors and metonymies, figures tied to their referents by the slenderest of threads. *Que parodia horriblemente:* since every parody disfigures its model, it is horrible. The phrase, consequently, is something of a pleonasm, but it serves to highlight an additional feature of festive imitations: because the connection with the model may be tenuous, a work of festive mimesis always tends, in varying degrees, toward self-consciousness; that is, such a work needs to identify itself, to tell us, as in this case, that what we are viewing or reading is a "horrible parody." It is not enough to depict a table full of snakes and bones and fire, for the reader or viewer may not connect these items with Don Juan's dinner table; there must also be some explicit "deictics" that point to the model (the *spectator* of the play, who does not have the stage directions before him, is therefore at a disadvantage when it comes to interpreting the banquet scene: he might mistake the copy for an original). A work of festive mimesis will reveal itself as an imitation. In order to compensate for its distance from the original, it will brand itself, expose its sources, give the reader or viewer guidelines for interpretation. Festive mimesis thus involves a three-part process of transformation (*se cambia*), substitution (*en vez de*), and identification (*que parodia horriblemente*). The original is changed; its features are replaced; and its status as model is revealed. This process might be seen as a two-way polar movement, as the festive text at once alienates and approaches its sources. As we will discover, this double movement provides a suitable conceptual framework in which to understand *Las galas's* alteration of *Don Juan Tenorio*. The *esperpento* emerges from the transformation, substitution, and identification of selected features of Zorrilla's play. This hypothesis, moreover, is less harmless than it sounds, for we will also discover that an examination of the operation of festive mimesis in Valle's play leads to a modification in the way we usually think of the *esperpento*. I will be arguing that, following the lead of Valle himself, interpreters of his work discuss the *esperpentos* with a language that betrays a "sculptural" bias, and that this language is insufficient to grasp how a text like *Las galas* comes into being.

— That *Las galas* imitates *Don Juan* self-consciously is easy enough to demonstrate. The prostitute's four words furnish a first clue; there are others. At three different points Zorrilla's play is explicitly invoked. Appropriately all three references have to do with Juanito's profanation of Galindo's grave, since this is the incident in the *esperpento* that most clearly recalls *Don Juan Tenorio*. The first two references occur in the cemetery scene. When Maluenda invites Juanito to dinner, he replies: "It seems that you are staging the Juan Tenorio. But there the dead dine for nothing" (p. 29). Moments later, when Juanito confesses that he intends to steal Galindo's Sunday suit, Maluenda says, "Not even Juan Tenorio was so foolhardy" (p. 30). The third reference, which occurs in the following scene, is prompted by Juanito's entrance into the inn wearing Galindo's suit. Echoing Maluenda, Ricote states: "Not even the renowned Juan Tenorio!" [*¡Ni el tan mentado Juan Tenorio!*] (p. 39). These allusions, of course, have been noted before.[3] What has not been noted is that in all three instances the characters assert *Las galas*'s independence from its model. Every time the *Tenorio* is invoked, the mention serves to point out some of the ways in which the copy diverges from the original. In two of the examples Maluenda and Ricote say that Juanito's foolhardiness surpasses even Don Juan's; in the other example, Juanito mentions the difference between the dinner scenes in each play. The *esperpento*'s act of naming, its *mentar,* embodies that double movement of attraction and repulsion typical of festive imitations. The *Tenorio* is simultaneously invoked and rejected. When Ricote states, "¡Ni el tan mentado Juan Tenorio!", his use of *mentar* evokes the dual meaning that the verb has in common speech; *mentar* is to name but also, by naming, to scorn or contemn. The repeated invocation of *Don Juan Tenorio* is *Las galas*'s way of *mentar el padre,* in the double sense of the expression.

The *esperpento* contains an additional act of naming that, while less explicit than the previous ones, is no less important. I refer to the title, which also alludes to the profanation incident. "The clothes of the deceased" carries a double referent. It refers, first of all, to the desecration of Galindo's grave; but it can be taken also as a reference to the despoiling of Zorrilla's text. The *difunto* of the title is Galindo, the Comendador character, the father figure; but it is also the parent text, the scriptive forebear. One might say, in fact, that when Juanito dons the dead man's finery he becomes an ambulatory emblem of Valle's transformations, for a parodic text behaves much like Juanito: it borrows the clothing, the external features of its model, while fitting them to an entirely different physique. Furthermore, Juanito not only steals Galindo's suit, he also lives off him as an unwelcome guest. Again the allegory is easy: a parodic text is also an unwelcome guest that sponges off its predecessor. The confusion that overcomes Galindo's wife when Juanito appears (wearing her husband's clothes) may then be compared to the reader's puzzlement before a text like this one: is *Las galas* an old story or a new one? How does one explain the sensation of *déjà vu* (or *déjà lu*) that it induces? Is Juanito Don Juan? Are *Las galas del difunto* and *Don Juan Tenorio* "the same"?

A familiar paradox gives the answer to these questions: if one concedes that the deceased of the title is Zorrilla's play, one must also concede that *Don Juan Tenorio* is alive and well (or medium-well, like the snakes at the banquet) inasmuch as Valle's naming keeps resurrecting it. As every reader of *Don Quijote* knows, a parody pays for the father's death with the father's life. For the travestied forebear, parody bestows a life in death, a half-afterlife, a kind of straw-man existence reminiscent of the puppets to which the *esperpento*'s personages are often likened. Once more attraction and repulsion, derivativeness and independence coincide in a simultaneous double movement. In order to affirm the differences between *Las galas* and *Don Juan,* one must grant their resemblance. As Ricote puts it, "One thing is clear: the dead cannot be killed" (p. 36).

This statement is made in a conversation that takes place just before Juanito arrives at the inn. To Maside's guess that Juanito has been surrounded by dead souls who—since they cannot be killed—are liable to fight with him all night, Maluenda replies by expressing his skepticism about such occurrences. Maside insists, nevertheless, that the dead behave just like the living—"There's correspondence" [*Hay correspondencia*] (p. 36). Like Juanito, I may be going too far, but I regard this exchange as a continuation of the play's implicit discussion of parody. Because of the symbolism of Valle's title, when Maside speaks of the "correspondence" between this world and the next I take his words as a statement about the correspondences between past and present texts, between, say, *Don Juan Tenorio* and *Las galas del difunto.* These are correspondences that depend, in part, on another sort of "correspondence"—Don Juan's letter to Inés, La Daifa's letter to her father. In this otherworldly light, the disagreement between Maside and Ricote on one side, and Maluenda on the other, turns on whether it is possible for texts to impinge on one another. Maluenda, who is cross-eyed, does not believe in ghosts: he is a formalist, a champion of "intrinsic" criticism, a defender of *la obra en sí.* For him there exist no other texts behind, beneath, or within the text. Life ends with the colophon. Although Maside is not cross-eyed, he is the one who sees double, for he asserts not only that Juanito is struggling with the dead but that the worlds of the living and the dead make a perfect match—"They dance together" [*bailan en pareja*], as Maluenda jokes (p. 36).[4] Maside is the anti-formalist critic, the one who believes in textual séances, in intertextuality, the precursor of Kristeva or Derrida. For Maside reality is double, with every text having its companion or dancing partner. And in this instance at least, the polemic is decided in his favor when Juanito, a walking intertext, comes into the room dressed in Galindo's suit.

This self-conscious dimension of *Las galas* has a precedent in *Don Juan Tenorio,* and not only because Zorrilla's play also includes recursive elements or because I have developed the notion of festive mimesis from an incident in part 2. I mean rather that *Don Juan Tenorio* enacts some of the fundamental gestures of the parodist's art. Since the play deals with profanation, mockery, transgression, murder, Valle-Inclán's parodying is foreshadowed in the parodied text. His *burla* is a trick borrowed from Don Juan, the original *burlador.* Parody normally acts against solemnity or seriousness, but when the object of ridicule is itself brimming with *burlas,* the procedure becomes richly resonant and the contending works acquire an unusual closeness. *Las galas* does not achieve the customary aesthetic distance from its model because those very mechanisms of distancing only send the reader back to *Don Juan,* where they are already contained. One cannot label (or refuse to label) this *esperpento* a parody without first realizing the special intimacy that binds the two works, an intimacy in which every act of aggression of one against the other only cements their kinship. Just as Zorrilla could not "kill" his *Don Juan* without committing suicide, Valle cannot repudiate Zorrilla's play without drawing ever closer to it. In both of these instances the earlier and later texts stick to each other, and it becomes an impossible task to pry them apart. In this respect also *Las galas del difunto* and *Don Juan Tenorio* "bailan en pareja." (Later in this book we will find the definitive image for this adhesiveness—magma. For now, suffice it to remark, first, that "limen" goes back to an Indo-European root that generates several words having to do with stickiness: slime, loam, and the archaic "liming," "gluing or cementing together"; and second, that according to Alberto Lista in the passage that I have used as an epigraph for part 1 of this book, Zorrilla's play keeps us "stuck" to the mud of the earth [*pegados al fango de la tierra*].)

It may seem odd that I speak of a special intimacy between works that are so obviously different. Indeed, more than one critic has argued that the resemblances are minor and should not be unduly stressed. According to Rodolfo Cardona and Anthony Za-hareas, by studying this *esperpento* with one eye on *Don Juan* we "distort" and "falsify" the author's intention.[5] And Joaquín Casalduero maintains that without the overt allusions "no one would think of the *Tenorio*"; thus, "there is no parody."[6] The peculiar thing about these opinions, which hark back to the Maluenda school of literary studies, is that they point to another area in which Zorrilla has anticipated Valle-Inclán. As Casalduero's reasoning shows, the central issue is recognition, how one work is perceived as an extension or copy of another. The first recursive twist appears once *we* recognize that both the *Tenorio* and *Las galas* contain numerous recognition scenes; that is, both dramatize that decisive moment in which difference is reduced to sameness or foreignness dissolves into familiarity. Luis doffs his mask and Juan discovers his twin, or Diego uncovers himself and Juan discovers his father. All throughout the *Tenorio* recognition scenes proliferate: between Juan and Luis (several times), between Juan and Ana, between Juan and Gonzalo, between Juan and Diego, between Juan and Inés. The visit to the pantheon at the beginning of part 2 consists of a succession of recognitions: first Juan notices his father's statue, then Mejía's, then Gonzalo's, then Inés's—a string of anagnorises that recapitulates the principal recognition scenes of part 1. If only because it copies *Don Juan,* Valle's play also contains such scenes, the prominent ones being Juanito/Galindo's recognition by Ricote and company, by Doña Terita, and by La Daifa.

The second recursive twist appears when we ponder the usage of the word *conocer* in each text. In the *Tenorio conocer* is used in the sense of "to recognize," most notably in Diego's anathema to his son, "I don't know you, Don Juan" [*no te conozco, don Juan*] (1.1.12). In *Las galas,* however, the word refers to carnal knowledge. When La Daifa sidesteps Juanito's advances by saying, "Wait until we know each other better," he rejoins, "And when is that knowledge going to be?" [*¿Y cuándo va a ser ese conocimiento?*] (p. 21). She answers that on Monday afternoon. Thus, Valle-Inclán goes one up on Zorrilla by burlesquing the usage in *Don Juan,* with the result that Juanito's pun becomes still another recognition scene, still another way in which the copy re-cognizes, that is, recalls and recoils from the original.

The question then: how is travesty travestied? how does a mocking play mock a play about mockery? The initial episode in the *esperpento* will serve to illustrate. The work opens with as odd a transformation as one can imagine: La Daifa, who will subsequently play Ana and Inés, first appears in the place of Don Juan, like him composing a passionate letter. Valle begins in characteristic fashion by "prostituting" his original. La Daifa does not remain Juan for long, however, for as soon as Juanito shows up she slips into the part of Ana. Like Ana, she has a fiancé, Aureliano Rodríguez, who Juanito claims died in Cuba; and like Ana, she is "stolen" from her intended. Later in the play she will also play Inés's role, and it is with this mask that we last see her, as her fainting spell during the reading of the letter recalls Inés's. But these are not La Daifa's only disguises. Her name and profession take us back to another *Don Juan,* Zamora's, where Pispireta the gypsy is identified with the same rubric: "Caballeros, y la daifa, / Para que haya la chillona / Eche la jacarandaina."[7] It is interesting that these lines are apparently the inspiration for characters both in Zorrilla's *zarzuela* and in Valle's *esperpento,* two wildly different rewritings that share, nonetheless, the same revisionary animus. Even though Valle's borrowing from Zamora, to my knowledge, has not been noticed before, it is important, for it contraposes Zamora's and Zorrilla's plays. Although La Daifa is frequently mentioned as a prime example of the liberties Valle-Inclán has taken with his original, her presence in the *esperpento* is not a departure from the Don Juan legend but a retrieval of more primitive sources. It is as if Valle-Inclán had superimposed *No hay plazo que no se cumpla* and *Don Juan Tenorio* and instead of matching Inés and Ana with their counterparts in Zamora—Beatriz de Fresneda and Ana de Ulloa—he had mismatched them with Pispireta, also one of Juan's paramours, but the wrong one. The deformation of *Don Juan Tenorio* does not then result from willful distortion; it results rather from a kind of error in perspective or failure of matching parts. Valle's departure from one model testifies to his adherence to an older one. Acting as a filter or membrane through which Zorrilla's and Zamora's creations communicate and clash, *Las galas* situates itself between those two works in its representation of Don Juan's love interests. Not distortion but mediation, not errancy but eccentric faithfulness to tradition. Recalling van Gennep's vocabulary, one might say that *Las galas* marks a transitional or liminal stage between one work and the other.

The other character who appears at the beginning of the *esperpento* is an old hag. Since her task is to transport the letter, she takes Ciutti's place, though Juan's servant is not her only persona. She also acts the parts of Brígida and Lucía, the go-betweens in *Don Juan* (the witch is later labelled "la trotaconventos" [p. 24]). This character, in fact, offers a striking illustration of the transforming impetus of festive mimesis, for she not only conflates several characters from *Don Juan* but is constantly metamorphosing into a variety of winged creatures—owls, bats, crows: "The witch wrapped the shawl over her head and flew away transformed into a crow" (p. 13); "The voice grew distant. With a black flutter, the owl disappeared around the corner" (p. 25); "Like a bat pinned to the corners of the shawl, she twists into an angle" (p. 27). These transformations are appropriate because they project the characteristics of the letter onto its courier. This winged and metamorphic creature, who folds into her shawl as if it were an envelope and flies off, personifies the spirit of the letter— another odd, fleeting identification, for the character who principally fills that role in Zorrilla is Don Juan. The witch is motion incarnate; her first words (the first spoken words in the play)— "We're off to the end of the world!"—already convey her aptitude for unbridled displacement.

The last participant in the opening episode of the *esperpento* is the letter. As I have already mentioned, La Daifa's letter, like its predecessor, travels in an irregular circular route. If anything, here its journey is even more unpredictable and its effects more lasting than in *Don Juan,* whose part 2 rectifies most of the havoc wrought in part 1. In *Las galas del difunto* nothing undoes the letter's mischief: at the end Galindo remains in his grave, La Daifa has no prospects of leaving the brothel, and Juanito is unrepentant. But what of the letter's other defining feature, its poisonousness? As we saw in the first chapter, Don Juan's letter is a "philter," a "charm," an "amulet" that "fascinates" and "poisons" Inés. In Valle's play these attributes float away from the letter and find other embodiments; that is, in the translation to the *esperpento* the document's occult powers migrate from their original site.

Even though the references to magic, drugs, and the occult persist, they have found other locations. The witch offers a first example of this phenomenon, for she anthropomorphizes the letter's occult connection. As the letter's spirit, she personifies and gathers the *Tenorio*'s scattered allusions. Even so, as Galindo's collapse attests, the letter has not lost its powers; they have merely found a new niche in the witch. The second new location of the letter's magic is the pharmacy, and not just because it dispenses drugs (though this is an important link). The pharmacy itself is a magical place: "The witch, carrying La Daifa's letter, stops her flight in the glare of the magical pupil" (p. 22); "With an angular flutter, the owl has again come to rest in the magical iris that illuminates the sidewalk" (p. 26); "Two shadows on the sidewalk, against the magical light of the necromantic eye" (p. 41). The proximity of the witch seems to elicit the pharmacy's latent charms, for when she approaches the lights that are elsewhere called "globes" (p. 45) turn into magical pupils and necromantic eyes. A similar and similarly surprising relocation emerges when we reflect on Galindo's given name, Sócrates: he is Sócrates because, like his namesake, he succumbs to poison—that of La Daifa's words.[8]

Valle-Inclán has taken the *Tenorio*'s pharmacopoeia and concentrated it in a witch and a drugstore. I find the symbol for this dispersion and reconstitution in another object connected with the pharmacy, a big mortar that is mentioned several times. And I would suggest that if there is an artist figure in this *esperpento,* as there is in others, it is not only La Daifa, who writes, but also Galindo's assistant, who pounds: "A young man, with apron and *alpargatas,* pounds in the mortar" (p. 22); "The boy pounds in the great mortar" (p. 41). This portrait of the artist as a pharmacist's aid is noteworthy because it entails a view of the *esperpento* rather different from that which is commonly held. Students of Valle's aesthetics have often remarked on his mechanical, "dehumanized" deforming techniques. Valle-Inclán himself, presumably speaking through Max Estrella, is cited as the authority for this view, since, as Max states, the *esperpento* emerges from a deformation that is "systematic" and "mathematically perfect."[9] The famous metaphor of the concave mirrors supports this idea, for their curved surface creates a distortion factor, a coefficient of deformation, as it were, that operates uniformly. In other words, the mirror alters everything that comes before it, and it alters it all in the same way. It is nonselective and consistent. The icon of the mortar suggests, on the contrary, that the *esperpento* selects and recombines. The procedure is imaged not as a reflection from concave mirrors but as the manufacture of a new substance. And in light of the associate references to witchcraft and poison, it is no ordinary chemical reaction that takes place inside the mortar: magic instead of math; sorcery instead of system. To the mathematical, specular conception of the *esperpento* one could oppose a magical one. The *esperpento* would then result from an extravagant, inconsistent, improbable aggregation of ingredients rather than from the reflective virtues of the mirrors on the Calle del Gato.

The specular conception, it seems to me, is too lucid, too transparent, too classical in its own way to explain a work like *Las galas del difunto*. I am not surprised that some of the critics who hold this view have difficulty in recognizing this *esperpento* as a sendup of the *Tenorio*. Not even a concave mirror can produce the effects of dissemination and displacement that Valle's play instigates. A concave mirror might explain how Juan becomes Juanito; but it cannot explain how Juanito, in the scene where he breaks into the pharmacy, becomes the Comendador's statue. Neither can it explain how La Daifa conflates nonequivalent characters from two different works. Mirror effects, no matter how concave or convex the surface, fall within the logic of sculptural mimesis, since they still produce a portrait or semblance of the models. The likeness might be poor; the model might appear elongated or misshapen; but the resulting likeness remains a mirror image, a representation.

Las galas cannot be considered a portrait in this sense. Bearing witness to the lack of symmetry and precision, to the utter imperfection of festive mimesis, this work's distortions are unrepresentative and irreflective.[10] Festive mimesis spreads its effects, plants its imitations, in the most unlikely places. It does not simply deform or exaggerate; it splinters, recombines, disseminates. It turns a suitor into a witch and the witch into a letter. It takes the letter and recycles a pharmacy from it. Rather than deformation, the generative principle is metamorphosis, *trans*formation. When Juanito enters the tavern, the stage directions state that he appears "transfigured with the dead man's clothes" (p. 37). Transfigured:

that is, literally having changed form—like the place-settings at the grotesque banquet. Festive mimesis transfigures. *Las galas del difunto* is, in a strict sense, a transfiguration of *Don Juan Tenorio*.[11]

When employing Max Estrella's words in order to devise a theory of the *esperpento,* one ought not to forget the preceding statement by Don Latino: "You are completely drunk!" The whole passage, in fact, is bracketed by references to Max's inebriation, for after Max has finished expostulating, Latino asks, "And where is the mirror?"—to which Max retorts, "In the bottom of the glass."[12] The friction between the scientific tenor of Max's pronouncements and his state of mind is obvious. What is one to make of the fact that the canonical definition of the *esperpento* is formulated by a senile poet in a drunken stupor? *In vino veritas?* Perhaps. And what of the paradox that Max, who is blind, explains himself with optical metaphors? I would suggest that at least as far as *Las galas* is concerned Max's definition explains nothing; it amounts to little more than a drunken *boutade.* What does it mean, moreover, to deform with "mathematical perfection"? Cardona and Zahareas's painstaking efforts to elucidate the phrase make its vacuity all the more evident. The best they can do is furnish a circular gloss: "Thus Max, in order to render faithfully this absurd reality, will portray it with the 'mathematics' of a concave mirror, that is, perfectly, with all of the constitutive components of the deforming concave mirror."[13] To employ Max's mathematical metaphor, or to speak of the "equations" of *Las galas,* as another critic has done,[14] is to impose a false system on the work; it is, in effect, to de-esperpentize the *esperpento,* to convert it into a "desperpento." The proper context, the apt allusive framework for the *esperpento* is not mathematical or optical but narcotic. What is pertinent in Max and Latino's conversation are the references to intoxication, since they put this passage in contact with the drugs and poisons of *Don Juan Tenorio* and *Las galas del difunto.* And let us not dismiss those concave mirrors too hastily, for concavity has other uses: containing, for instance. Does not a mortar also have a concave shape? And doesn't the wine glass contain a drug?

Festive mimesis, thus, exploits and extends the atmosphere of carnival excess of Zorrilla's play. As befits a concept elaborated from prandial images, this variety of imitation is nourished by the unpredictable, unbridled energy of carnival.[15] One can contrast this rewriting of *Don Juan Tenorio* with Zorrilla's own revision. All of the *zarzuela* falls under the aegis of sculptural mimesis. As Zorrilla avowed, he was out to produce a *Don Juan* identical to the old one in everything except the "flaws." At the end of *Luces de bohemia,* in the conversation between Rubén Darío and Bradomín, Rubén refuses to read some of his verses because, as he puts it, they are still "a monster," not having yet been "purified."[16] In the *zarzuela* Zorrilla limits himself to purifying the original, to correcting its monstrosity. Valle-Inclán, by contrast, adopts a different approach, since he has only compounded, multiplied, the monstrosity of the original. He responds to the improbabilities and anomalies of the *Tenorio* with a play full of fantastic transmutations and eccentric equivalences. Strangely, the slavish, sculptural copying of the *zarzuela* is less faithful to the original than the farfetched, festive parody of the *esperpento.* In this respect *Las galas* is both a parody and a panegyric: a poisoned letter—of praise.

The *esperpento* features an additional image that helps us visualize the result of the transformations operated on *Don Juan.* The image, which is that of an entangling or enmeshing, surfaces already in the first phrase of the play: "The house of sin, in a tangle of alleys [*un enredo de callejones*] near the old dock" (p. 12). After this the image recurs three other times. Waiting for Juanito, Ricote and his friends find themselves "entangled in the wait" [*enredados en la espera*] (p. 36); when Juanito shows up in Galindo's attire, La Daifa's reaction is, "What an entanglement!" [*¡Qué enredo malvado!*] (p. 57), a feeling echoed moments later by Juanito, "¡Qué enredo macanudo!" (p. 59). Not unexpectedly, this image goes back to *Don Juan,* though with some alteration: Brígida, describing Inés, declares, "I have trapped her in my net [*red*]" (1.3.3); Inés, describing her own confusion, says,

Me estás confundiendo,
Brígida . . . , y no sé qué redes
son las que entre estas paredes
temo que me estás tendiendo. (1.4.2)

(You are confusing me, Brígida . . . and I don't know what traps you are setting for me inside these walls.)

The transformation of *Don Juan* into *Las galas,* of a romantic melodrama into a modern *esperpento,* can be summarized as the passage from a *red* to an *enredo,* from a net to a knot. What in Zorrilla was already an improbably complicated skein becomes in Valle-Inclán a dense tangle. (One might phrase the moral of the two works' interrelationship thus: it takes two to tangle; or, remembering Maluenda's "bailan en pareja," to tango.) The art of *Las galas* is to heap complication on complication, to counter excess with excess.

In *Don Juan Tenorio* the references to ensnaring all focus on Brígida, a kind of Arachne. In Valle's play, however, the corresponding allusions, like the letter's poison, are spread out. They surface once in the stage directions and subsequently in the mouths of three different characters, as if every personage in the play, and not just the female protagonist, were trammelled in the web. One character, nonetheless, might be considered the spiritual source of the network. Once again I am thinking of the witch, one of whose prototypes is precisely Brígida; and I call her the source not just because her errand gets things started, but because of the way she is depicted before and after the delivery of the letter. Before: "Showing the letter, [La Daifa] signalled to the witch who was mending her stocking in the poorly lit staircase. The old whore bites the thread, and pins the needle to her shirt" (p. 41). After: "The hag, who mends her stocking under the staircase, whispers and winks, cutting the thread" (p. 58). The witch's sewing and cutting—a transfiguration perhaps of the labor of the fates of classical mythology—is yet another instance of the net-work of the play. In addition, given the traditional connotations of her activity (*texere* > text) and the reference to apparel in the title, it is not difficult to see the witch as another writer figure. Her before and after pictures also limn the portrait of an artist. She may be darning her stockings, but the result is a dead man's suit.

Las galas del difunto depicts two repetitive chores, repetitive both by their nature and by their recurrence in the play: pounding and patching. Both are symbols of Valle-Inclán's transformations, of the recreative labor of festive mimesis. The author of an *esperpento* is either an apprentice who pounds or a witch who patches. Writing is blending and mending. Writing is mixing and fixing. Writing is smashing and patching: an ounce of this, a pinch of that; a stitch here, a loop there. The carnival principle of motley, rather than the geometrical principle of concavity, generates the *esperpento*'s tangled, intricate design.

Part Two

CHOTEO

. . . faustos y fábulas del trópico.

(. . . tropical feasts, tropical fables.)

RAMÓN DEL VALLE-INCLÁN,
La hija del capitán

4

Riddles of the Sphincter

Indagación del choteo, Jorge Mañach's inquiry into the "idiosyncrasies" of the Cuban character,[1] is one of those "classic" texts that one frequently mentions, just as often quotes or paraphrases, but seldom submits to sustained analysis. Part of the reason has to do with Mañach's subject. As he acknowledges at the beginning of the essay, *choteo* does not seem to be a topic that deserves concentrated scrutiny; besides, like other sorts of humor, it is an elusive phenomenon more easily recognized than defined. The other part of the reason has to do with Mañach's essay itself. Originally delivered as a lecture before the Institución Hispano-Cubana de Cultura and written in an unpretentious, conversational style, *Indagación del choteo* carries the reader along without obstructing his path with detours of meaning or barriers to understanding. This quality has led readers of the essay to "apply" its ideas rather than probe into them.[2] The transparency of the exposition, even as it guarantees the success of the application of Mañach's criteria to other texts, preempts close textual study of the essay itself, which seems exhausted by quotation and paraphrase. It is not surprising, then, that even though over half a century has elapsed since its original publication, *Indagación del choteo* remains the definitive word on the subject.

This approach, in my view, both overestimates and underrates Mañach's achievement. It overestimates his achievement by imputing to the essay a finality it does not possess (Mañach calls it "a first inquiry" [p. 13]); and it underrates his achievement by ignoring the evasions and ambiguities, the dead ends and back alleys of Mañach's argument. For *Indagación del choteo* is not the straightforward, unencumbered exposition that it might at first appear to be. Although its argument seems to unfold smoothly and coherently, a closer look reveals twists and turns that complicate (and hence enrich) the attempt at definition. In this respect the essay surprisingly resembles its subject matter, since *choteo,* as Mañach points out, also conceals unsuspected complexities—"alcances sociológicos insospechables" (p. 11). I say "surprisingly" because this is one text where one would not expect any mimesis of form and content. Mañach is generally hostile to *choteo,* which he regards as a noxious and obnoxious trait in the Cuban character, an idiosyncrasy that his essay strives to eradicate. In fact, the decision to study *choteo* already entails an attack against it, for this phenomenon originates in a lack of attention or concentration (p. 19). The title of the book contains something of an oxymoron: to inquire into *choteo* is to attend to inattention, to concentrate on Cubans' apparent proclivity not to. Mañach's is a meditation on impremeditation, a seeming betrayal of the spirit of the subject—"el diablillo del choteo" (p. 64)—by the seriousness of the treatment. But this does not mean that there are no lapses of attention, no hesitations in the meditation. On occasion even Mañach, Cuban after all, wanders from his path.

The first thing to remark is Mañach's indecisiveness in grasping the subject. He states at the outset that he will proceed by "conjugating an empirical method with a logical one" (p. 15); what happens, though, is that his empirical sense often contradicts his deductive reasonings. No matter what the angle of approach to *choteo,* and there are many—etymology, psychological causes, environmental influences, social consequences—Mañach proceeds by first making distinctions and subsequently placing *choteo* on both ends of the dichotomy. One major example: much of *Indagación* is given over to a discussion of whether *choteo* is pernicious or salutary; after weighing both alternatives, however, Mañach concludes that it is both. He concludes, in fact, that *choteo* divides into two strains, one "benign" and the other "toxic." These strains have diverse etiologies. Toxic *choteo* springs from a congenital inability to acknowledge any sort of authority. This kind of *choteador* suffers from "a vice of mental optics or moral sensibility" (p. 21); it is not that he recognizes authority and chooses to disregard it, but that he finds himself constitutionally incapable of having any concept of what authority is. He is blind to hierarchies and insensitive to distinctions of class or culture or wealth, no matter how ingrained or how apparent.

By contrast, benign *choteo,* according to Mañach, consists in a selective disrespect for those kinds of authority that one thinks illegitimate. Since it exposes falsity and pretentiousness, benign *choteo* can fulfill a salutary function in society. Its cultivators suffer not from moral blindness but merely from "a vice of behavior" (p. 20), an external malaise that can be treated. Unlike the congenital *choteadores*—"the professional nay-sayers, the inveterate skeptics, the extreme egoists" (p. 22)—this type of person can be reasoned with and reformed, since he acknowledges the existence of some authority. Benign *choteo,* thus, is "light, healthy, almost purely external" (p. 23), while its pernicious counterpart is "deep and skeptical," a "perversion" of one's inner faculties that originates in "a real collapse in the sense of authority" (p. 23).

Clearly, Mañach wants to have his cake and eat it too. If his analysis is correct, *choteo* is both internal and external, congenital and learned, habitual and sporadic, malignant and benign; it is both a virtue and a defect, both sickness and health. I find it difficult to comprehend a phenomenon that undercuts such familiar oppositions as that between inside and out or sickness and health. Moreover, how does one decide whether a particular instance of *choteo* belongs to the benign or the malignant strain? Mañach would answer, I think, that the identification will depend on whether the ridicule is warranted or not. Outwardly both strains behave alike in that both act to subvert authority and level hierarchies. The discrimination between them can only occur at other levels: either genetically, by differentiating between the two psychological profiles; or pragmatically, by examining the *choteador's* victim. Although the two strains have differing etiologies and dissimilar targets, in the interval between origin and destination— that is, in the interval in which *choteo* materializes as word or gesture—the two strains are indistinguishable. Even though Mañach talks at some length about the sources and consequences of *choteo,* about the act itself he says relatively little, as is indicated by the dearth of illustrative examples in the book. Phrasing the problem in linguistic terms, one could say that Mañach focuses on the sender and the receiver rather than on the message. His discussion of the *choteo*-act concentrates on the interaction of speaker and addressee rather than on the characteristic properties of the "message" that passes between them. Indeed, one of his first definitions states that *"choteo*—a familiar, slight, and festive thing—is a type of relation [*forma de relación*] that we consider typically ours" (p. 11). Since Mañach is primarily interested in social psychology, his attention veers away from the "thing" and toward the social matrix in which it is embedded.

What he does tell us, nevertheless, is that *choteo* consists of a systematic opposition to authority. Let us look a bit more closely at each of the terms in this description. *Systematic:* the most important feature of *choteo,* says Mañach, is its systematic or habitual character: *"Choteo* is, then, an attitude hardened into a habit, and this habitualness is its most important characteristic" (p. 18). The *choteador* is an "opositor sistemático" (p. 17) who pays no attention to the objects of his scorn; everything is fair game. (From this it is evident that Mañach privileges pernicious *choteo,* for the benign strain is not habitual; its sporadic incidence is precisely what distinguishes it from the other strain.)[3] *Opposition:* as a form of uncivil disobedience, *choteo* involves an affirmation of the individual will in the face of collective strictures: "the mockery has its origin in this impatience of our temperament toward any impediments placed in the way of our free expansion" (p. 38). *Authority:* rather than concrete governmental or political power, Mañach means "any state of harmony and order" (p. 32). In fact, before the kind of authority with the means to enforce its dictates, the *choteador,* being essentially passive, will submit (p. 40).

Putting these elements together, Mañach finally arrives at a formal definition: *"Choteo* is a desire for independence that is externalized in a mockery of every non-imperative form of authority" (p. 41). This definition is fine as far as it goes. Its shortcoming, in my view, is that it does not go far enough. Since it addresses less the content than the form of *choteo,* Mañach's definition suffers from insufficient specificity. Although Mañach describes the social context in which this phenomenon materializes, he says nothing directly about its specific content. He studies *choteo*'s natural habitat, as it were, without dissecting the beast itself. There exist, after all, other varieties of *burla* that would meet his loose criteria. A habitual disregard for authority, for example, characterizes a *burlador* like Don Juan as well as it does the *choteador*. Only an analysis of the *substance* of the phenomenon will adequately differentiate *choteo* from *burla*. But, as we will see, it is precisely *choteo*'s substance that Mañach is reluctant to confront.

The couple of examples that Mañach adduces serve to illustrate different aspects of his definition. The first example comes from an anecdote related to him by a friend:

A Cuban friend of mine, someone devoid of intellectual malice (though not of the other sorts), once related to me his impression of a storm at sea. What seemed to have impressed him most was the displacement of the cargo, which had not been fastened securely, with the rocking of the ship: "The barrels—he said—the packages, the boxes, everything was tossing from side to side: the whole thing was a *choteo*." (p. 32)

In the unloosening of the cables that kept the cargo in place, Mañach finds a symbol of the relaxing of social structures and strictures caused by *choteo* and a motivation for the word's vulgar doublet, *relajo:* "A *choteo*, that is to say, confusion, subversion, disorder:—in sum: *'relajo.'* For what does this word mean if not that, the relaxation [*relajamiento*] of all of the connections and junctures that give things an articulate, integral aspect?" (pp. 32–33).[4] The incident also demonstrates *choteo*'s systematicity, for everything in the ship becomes unmoored—barrels, packages, boxes: "*everything* was tossing from side to side."

The second example illustrates *choteo*'s mockery of death: "On a certain occasion, some Cubans were visiting the Municipal Crematorium in Paris. On seeing a corpse go into the incinerator, one of our compatriots remarked, addressing the somber operator: 'Once over, please' [*Démelo vuelta y vuelta*]. With doubtful taste but undoubted cleverness, he reduced those human remains to the category of a steak" (pp. 35–36). Because death imposes a fundamental limitation on the individual's freedom of action, it is one of the *choteador*'s favorite targets. In conceiving of the corpse as a piece of meat, the Cuban in the joke devalues death. His *boutade* erases the distinction between the human and the nonhuman and, by implication, denies death: old people never die, they simply turn into steaks.

These two examples exhibit an additional feature not mentioned by Mañach. In both instances *choteo* entails movement. The account of the storm at sea centers on the word *desplazamiento;* according to Mañach, what most impressed his friend was "the displacement of the cargo." The other example, though adduced in an unrelated context, makes the same connection, since the Cuban asks that the body be turned over. The humor, in fact, resides less in the request than in the phrasing. Had the Cuban said, "Medium rare," the request would have been essentially the same but the joke would not be as funny. The source of the humor lies not in the depiction of man as meat but of death as movement. The fundamental incongruity resides in the association of death and motion. The grave is a resting place; death is stasis. But *choteo* takes resting remains and sets them spinning. Death is mocked here less by the dehumanizing metaphor, as Mañach thinks, than by the violation of the body's inertness.

This association of *choteo* and movement connects with Mañach's bipolar definition, for Mañach finds that this species of mockery oscillates, moves between mutually exclusive alternatives. Like the cargo that tosses from one side to the other, *choteo* alternately occupies different positions within the same pair of opposed terms. At one moment in the *Indagación* it is considered salutary and at the next, pernicious. Mañach himself seems cognizant of this slipperiness when, at different points, he brands *choteo* as "evasive," "fluid," "multiform," "variable" (pp. 13, 23). *Choteo* for Mañach is a kind of "floating" signifier (floating like the cargo) that alights on a plurality of signified objects. This, then, is the first, modest addition that one can make to Mañach's inquiry: Cuban mockery *moves*—both in its theoretical elusiveness and in its concrete manifestations, which involve a displacement of some sort. A look at another joke, this one not found in *Indagación*, will take us further along the track of *choteo*'s movement.

The joke is entitled "Los payasos" and I take it from a collection by Guillermo Alvarez Guedes, a popular Cuban-exile comedian:

Los dos payasos estaban en el circo y un payaso le
decía al otro:
—¿A que tú no sabes qué es lo que más me gusta a mí

de las mujeres?
Y dícele el otro payaso:
—El pelo.
Y dice el payaso:
—No, no, no. Más p'abajo.
Y dice el payaso:
—¿La frente?
—No, no, no. Más p'abajo.
Y dice el otro payaso:
—¿La boca?
—No, no, no. Más p'abajo.
Y las mujeres en el circo empezaron a ponerse de pie,
porque pensaban que el payaso iba a decir una grosería.
Se estaban poniendo de pie cuando dice el otro payaso:
—¿El ombligo?
Y dice el payaso:
—No, no. no. Más p'abajo y más p'atrás.
Siguen las mujeres poniéndose de pie y sale un sargento
que estaba a cargo del orden, y grita:
—¡No se me levante nadie, que nada más estoy esperando
a que diga culo para darle una entrada de leña a éste!

(The two clowns were in the circus and one clown was saying to the
other one: "I bet you don't know what I like best in women." And the
other clown says, "Their hair?" And the clown says, "No, no, no.
Lower." And the other clown says, "Their forehead?" And the clown
says, "No, no, no. Lower." And the other clown says, "Their mouth?"
And the clown says, "No, no, no. Lower." And the women in the
circus began to get on their feet, because they thought the clown was
going to say an obscenity. They were getting up when the other clown
says, "Their bellybutton?" And the clown replies, "No, no, no.
Lower, and back." The women were still getting up when out comes
a sergeant, who was there to keep order, and screams: "Don't anybody
get up. I'm just waiting to hear the word 'ass' to give that clown a
beating!")[5]

"Los payasos" not only meets Mañach's criteria; it would, I believe, be identified by the "average Cuban" (more on him later)
as an example of *choteo*.[6] As Mañach points out, most humor results from a nondeliberate or unexpected self-ridicule. In "Los

payasos," instead of the proverbial slip on the banana peel, we
have the equally proverbial slip of the tongue, since by uttering
"culo" the policeman violates the very decorum he is charged with
maintaining. Mañach would define his slip as "the accident that
undermines one's desire to behave circumspectly" (p. 30) and
would regard it as an example of the "self-contradiction" that lies
at the root of the comic (p. 27). But it is difficult to be circum-
spect in the circus. What happens in the joke, in fact, is that the
policeman unintentionally gets into the act, for the self-inflicted
choteo of his authority involves a transmutation in identity: the
gag in the gag order is that the cop turns into another clown. By
saying "culo" he becomes, so to speak, the butt of the joke, the
protagonist of the clowns' routine. His order acts as a counter-
performative, by which I mean both that it aims to censor the
clowns' routine and that it accomplishes the very thing it inter-
dicts. Three different sets of characters participate in the performance: the two clowns, the women in the crowd, and the sergeant. The sergeant's job is to provide a buffer, a kind of sanitary
cordon between performers and spectators. As the "keeper of order," he has to protect the women from verbal aggression, and
thus his only words are a command, for authority-figures live in an
imperative mood (as Mañach mentions, "to order" means to make
an order as well as to keep order). When the cop delivers the
punch line, however, he passes from interested bystander to active
participant. As a result not only is the policeman's authority ridiculed but the distinction between actors and spectators is subverted
as well.

Seen in this light, "Los payasos" bears a striking resemblance to
another performance I have already discussed at some length—the
wager between Juan and Luis. Both performances center on a pair
of nearly identical characters: two anonymous clowns, and Juan
and Luis. In each instance the performance involves a game or
competition—"un juego ilusorio," in Avellaneda's phrase (*Don
Juan Tenorio*, 1.1.16).[7] The competition, furthermore, has to do
with women, and we may even detect a trace of Juan's and Luis's
catalogues in the clowns' anatomical enumeration. But the most
interesting parallel lies in the fact that both joke and wager depict
metatheatrical scenes, for both bring the spectators into the act.

Just as the wager scene makes room not only for the two protagonists but also for the onlookers that crowd around the table, the
joke incorporates the women in the audience. Given that the two
performances climax with the intrusion of someone from the audience—Diego and Gonzalo, the sergeant—one could say, indeed,
that the real subject of both wager and joke is the tenuousness of
the boundary between actors and spectators, between "art" and
"life." In both situations, moreover, the intrusion has the same purpose: to abort the performance, to reestablish the order disrupted
by the competition. The fathers in *Don Juan* are no less agents of
law and order than is the cop. Their words, as we have seen, are
also counter-performatives. And yet, since Gonzalo's and Diego's
intromission only makes Juan brazen enough to bring Inés into
the bet, what happens to the cop happens also to them. In both
cases authority aids in its own undoing.

These similarities are perhaps explained by the inner dynamics
of what we call a "circus atmosphere." The phrase is used to label
a situation typified by confusion, role-playing, unruly activity. All
of these are certainly elements in both joke and wager. More ab-
stractly, a circus atmosphere obtains its peculiar coloration from
the abolition of distinctions: distinctions between what is licit and
illicit, between what is decorous and indecorous, between what is
authentic and faked, between demeanor and disguise. In a circus,
where a clown will take up a seat in the audience, where bucketfuls
of confetti—water in disguise—periodically rain down on the audience, where the trapeze artist, ever in danger of falling, gyrates
above the spectators' heads, distinctions between actors and spectators and between reality and illusion are temporarily suspended.
Part of the thrill of the circus, undoubtedly, inheres in this unusual
blurring of boundaries. It is then appropriate that "Los payasos" is
set in a circus, for in no other environment would the cop's slip be
so natural. A skeptic in the crowd might wonder, in fact, whether
the cop was not a "plant"—a third clown dressed as a police offi-
cer—and the impromptu obscenity actually a well-rehearsed line.
This possibility, it should be noted, would accord with Mañach's
analysis, which emphasizes that more often than not *choteo* invents
its own pretexts; it is "a kind of mockery that makes up its own
motives and that, to use the Cuban phrase, 'pins a tail' on a serious

object" (p. 28). Like the wager, *choteo* is a game of illusion. Just as Juan and Luis set up guidelines and deadlines, *choteo* sets up punch lines.

On a more general level these parallels point to affinities between *choteo* and carnival, affinities already implicit in Mañach's passing reference to the "festiveness" of the phenomenon (p. 11). Indeed, when he defines *choteo* as a levelling impulse, his definition fits carnival equally well, since it too vents its energies against hierarchy and authority. The topsy-turvy world of carnival and the "confusion, subversion, disorder" of *choteo* seem allied phenomena. And although I realize I may be stretching it, I even see the "Démelo vuelta y vuelta" of the crematorium joke as an instance of the carnival topos of inversion. At least this much is certain, nonetheless: both carnival and *choteo* are forms of festive behavior during which, as Mañach puts it, the connections and articulations of society become relaxed.

The differences between the two phenomena have to do, first, with their diffusion, and second, with each one's medium of expression. *Choteo* is pernicious because of its ubiquity. Any time, place, and occasion will serve the *choteador*. The more inappropriate the situation, the more effective his assault. By contrast, carnival is narrowly circumscribed: it unfolds at a prescribed time and its activities obey a set pattern (specific types of games, disguises, etc.). In this respect carnival is less unruly than *choteo*. One traditional theory holds that by providing an escape valve for societal tensions, carnival and other festivals reaffirm, not undermine, the social order. They constitute a "tolerated margin of mess," in Aldous Huxley's phrase, a controlled, cathartic outpouring after which the status quo reemerges.[8] The same could not be said of *choteo,* for the ripples of derision that the *choteador* sets in motion extend indefinitely. When Mañach speaks of a "benign" *choteo,* in fact, he seems to have in mind something like carnival—a controlled disorder or ruled unruliness, the kind of situation enjoined in the Cuban idiom, "que el relajo sea con orden." *Choteo* turns toxic when it oversteps its bounds and becomes disorderly, "desbordante" (p. 59).

The second difference between carnival and *choteo* lies in the latter's limited expressive resources. What carnival lacks in exten-

sion it makes up in comprehensiveness. Carnival celebrations involve almost every aspect of human culture. All of man's sign
systems, to put it another way, come into play: garb, language,
ritual, religion, gesture, dance, etc. *Choteo,* on the contrary, is exclusively verbal or paraverbal. In Fernando Ortiz's opinion the
word derives from an African root meaning to speak, an etymology
corroborated by the related term, *chota,* Cuban for snitch.[9] The
choteador, like the *chota,* is one who speaks when he ought not to.
Being a spectacle, carnival evokes visual images.[10] *Choteo,* however,
is not seen but heard. Even when the setting is a circus (a spectacle
if there ever was one), *choteo* materializes in a word.

   In a recent essay Severo Sarduy has argued for the preeminence
of the phonic in Cuban culture—"privilegio, en lo cubano, de la
audición."[11] Departing from a line in one of Gertrudis Gómez de
Avellaneda's sonnets—"Tu dulce nombre halagará mi oído"—
Sarduy traces the phonic boom in Cuban literature from the letters of Columbus to the poetry of Lezama. In *choteo* we may have
the popular side of this proclivity, a "low-culture" manifestation
of that same insistence on the sonorous. This is especially so if we
recall that *choteo*'s ultimate resource—what Mañach terms its
"tremendous weapon"—is the *trompetilla:* "In the entire repertoire of despective gestures and emissions, there is nothing so
powerful as the *trompetilla,* perhaps because it is loaded with
abject allusions. There is no gravity, no matter how imperturb-
able, that is not penetrated by this spray of disdain. You can stick
your tongue out or spit at someone and it will have no effect; but
the *trompetilla* is an arrow that always hits its mark—the center
of gravity—flaunting the banner of ridicule" (p. 66). The *trompetilla,* a dark cousin of the English raspberry, is produced by
pressing one's palms against one's mouth and squeezing out air.
The sound emitted is indeed, as Mañach says, loaded with abject
allusions, for the *trompetilla* is simply the fart of the upper body.
One blast will cut down to size the most exalted personage, will
expose the most inveterate kind of pretentiousness. A popular
Cuban song of some years ago made fun of snobs and pedants by
mimicking their affectations and then adding, after each snippet
of affected speech (and with the appropriate acoustic accompani-
ment), "Y sonó la trompetilla." In *choteo* all of carnival's varie-

gated ruses are finally reduced to this one stratagem of phonic assault. The *trompetilla* is the *choteador*'s all-purpose weapon, effective regardless of the pretext or the provocation.

But let me return to the circus. In order to appreciate fully the kinship between *choteo* and the *trompetilla,* between a disordering impulse and an abject sound, we must get to the bottom of the joke; we must, that is, reach the cop's *culo*. On our way there let me note, first, that "Los payasos" once again associates *choteo* and movement. Since the clowns take their audience on a quick tour of the female body, the joke has the structure of an itinerant narrative or picaresque romance in which anatomy has replaced topography. Instead of travelling from town to town, the clowns go from part to part of the body. The journey does not come to its rear end until the cop acts to stop movement—and not just by putting an end to the enumeration, but also by telling the women to stay put. There is a nice play of symmetry here: as the clowns descend, the women rise; the further down the clowns go, the greater the ascending impetus. The sergeant's intervention arrests these polar movements. His first words are, "No se me levante nadie." Authority immobilizes, a fact conveyed in the double meaning of "to arrest." And had the clowns gone ahead and uttered the word *culo,* they also would have been immobilized—by a beating, "una entrada de leña."

We know, however, that the journey will not stop, but it does suffer two important detours. The first concerns the uttering of *culo;* when one has been led to expect that one of the clowns will mouth the obscenity, the forbidden word is heard, but it comes from somewhere in the audience. The narrative perspective, what in Spanish is sometimes called *el punto de hablada,* shifts offstage, from clown to cop. The second detour involves a change in the trip's itinerary. After having repeatedly replied to his questioner with the words, "Más p'abajo," with the last question the clown expands his answer to, "Más p'abajo y más p'atrás." The substance of *choteo,* all of its abjectness, is subsumed in that reply. *Choteo* is not, as Mañach says, "aimless laughter" [*una risa sin rumbo*] (p. 29). The two clowns demonstrate that mockery's movement has a direction—down, and back. Mañach's inquiry, for all of its insightfulness, fails to recognize *choteo*'s downward tropism, its scatological compass. There is not enough anality in his analysis. Even though he acknowledges the pertinence of the *trompetilla* with its "abject allusions," he does not pause to consider the implications of *choteo*'s connections with abjectness. Yet given the link between authority and repression on the one hand, and between permissiveness and anality on the other, these connections are hardly surprising.[12] They are also not surprising in view of *choteo*'s carnival affinities, for carnival is likewise a celebration and liberation of the forces of the lower body. A "mighty thrust downward," according to Bakhtin, characterizes carnival images.[13]

→ The key to *choteo* lies in that step to the rear pictured in the joke. The point at which the turn occurs is significant. The detour does not take place until the clowns' enumeration has reached the navel, the part of the body that has traditionally been considered its center. The movement from navel to anus displaces from the center to the margins. But this was also the direction of the other detour, which took us from the circus stage, where the clowns were, to the wings, where the cop stood. *Choteo* may then be described, *more geometrico,* as a movement toward or assault from the margins. Mañach's notion that *choteo* consists of a "forma de relación" is correct, except that the relation is not only between individuals but between a center and a periphery (though individuals may, of course, occupy these positions). Let us recall part of Mañach's description of the *trompetilla:* "the *trompetilla* is an arrow that always hits its mark—the center of gravity—flaunting the banner of ridicule." Let us recall also Mañach's initial observation that *choteo* results from a lack of attention or concentration. The liminal structure underlies both of these remarks. Just as the *trompetilla* attacks the "center" of gravity, the *choteador* cannot converge on the "center" of attention, cannot "concentrate."

Mary Douglas's reflections on the relationship between dirt and marginality may be helpful here. According to Douglas, dirt is essentially disorder, "matter out of place," and implies two conditions: "a set of ordered relations and a contravention of that order."[14] Persons in a marginal state, however, are also out of place, either because they violate personal or social strictures or because they are perceived as threatening and ostracized (or both, as is clearly the case with the *choteador,* who constitutes one type of "marginal"). Thus marginal people are also "dirt."[15] (We have

all heard misfits of various types labelled "trash," "rubbish,"
"refuse," *escoria,* and so on.) Douglas's discussion points up on the
one hand the connection between dirt and disorder, two of the
indicia of *choteo,* and on the other the connection between liminality and dirt, that is, between *choteo*'s trajectory and its destination.
Not only is the backside a marginal site; as my discussion of *Juan
Criollo* will bear out, a displacement toward the margins always
takes us, sooner or later, to the dungheap. There is always slime
in the limen, an association borne out by both words' etymological
relation to *limus,* Latin for mire and margin.

The turn from bellybutton to buttocks has the force of a scatological implication. And anatomically, of course, the liminal distinction between what is within and without merges with the
topographical distinction between what is above and below, since
the normal way out of the body leads down. *Choteo* comprises a
three-term equation whose members are disorder, dirt, and marginality. By insisting on the first of these, Mañach taps only one of
the constants in the equation. "Los payasos" calls attention to the
other two terms.

We should notice, though, that the joke's turn toward the anal
also signifies a turn *away* from the genital, from those areas of the
female anatomy that would have been encountered had the clowns
proceeded straight down. In some ways the biggest surprise in the
joke occurs not when the sergeant slips up (or down), but when
the clown changes direction. I have been in an audience before
whom Alvarez Guedes was telling this joke and have sensed the
very perceptible relief all around when the clown adds, "y más
p'atrás." A large part of the women's nervousness (in both the
real and the fictive audience) stems, it seems to me, from the anticipation of a genital "grosería." The turn toward the backside,
even as it violates certain rules of propriety, abides by others, thus
relieving some of the tension that the joke's incremental structure
builds up. For all its transgressive qualities, *choteo* is often scatological but seldom genital. These are not "dirty" jokes in the usual
sense of the word, but only because they deal with real, not figurative, dirt. This kind of humor would not find its way into most
pornographic literature, for it contains too much smut and too
little sex. References to sexual activity play a relatively minor role

in *choteo;* most of the time they are carefully (and hence obtrusively) skirted. By contrast, excrement is everywhere.⌉

Let me give another corroborative example, one that will take us from the circus to a church. This joke is entitled "El pecado," and once again I take it from Alvarez Guedes's repertoire.

Un joven, muy pecoso, se confesaba. El cura comenzó
diciendo . . .
—Ave María Purísima.
—Sin pecado concebida, dijo él.
—¿Pecas?, preguntó el cura.
—Hasta en el culo, Padre, contestó él.

(A young man with a lot of freckles went to confession. The priest began: "Hail Mary." "Full of grace," the young man replied. "Sins?" [or, "Freckles?"] asked the priest. "Down to my ass, Father," he replied.)[16]

In the young man's smart-ass comeback, we find again the familiar disrespect for authority, in this instance religious authority as personified in still another "father," that helps typify *choteo.* More important, however, the disrespect once more involves a downward movement from face to anus, for in replying to the confessor's question the sinner transfers freckles from their usual location— the face—to the lower body, a move that obeys a certain inverted logic, since buttocks have often been regarded, in myth and folklore, as the "face" of the lower body.[17] Like "Los payasos," "El pecado" substitutes the lower for the upper; and as in the first joke, the substitution takes place with the unexpected utterance of the word *culo.* What I find most interesting in this joke, though, is that by punning on *pecas* the sinner turns the confessional back into what a Freudian might see as its sublimated model—a latrine. A psychoanalytic reading might say that the joke reveals the anality behind religion's sublimation. But one need not be a devout Freudian to perceive the corrosive associations triggered by the pun, associations already hinted at in the common euphemism for a john—" a holy place."[18] Both latrine and confessional are private places into which one enters periodically in order to unburden oneself, to cleanse the body or the soul. Both cubicles are shrouded in secrecy: no one is privy to what goes on in the confessional; no one

will confess to what he (or she) does in the privy. The requirement of periodic confession finds an echo in the belief in the
salutary effects of regular bowel movements. In addition, both
latrine and confessional share a similar isolation, for both are
"marginal" sites, secreted in the corner of a nave or a house (or
even outside it: the outhouse).[19]

Besides subverting the sanctity of the confessional by equating
it with a latrine, the pun also involves a *choteo* of the doctrine of
the Immaculate Conception. Having activated the *peca* in *pecado,*
the joke suggests that Mary was conceived not without sin but
without freckles: *sin pecas concebida.* This suggestion is reinforced
by the double resemblance between *pecas* and *pecado,* aural and
semantic, for just as sins are blemishes on the soul, freckles are
blemishes on the skin. "El pecado" illustrates, thus, that *choteo*
consists of a downward displacement in which intellectual, spiritual, or aesthetic entities revert to their material grounding: con-
fessionals become commodes, sins become freckles. Mañach is
quite right, therefore, to insist that *choteo* is not a form of wit, for
wit displaces upward.[20] The *choteador* is anything but subtle; he
has no talent for clever repartee or verbal fencing. Crass invective
is more his speed: not the refined irony of a Voltaire but the scatological mud-slinging of a Swift. Not wit, shit. As Mañach expresses it, a bit more decorously, "*choteo* is so unintellectual that,
confronted by an ingenious sally, it can only answer with another
exasperating jeer. It is not a variety of dialectics, but of assault"
(p. 47).

Another of Alvarez Guedes's texts, my favorite, provides the
paradigmatic example—and the last to which I'll subject my
reader—of *choteo*'s bluntness. It is a song entitled "Cada vez que
pienso en ti," which begins as a sentimental *bolero* where the
speaker laments spending another Christmas far away from his
loved one:

Cada vez que pienso en ti
en esta época del año,
siempre tengo que admitir
cuánto te extraño.
Y ahora para aumentar

esta desdicha completa
hoy recibí tu tarjeta,
ay, cuánto me ha hecho llorar.
Cuando yo veo un arbolito
con sus farolitos
yo no sé qué hacer,
y cuando sirven la cena
en la Nochebuena
no puedo comer.
Y después del quinto ron
para tratar de olvidarte
al fin yo logro arrancarte
de mi pobre corazón.
Y canto así . . .

(Every time I think about you at this time of the year, I always have
to admit how much I miss you. And, to make my misery complete,
today I received your Christmas card—oh, how it's made me cry. I
look at the Christmas tree with its little lights and I don't know what
to do; Christmas dinner is served and I can't eat a thing. Finally,
after drinking five rums to try to forget you, I manage to tear you
away from my heart. And I sing . . .)

At this point the song shifts gears. The beat speeds up; sentiment
dissolves into *salsa;* and the speaker modulates from kitsch to crud.
The refrain that follows is repeated at least four or five times before the song ends.

. . . Y canto así:
Me cago en el Año Viejo.
Me cago en el Año Nuevo.
Me cago en el arbolito
y me cago en ti.
El fin de año me recuerda
lo mucho que nos quisimos,
pero ya nos aburrimos,
por eso, vete a la mierda.
Me cago en el Año Viejo, etc.
Yo de tu lado me fui
porque tu cariño es malo,

por eso me doy dos palos
y después me cago en ti.
Me cago en el Año Viejo, etc.

(I shit on the Old Year, I shit on the New Year, I shit on the Christmas tree, and I shit on you. The end of the year reminds me of how
much we loved each other; but now we bore each other—you're really
a piece of shit. I shit on the Old Year, etc. I left your side because your
love was evil, so I'll have a couple of drinks and then I'll shit on
you. I shit on the Old Year, etc.)[21]

Mañach would perhaps remark that these lyrics evince *choteo*'s
systematic character. The speaker shits on everything: the old year,
the new year, his fickle girlfriend. He even shits on what dogs de-
cently avoid—Christmas trees. Mañach could also remark that this
invective attacks one of our most serious and solemn festivities,
the celebration of the birth of Christ. What Mañach would not
mention, to judge from his essay, is the *substance* of the attack, the
excrement that Alvarez Guedes's jilted lover flings indiscriminately
at the world.

My first point, then, is that *Indagación del choteo* scants *choteo*'s scatological specificity. Geoffrey Hartman's affirmation of the
duplicity of poetic language—and perhaps of all language—is pertinent here: "What we get to see is always a palimpsest or a contaminated form of some kind: a stratum of legitimate, sacred, or
exalted words purifying a stratum of guilty, forbidden, or debased
words."[22] This duality describes precisely the situation in *Indagación*. Mañach attempts a "purification" of *choteo,* a filtering out of
its baseness or filth. Deliberately or not, he acts to cleanse or edul-
corate his subject by glossing over its scatological subtext, its bottom lines.

One could say, in fact, that Mañach takes the position of the
cop in "Los payasos." The author of *Indagación del choteo* is no
less an authority, no less a father figure, no less an agent of propriety than the sergeant. Note how he begins his inquiry:

If we ask the average Cuban, the man on the street [*el cubano de
la calle*], he will give us a simple answer, but one that comes close to
being a definition, since it logically implies everything that we find in
the most typical manifestations of this phenomenon. He will tell us

that *choteo* consists of "not taking anything seriously." If we press him a bit, he will explain—with a phrase that is not usually used in front of ladies, but one that you must allow me to use, however sparingly—that *choteo* consists of "making fun of everything" [*tirarlo todo a relajo*]. (p. 17)

Just as the joke can be superimposed on the wager, this excerpt can be superimposed on the joke. Three sets of characters figure in this passage: the average Cuban, Mañach, and the women in his audience. The match with the cast of "Los payasos" is nearly exact. The *cubano de la calle* has the part of the clowns, Mañach has the part of the sergeant, and the women's identity remains unchanged. Like the cop, Mañach acts as a buffer. In order both to explicate and expurgate street slang (the two operations amount to the same thing), he places himself between the man on the street and the "ladies" in his audience. The word *relajo* will be admitted, but it will be used sparingly (actually Mañach will use it only once more). *Indagación del choteo* thus begins by sketching a scene in which *choteo* is brought up from the street to the lecture hall, a scene where the author plays the part of cultural commissar or censor. On one level we have *choteo,* the legitimate word; on another, *relajo,* the debased word. Mañach's job is to keep his conceptual cargo under such tight control that it cannot break loose and create "confusion, subversion, disorder: in sum: '*relajo.*' " He must purify street slang so that it becomes suitable for women's ears.

Ironically, only a few paragraphs earlier Mañach had chided earlier studies of the Cuban character for avoiding the word *choteo:* "The few Cuban books that deal with our psychology have contented themselves, at most, with a passing allusion to the topic of *choteo.* Because this vernacular name [*esta denominación vernácula*] has almost always been avoided, the peculiarities of the phenomenon have been ignored and *choteo* has been confused with other, more generic qualities like levity [*ligereza*], cheerfulness [*alegría*], and such" (pp. 11–12). Yet Mañach engages in a similar evasiveness. If other writers substitute *ligereza* for *choteo,* Mañach substitutes *choteo* for *relajo.* If other writers tend to elide the specificity of the phenomenon, Mañach does also by formulat-

ing criteria that are "generic" indeed. One could say, in short, that
Mañach overlooks the *culo* in *lo vernáculo*.

My second point is that this evasiveness does not quite succeed.
Again like the sergeant, Mañach infringes on the very decorum
he intends to protect. Even if the word *relajo* is censored, there are
moments in the essay when the vulgarity of the phenomenon slips
through. One such moment arises from Mañach's insistence on
the "lowness" of *choteo*. As "a very low form of mockery" (p. 27),
choteo stands just a notch above the despective grimace and well
below parody, satire, and irony in the scale of mockery. It differs
from these higher species of humor in that the latter presuppose
some sort of community between the attacker and his victim. In
the upper end of the scale, in fact, the derision is so subtle, so ex-
quisite, that it takes on the appearance of a "delicate form of
solidarity and respect" (p. 27). The ironist and his victim, for example, stand on an equal plane; because irony, "the highest species
of humor" (p. 27), implies bonds of solidarity and respect, it only
strengthens the social fabric. Compare, however, the action of the
grimace—"the purely instinctive grimace [*mueca*] of the child
toward his father or teacher" (p. 26)—which, like *choteo*, aims at
higher-ups. The *mueca* resembles *choteo* and differs from irony in
that it serves not to cement but to subvert the social order upheld
by authority figures like parents and teachers. One can infer that
only *choteo*'s recourse to language separates these two "low" forms
of ridicule; one can also infer that in Mañach's view the *choteador*
behaves much like the grimacing child. Indeed, Mañach attributes
the prevalence of *choteo* in Cuba to the youth of the Republic—
"nuestra primitiva aldeanidad de pueblo joven"—and affirms that
with the onset of political maturity the conditions that breed *choteo* will disappear (p. 75). The contrast with the subtlety and
refinement of irony, which finds fertile soil in old and tradition-
laden nations like England (pp. 57–58), could not be sharper.
With each gradation in the hierarchy of humor one progresses
from reflex to reason, from childhood to maturity, from improvisation to tradition, from anarchy to order. *Choteo* is the dialect of
the inarticulate. As in the *trompetilla*, the *choteador*, child that he
is, counters the ironist's feints with elemental insults.

But *choteo* is doubly low: it is a "low" humor that "lowers" its victims. Its action is rendered with verbs that communicate a downward movement: "rebajar" (pp. 36, 65); "allanar" (pp. 48, 56); "bajar" (p. 67); "minar" (p. 72). This emphasis on *choteo*'s gravitational pull connects with my previous remarks on the jokes. What is missing from this language is the anatomical figure explicit in Alvarez Guedes's texts. Mañach considers lowness only in its social, moral, or aesthetic senses; he "sublimates" lowness, one might say, much as the confessional sublimates the commode. It is still possible, nonetheless, to infer the presence of an anatomical subtext in *Indagación. Choteo* is a "desahogo" or "descarga" (p. 27), a "descongestionador" (pp. 64, 68), a "válvula de escape" (p. 64) that releases something "tóxico y desbordante" (p. 59) and fills the air with "gases asfixiantes" (pp. 70, 72). Then there is, of course, the *trompetilla* with its abject allusions. Since the picture behind or beneath these words is that of an uncontrolled bowel movement, this language cumulatively recovers *choteo*'s specificity as a scatological explosion. The last insinuation is given in Mañach's antidote to this form of mockery; *choteo*'s will to stink can be controlled only by perfuming the air—"saturating our environment with those subtle essences of respect that are the antidote to excessive mockery" (p. 76).

This network of covert anatomical allusions tends to turn *Indagación del choteo* into self-parody or auto-*choteo,* for Mañach, like the cop, unintentionally undermines the "purity" of his language. The disguised but persistent anal references contaminate his exposition by bringing the "low" in touch with the "high," by suggesting, in effect, that highness is nothing more than relocated lowness. (Decorum is dirt out of place.) If my discussion of *Don Juan Tenorio* focused on four-word letters, then, this consideration of *choteo* must rest on four-letter words, the most prominent of which, to be sure, is not *culo* but *Cuba.* But four-word letters and four-letter words are nearly interchangeable, as is shown by the relevance here of Lista's remark about Zorrilla's play: "When on the wings of an idea our imagination wants to fly to the empyrean, an incorrect expression, an improper word, a harsh sound, a gallicism, or an insufferable neologism reminds us that we are mired in the mud of the earth."[23] *Choteo* also keeps our noses in the dirt, and it does so by means of "improper words" (like *culo*) and "harsh sounds" (like those of a *trompetilla*). This indecent descent from the empyrean to the dungheap describes exactly *choteo*'s trajectory. *Choteo* is a tropical tropism that unmasks the *culo* behind every *cara*, that bares the other cheek; it is this anatomical downturn that Mañach's essay attempts, but does not quite manage, to arrest.

5

※

Don Juan in the Tropics

Juan Criollo is in several respects the perfect companion piece to *Indagación del choteo*. Published in the same year as the essay,[1] Loveira's novel also undertakes a study of the defining features of the Cuban temperament. Novel and essay complement and illuminate each other. Juan Criollo, Loveira's protagonist, is precisely that "cubano de la calle" evoked by Mañach at the beginning of his essay. Juan possesses all of the qualities that Mañach identifies as characteristic of the average Cuban: sensuality, lack of foresight, a taste for gambling, skepticism, mental quickness, generosity, independence.[2] More narrowly, Juan behaves like a typical *choteador*. One of the climactic scenes in the novel relates how he breaks up the appointment of a judge to the High Courts with a mortifying, sarcastic laugh—"una carcajada de mortificante intención, de desbordante sarcasmo" (p. 422). All of Mañach's ingredients for *choteo* appear in this scene. For Juan, who has no respect for social hierarchy, no sense of the solemn, the ceremony is nothing more than a "sublime trifle" (p. 422). As his target, Adolfo Ruiz y Fontanills, realizes, Juan's laughter constitutes a "mockery" (*burla*) of Law and Morality (p. 422). Earlier in the novel, his jokes at the expense of another member of the Ruiz and Fontanills family had met with a similar retort: "Listen, I won't be ridiculed by you [*tú sí que no puedes chotearme*]. We're not equals. You upstart! [*¡So parejero!*]" (p. 76). In the later scene Juan evinces a similar disregard for distinctions of class. His mere presence at the ceremony, among lawyers, academics, high-ranking church and government officials, is already an act of *parejería,* for Juan cer-

tainly does not belong in such company.[3] That he not only attends
the ceremony but makes fun of it demonstrates the *choteador*'s
typical repugnance toward restraining decorum, what Mañach
terms his "impatience" with limitation (*Indagación*, p. 38).
In this sense essay and novel relate as precept to example. Because *Indagación del choteo* offers so few concrete illustrations, its
argument profits from being conjoined to a book like Loveira's,
with its naturalistic wealth of detail. While in Mañach the "cubano de la calle" figures only as an initial pretext, in Loveira he
traverses the entire text. If Mañach takes *choteo* away from the
streets and into polite company, Loveira situates it back in its own
element. The passage from essay to novel, from precept to illustration, follows a descent into the mud like the one described by Lista.
It is already symptomatic that the first scene of the novel places us
in a slum: "He lived with his mother in a wood and zinc shack in
what were then the outskirts of Havana: Príncipe Street, near the
shore, which in those days lacked asphalt, levees, and great mansions, but did have an abundance of puddles, trash heaps, and
shacks like this one" (p. 1). Here the urbanity of the essay gives
way to the sub-urban filth and squalor of Juan's surroundings.
Since Mañach orients his discussion by dropping such names as
Ortega y Gasset, Américo Castro, Bergson, Simmel, and William
James, *Indagación del choteo* evokes a world of civilized, cosmo-
politan discourse. In contrast, Juan emerges from an environment
lacking in even the most rudimentary furnishings of civilization.
As Mañach himself realizes, this is the kind of environment that
breeds pernicious *choteo*.

But the pertinence of *Juan Criollo* for my argument does not
reside alone in the novel's dramatization of Mañach's ideas. Just as
pertinent, *Juan Criollo* offers still another elaboration of the Don
Juan theme. Loveira's protagonist is a tropical reincarnation of his
Andalusian namesake; Juan Criollo is a Don Juan *criollo*. This
assertion does not, however, take us completely out of *Indagación
del choteo*, where the conjunction of *choteador* and *burlador* is
implicit in *choteo*'s connection with *burla*. The same conjunction
also underlies Mañach's observation that Cuban jokers often mock
death; and when he states that "the man who is easily impression-
able, or extroverted, or who has a wandering curiosity, is generally
a disrespectful man, a great candidate to *choteo*" (*Indagación*,

p. 19), this personality profile fits el burlador almost as well as it describes *el choteador*. If only for this reason, in *Juan Criollo* donjuanism is inevitable and pervasive. Indeed, according to Loveira, it constitutes "the primordial *leit motiv* of creole life" (p. 158). Not only the protagonist but most of the male characters suffer from this "endemic erotic mania" (p. 406). One typical case is that of Don Roberto, the aging patriarch of the Ruiz y Fontanills clan, one of whose many concubines was Juan's mother. Don Roberto's death is a mirror of his life: he collapses late one night in a lovers' hideaway, and for many hours afterwards "an unyielding priapism" (p. 212) prevents his casket from being closed.

In its acculturation in Cuban soil peninsular donjuanism has acquired a popular flavor. The honorific *don* vanishes and a generic epithet is tacked on; the individual trait of one nobleman becomes a defining attribute of a whole nation. (Significantly, the original title of the novel was *Uno de tantos*.) Since one of Don Juan's traits is his uniqueness, this distribution of donjuanism over a whole population necessarily involves some redefinition of the concept. Juan's wager with Luis turns, in fact, on the claim of uniqueness. The successful completion of the wager means that Juan has no rival, that he is in no sense "one of many"; as he puts it in the *zarzuela:* "I don't take it well, Don Luis, / when someone tries to equal me."[4] Thus to take donjuanism and attribute it to a whole nation involves some denaturing of the model. More accurately, this affiliation involves a reduction of the model to its lowest common denominator, skirt-chasing, what Loveira likes to call "erotomania" (pp. 165, 296). The transformation of *donjuanismo* into *juancriollismo*[5] constitutes a vulgarization, both in the sense of impoverishment and in the primitive meaning of diffusion among the *vulgus.* To the extent that the donjuanism in the novel is restricted to the erotic, the creole Don Juan echoes the original only faintly.

Yet the most interesting connections between novel and antecedent legend have little to do with donjuanism in this restricted sense, and they are established, concretely, between Zorrilla's and Loveira's works.[6] For it turns out that *Juan Criollo* also focuses on a love letter, or rather a packet of love letters written by Nena (Don Roberto's granddaughter) to Juan when they were both adolescents and Juan lived in the Ruiz y Fontanills mansion. As in Zorrilla's play, these love letters become a recurring motif that draws the attention of many of the principal characters. When one of her uncles discovers Juan and Nena's flirtation, Juan claims that he has destroyed the compromising correspondence, though the letters go with him, hidden inside his trunk along with other memorabilia, when he is sent off to the sugar cane plantation. From this point on the letters will accompany him for most of his life. They will travel to Mexico with him; return to Cuba in the care of a trusted friend, Julián; and go back to Juan upon his return to the island. Finally, in the last scene of the novel, Julián asks Juan what should be done with "that famous packet of amorous papers" (p. 437). In a fit of cynical generosity Juan rejoins that it should be destroyed, since Nena should not have to pay for what was only an episode of youthful indiscretion. Loveira thought the *papelitos* (they are identified as such on pp. 115, 127, 262, 362) significant enough to make the novel's conclusion coincide with their destruction, as if the two texts were interlocked and the end of one entailed the end of the other. Both *Don Juan Tenorio* and *Juan Criollo* insinuate the importance of the *papelitos* by their placement: the play begins, and the novel closes, with letters.

The two sets of documents differ mainly in that Don Juan's epistle is visible to both characters and readers (or spectators), while Juan's packet is visible only to the reader. The contrast between the prayer book where Juan inserts his letter and the trunk where Juan hides his packet accounts for this difference. The *horario* discloses its contents; Inés opens it and the letter slips out. The trunk, however, shuts everything in; its double bottom ensures the invisibility of its contents. For this reason when Nena's uncle comes into Juan's room looking for the packet he cannot find it, even though he rummages through all of Juan's belongings. The corresponding but opposite scene in *Don Juan* occurs when Gonzalo rushes into Inés's cell and immediately notices the letter lying on the floor. Don Juan circulates his letter the way an adolescent flaunts his sexual development, but Juan Criollo holds on to his mementos the way an infant hoards his feces.

That double bottom in Juan's trunk will repay further scrutiny. Unlike the prayer book, which means nothing to Don Juan, the trunk where Juan keeps the packet encloses as many memories as the letters themselves. Having originally belonged to his father, and then to his mother, the trunk—"practically the only thing that made him a human being, with the right to inhabit a piece of the earth; the only possession that linked him materially to his dead parents" (p. 233)—constitutes the whole of Juan's inheritance. The peculiar thing about this whole is that its value resides in a hole. Juan's mother instructs her son on her deathbed: "Take this. This key opens a secret compartment in the trunk. Look for the little hole under the lining, in a corner at the bottom. And put away the key. Just in case. There you'll find your father's picture along with some of our things. And letters and papers. At least, some day you'll be able to prove that you had a father . . . and a mother" (p. 65). Like the letters, which constitute "material proof" of Nena's wrongdoing (p. 109; a reminiscence of the "written proof" of *Don Juan Tenorio*), the trunk is itself a kind of proof. Hidden away in the double bottom, in the hole within a hole, is Juan's birthright. To the world he is little more than "a child of the streets" (pp. 15, 287, 289) or, what is worse, one of Don Roberto's bastard offspring. But the documents in the hole prove that he was born legitimately of known parents. The trunk represents Juan's "inner" self, a private identity that he opposes to his public persona. Its double bottom suggests that Juan himself is double—a duplication rendered on another level by his two sur-names: Cabrera, the family name, the one that links him to his father; and Criollo, his public pseudonym. As we will see a bit later, much of the novel turns on this splitting of Juan into Cabrera and Criollo. The trunk's "interior duplication" furnishes an early emblem of that division.

But the double bottom signifies also in another direction. Juan calls it "a hidden hole" [*un güeco escondío*] (p. 175) where he keeps his "dark and hidden treasure" (p. 109), his "guaca" (Cuban for buried treasure; p. 130). Consider also the compulsiveness with which he saves Nena's mementos: "he takes to his chest, to that secret compartment his mother told him about before her death, everything the girl gives him: flowers, postcards, religious memen-tos, and any papers with her handwriting" (p. 109). He even hides a couple of books—the hole must be a big one—only because Nena has annotated them. This hoarding of objects in a trunk that goes back to his earliest days reflects a regressive, infantile, "anal" re-

tentiveness. Juan, *choteador* that he is, does not mature emotion-
ally. He is a child who treasures his *papelitos* as if they were his
own feces. Indeed, the papers would seem to bear out the well-
known Freudian equation between excrement, gold, and gifts: they
are a gift from Nena; Juan thinks of them as his treasure; and he
keeps them in a "hidden hole."[7] The double bottom is no less a
"holy place," no less a site unseen than the confessional of the last
chapter, for it serves as the secret deposit for Juan's "dark" treasure.

The fecal quality of the papers goes along with their uselessness.
Julián finds it "incomprehensible" (p. 403) that Juan should
want to retain them, since they have no practical value (a judgment borne out by the failure of the blackmail scheme). Neither
do they fulfill any significant role in the novel's plot. To most of
the characters they do not even exist, either because Juan does not
reveal their existence or because he claims to have thrown them
away. The visibility of the letters, their public career, as it were,
ends the moment Juan buries them in the bottom of the maternal
trunk. After that the letters are constantly alluded to but seldom
surface in the plot. Unlike Juan's epistle, without which the action
of Zorrilla's play is unthinkable, the letters in *Juan Criollo* remain
on the periphery. For most of the novel they are a motif without a
motive, a resource without a reason.

This contrast between the letters in *Don Juan* and in *Juan
Criollo* is all the more striking given that Loveira's novel transforms Don Juan's single letter into a whole correspondence and
assorted memorabilia. Yet even though the documents proliferate,
their functionality diminishes. Something similar had happened
with the novel's donjuanism, for here also the model was frac-
tioned and, as a result, diminished. In both instances the multiplica-
tion of exemplars carries with it an impoverishment or loss of
value whose organic equivalent is excrement. It is as if the artistic
and cultural products of the Americas germinated, maggot-like,
in the cultural debris of the Old World; as if those dungheaps and
mud puddles evoked in the novel's opening paragraph ("Príncipe
Street, near the shore, which in those days lacked asphalt, levees,
and great mansions [*huérfano de asfaltado, malecón y palacetes*],
but did have an abundance of puddles, trash heaps, and shacks")
were actually the New World's cultural inheritance, which had

washed up on its shores like so much flotsam. In this respect the "orphanhood" mentioned in this passage refers figuratively not only to Juan's condition but to the New World's. As a form of debris or useless trash, the Americas, an orphan continent, remain outside the Old World's family. This points up once again the difference between *Juan Criollo* and *Indagación del choteo,* for the latter work, from the dedication on, places itself in a genealogical line that remands us to such Old World figures as Ortega y Gasset and Bergson.[8]

One can say, then, that one mode of connection between *Juan Criollo* and *Don Juan Tenorio* is excrementalization, the carrying over of elements from the earlier text but in a useless, fossilized condition. This is not, however, the only connective mode in the novel. Equally important is a kind of transformation that I will call "creolization," that is, the rendering in "Cuban" or "creole" terms of elements in Zorrilla's play. If the first connective mode made us see the novel as a dungheap, the second one draws our attention to the native flora that may arise from such ordure. The second procedure is contained, in germ, in the following statement: "Then the great meal arrived, or, not using the creole word [*no hablando en criollo*], the great repast" (p. 120). The novel is *Don Juan* "en criollo," that is, *Juan Criollo.* I pick out this sentence because of the pertinence of its context; since the sybaritic repasts of the Ruiz y Fontanills could well be one of those elements that has been translated from the play (where banquets, of course, figure prominently), the sentence, even as it names the process of translation, gives evidence of it. And it is on the day of this meal that Domingo, Nena's uncle, labels Juan "the local Don Juan" [*el flamante Don Juan de la casa*] (p. 124).

A more extended example of creolization is evident in the novel's elaboration of Don Juan's boast that his conquests have run the whole social gamut:

Desde una princesa real
a la hija de un pescador,
ha recorrido mi amor
toda la escala social. (1.1.12)

(From a royal princess to the daughter of a fisherman: my loves have traversed the entire social scale.)

The "mixed-up ethnic composition" of the tropics (p. 421) makes Don Juan's boast change complexion: the different rungs on the social ladder become the varying shades of the racial spectrum. To be sure, the creole Juan also runs the social gamut, from Nena the aristocrat to Julia the prostitute. But as Julia herself realizes, the overriding distinction is not between social classes but between shades of skin color. In a statement reminiscent of Don Juan's boast, she says that Juan is capable of taking to bed women of every race and condition—"capaz de apechugar con toda clase de carne con faldas: negra, india, vieja, o 'podrida'" (p. 322). In the creole version "toda la escala social" turns into "toda clase de carne con faldas." Juan's romantic entanglements bear out the truth of her assertion: Nena, Julia, and Julita (his Cuban wife) are all white; Petra, the girl he romances while at the sugar cane plantation, is mulatto; and Marta, his Mexican wife, is *mestiza*. The other seducers in the novel evince similar inclinations, normally by taking on a white wife and black or mulatto concubines (as is the custom with the male members of the Ruiz y Fontanills clan). Juan himself offers living proof of miscegenation, since his father was a Spaniard and his mother a mulatto from Camagüey.

Two other creolized elements in *Juan Criollo* are the related motifs of orphanhood and exile. In order to have a term of contrast, let us consider for a moment the function of these motifs in *Don Juan Tenorio*. One of the paradoxes of Zorrilla's play is that fathers are seemingly everywhere and yet Don Juan is an orphan—and an orphan twice over. He first becomes one when Diego, outraged at his son's behavior, refuses to recognize Juan as his son, affirming instead that Don Juan must be the devil's offspring; and he becomes an orphan again moments later when his insolence causes Diego to say that Don Juan has "killed" him (significantly, after this scene Diego disappears from the play). Thus Juan's orphanhood, though figurative and mentioned only in passing, is doubly determined, as it results from both parricide and disinheritance.

Like his orphanhood, Don Juan's exile also appears unobtrusively in the play, and yet it too is central. And I intend "central" here in almost a material sense, for his exile is situated exactly in the middle of the play, between the first and second parts—an interval longer by far than either of the sections that surround it. In

an illustration of the reversible nature of the center-periphery relation, Don Juan's territorial marginality is, structurally and themati-
cally, the center of the play. Like a protracted parenthesis with
nothing inside it, Don Juan's exile is precisely located but nowhere rendered: inscribed rather than described. Even though his
feats abroad earn him the right of repatriation, his exile is itself
banished to the interstices of the play. Yet without Juan's exile the
events in part 2 would not have taken place. Even his narration of
his experiences as an expatriate occurs between acts 1 and 2 of
part 2: both the event and the account of it are elided, inserted
"between and betwixt" acts and actions.[9] But if one ignores Zorrilla's emphases and counts the exilic interlude as one of the
"parts" of the play, the *Tenorio* follows the archetypical tripartite
pattern of banishment (part 1), exile (hiatus between parts 1 and
2), and return (part 2); or, in van Gennep's terms, of separation,
limen, and reaggregation. As in other rites of passage, Don Juan's
accomplishments abroad—what he calls his "thousand adventures"
(2.1.3)—justify his reaggregation into Spanish society. Don Juan's
much-discussed religious salvation, effected in the last scenes of the
play, is thus preceded and made possible by a secular, civil salvation that entitles him to step again on native soil.

Now in *Juan Criollo* the protagonist's orphanhood becomes literal and the pattern of exile and return turns into the fundamental
plot mechanism. The novel also shows us how closely intertwined
the two motifs are. For Juan the loss of his parents and his expulsion from native soil go hand in hand, as is demonstrated by his
feeling that the trunk not only links him to his parents but gives
him "the right to inhabit a piece of the earth." Not surprisingly
then, after the death of his mother his life becomes a succession of
geographical displacements. First he is taken away from the neighborhood where he grew up, and then he is thrown out of the Ruiz
y Fontanills mansion and sent to the country. After some years in
Los Mameyes he has to flee back to Havana, only to depart for
Mexico a few months later. In Mexico history repeats itself, for
once again Juan is expelled from the Ruiz y Fontanills household,
and once again the reason is his liberties with Nena. The punish-
ment remains banishment from the city: "Now Adolfo repeated
the words that his father had said several years ago: 'Get ready,
tomorrow you are leaving for the country'" (p. 287). In the

country the repetition of events continues when Juan—as he did in *Los Mameyes*—gets involved with one of the natives and has to return to the city. The final ironic turn in this pattern of displacements is that in the end Juan does go back to Cuba, though only because he is thrown out of Mexico for being a "pernicious foreigner" (pp. 338, 349). Paradoxically, his periplus concludes with an expatriation that is also a homecoming—as if one could be exiled to one's native country or thrown into one's home.

The reappearance of "perniciousness" in this context serves to remind us that the centrifugal impetus of Juan's life may also reflect the novel's connection with *choteo,* which also consists of a displacement toward the periphery. As a detour toward or an assault from the margins, *choteo* inscribes a double movement comparable to the pattern of exile and return. Even Mañach's description of the *choteador* as someone with a "wandering curiosity" suggests the peripatetic inclinations of the phenomenon, inclinations also manifested in the clowns' anatomical pilgrimage. Now we find that Juan, in addition to exhibiting *choteo*'s liminality, also shares its perniciousness, since he possesses similar pathogenic powers. When Juan's relationship with Nena is initially discovered, he is accused of being a "stranger" who has brought into the house his "street infections" (p. 134) and performed "monstrosities" with Don Roberto's own flesh and blood (p. 135). Just as *choteo* permeates the body politic with the "germs" of a toxic fermentation (*Indagación,* p. 59), Juan inflicts on Nena his street infections. If Juan is an "intruder" (p. 422), *choteo* is a "contumacious guest" (*Indagación,* p. 46); if Juan breeds monsters, so does *choteo* (*Indagación,* p. 29). In both texts the intrusive force, the liminal element, is regarded as a threat to social organization, whether of a family or of a nation. The consequent expulsion responds to a desire for social hygiene.

But Juan's many returns show that the danger of infection is chronic: he is banished from Havana and he returns; he is banished from Mérida and he returns; he leaves Cuba and he returns. And at no time does Juan's return mean that he has been cured. Near the end of the novel, in the ceremony to appoint a judge, Juan remains as much an unwelcome guest or pernicious stranger as he ever was. Unlike his namesake, Juan is never saved by reincorporation into a social or religious community.[10] As Juan will acknowledge, in his public life he is nothing other than a parasite feeding off the body politic (pp. 432–33); and in his private life he is as rootless at the end as he was at the beginning, a condition symbolized by the fact that he owns—and lives in—ten different houses. The creole Don Juan then differs from his peninsular counterpart in that his exile is not part of a rite of passage, a temporary period of purification or errancy, but a permanent state. As befits an orphan born in an orphan continent, Juan is never not in exile. Even at home is he homeless. Like *choteo* itself, he subsists in a perpetual pendular swing between the center and the periphery (Cuba–Mexico; the city–the country; his wife–his lovers, etc.), so much so that one wonders whether, at least in Juan's case, the terms "center" and "periphery" are not interchangeable: when Juan is banished from Mexico to Cuba, is he leaving or approaching the center? when he goes from house to house and from woman to woman, is he oscillating from a fixed center or rather moving in a circuit, each of whose relays is both center and periphery to all the remaining ones?

In light of these continual displacements, one can say that *Juan Criollo* emerges from the interstices of Zorrilla's play, from that structural exile within which Don Juan's homelessness is contained. Loveira spins his novel from a void, dilating on the very topics that Zorrilla elides. Thus *Juan Criollo* fits exactly in the middle of *Don Juan Tenorio,* between its two halves, in the manner of a folded letter. (Need I remark, in my role as Brígida, that Loveira's novel also occupies the exact middle of my book?) Following Loveira's lead, perhaps one should look upon New World texts as liminal letters that slip or are cast out of holy books, out of a canon. Creole literature is a letter lodged in a book of hours. The letter is an emblem of New World detachment. That the literal prototype for this detachment is a text written by a fractious son in defiance of his father only enhances the appropriateness of the conceit.

Loveira's creolization of the twin motifs of exile and orphanhood is also noteworthy because it shows that, if given narrative form, the Don Juan story becomes a picaresque novel, though one with a difference. *Juan Criollo*'s principal literary antecedents are on the one hand *Don Juan Tenorio* and on the other the picaresque tradition. If the play provides Loveira with the building blocks of his novel, the picaresque tradition, and particularly *Lazarillo de Tormes,* gives him a plan, a blueprint for their arrangement. *Don Juan Tenorio* is the contentual, and *Lazarillo* the structural, model. Thus *Juan Criollo* sports all of the trappings of the genre—an episodic plot, a protagonist of low origins, indenture to a succession of masters, the portrayal of the lower strata of society, and so on. It has all of the trappings, that is, but one, for Loveira's novel, unlike most picaresque narratives, is not a first-person account. But here also the divergence from the peninsular prototype grows out of the phenomenon of creolization, which operates in this instance in the area of narrative perspective. Behind the novel's seeming disregard for this generic convention there lies a reasoned attempt to acculturate, to render *en criollo,* the traditional way of presenting a picaresque tale.

Since most of the novel's commentators have taken for granted that the story is delivered by an undramatized, omniscient narrator close to Loveira himself, the narrative perspective of *Juan Criollo* has elicited little comment. A perusal of the text reveals, however, that the narrator is not omniscient, since he has access to the mental operations of only one character, the protagonist. All throughout the novel, with unexpected Jamesian scrupulousness, the narrative voice limits its information to what Juan knows and thinks. The novel is presented, in fact, as the text of Juan's reminiscences many years after the events took place: "His earliest memories, fixed in firm and clear images, of his extraordinary life, go back forty years, to when he was six years old" (p. 1). On occasion it even seems that what we are reading is a transcription of a memoir of some sort: "For a long time his life was simply that of a true bureaucrat: a resigned, monotonous, deadening existence that he has wanted to remember only in broad strokes, years at a time— just the opposite of the chapters dealing with his past, always reproduced with flowing, warm, evocative words" (p. 391).

In view of these statements and others like them (pp. 232, 258, 288, 363), one can posit that the novel emerges from the redaction, by an impersonal narrator, of Juan's recollections—the kind of narrative perspective labelled by Friedman "selective omniscience."[11] A different hypothesis is also possible: one can maintain that in keeping with its picaresque lineage the novel is an autobiographical memoir after all, but one in which the author speaks about himself in the third person. Hence, the implicit *yo* that speaks to the reader is the same person as the *él* on whom the story focuses; both are Juan Criollo. This hypothesis accords not only with the limitations of the narrator but also with the novel's theme. *Juan Criollo* narrates the protagonist's rise to the top, a rise propelled by all sorts of trickery and corruption. Like Lázaro de Tormes, Juan eventually scales "the summit of all good fortune."[12] If one accepts the notion of a displaced first-person account (displaced like Juan himself), one could then say that by telling his life's story Juan intends to exculpate himself, to explain how he became what he is.

Several critics have remarked on the abrupt conclusion of the novel; toward the end, almost twenty years of Juan's life are crammed into the space of a few pages.[13] What has not been noticed is that this sudden condensation is a quirk that *Juan Criollo* shares with *Lazarillo de Tormes,* the brevity of whose last *tratados* has elicited much critical debate.[14] The reasons that students of the *Lazarillo* commonly adduce to explain this condensation also elucidate Loveira's abrupt ending. Since Juan, like Lázaro, wants to exculpate himself, he emphasizes not his corrupt rise to the top but his formative influences—those people and circumstances responsible (or so he claims) for his degradation. The largest part of the novel, therefore, is taken up by his unfortunate childhood and adolescence. In *Lazarillo de Tormes* this distinction between venal narrator and innocent actor is rendered in part by the onomastic discrimination between the young Lazarillo and the adult Lázaro.[15] In *Juan Criollo* we find a similar discrimination: Juan the actor is Juan Cabrera; Juan the author, the narrator, is Juan Criollo. Furthermore, since Criollo is his *nom de plume,* the name he uses when he writes for the newspapers, it fits the narrator of the novel precisely. Juan Criollo is as much a signature as a title, and the novel as a whole may be considered the process whereby a title becomes a signature, or whereby Juan evolves a writerly self.[16]

The novel's ultimate act of "creolization"—Juan's assumption of the epithet *criollo*—is lexical or onomastic. This renaming provides the key to the splitting of the protagonist into a *yo* and an *él.* The recourse to the third person suggests that Juan Cabrera is the narrator's superseded identity, his old self. Juan Criollo is the new man

Juan knowingly becomes. By dropping his surname he accepts his orphanhood, substituting for the imperatives of genealogy the privileges of self-begetting.[17] But this forging of a new identity from an old one, of a Criollo from a Cabrera, also names the process whereby *Juan Criollo* the novel emerges from *Don Juan* the play. The protagonist's recreation of himself coincides with the novel's recreation of the Don Juan story, a recreation largely effected by merging elements of the Don Juan story with the conventions of the picaresque. Cabrera, the name of the (Spanish) father, is replaced by Criollo, a term that originally described those born in the New World of Spanish parents—a term, therefore, that fits the text as well as the character. Thus the distance between Cabrera and Criollo, and between the third and the first person, is an emblem of the separation of the novel from its peninsular prototypes.

In *Recuerdos del tiempo viejo* Zorrilla relates that during his wanderings in the savage wastes of the New World, he accidentally came upon a performance of *Don Juan* in which the play was so changed that he did not recognize it: "My Don Juan was such / that even I did not know him."[18] This statement, which paraphrases that crucial scene in *Don Juan* where Don Diego disowns his son with the words, "I don't know you, Don Juan" (1.1.12), is prompted by Zorrilla's perception that his play had been translated into a "jargon wrought by the devil" [*jerga que el diablo urdió*]—and this again echoes Don Diego, who says that *his* creation, Juan, must be the "son of Satan." These twin incidents help us situate Loveira's novel in the Don Juan family. For *Juan Criollo* is that bastard, butchered American version of the play, written in a creole jargon that the author of *Don Juan* would find unrecognizable. Loveira tampers with his sources in such a way that the family resemblance of his creation has all but disappeared. As we have seen, the "central" issue raised by the novel has to do with the modes of connection between Cuban/American cultural products and their Spanish/European ancestry. If, as Mañach says, *choteo* breeds monsters, one can perhaps conclude that this connection materializes as *choteo*. *Juan Criollo* is a *choteo*, a monstrous imitation of its originals. What I have called creolization and excrementalization may then be seen as the two interacting mechanisms in this type of imitation.

Let me make my meaning clearer by pondering for a moment *choteo*'s mimetic dimension. This dimension has been implicit in my discussion all along, for *choteo* is a mimetic phenomenon in exactly the same sense in which *culo* is the festive underside, the carnival copy, of *cara*. In *Juan Criollo* this dimension figures explicitly in the phrase "choteíto mimético" (p. 405) as well as in Juan's penchant for imitation (examples may be found on pp. 1, 14, 365–66, 434); more importantly, it also appears in *Indagación* when Mañach twice alludes to the myth of Narcissus: "In the solitude of a study, or in the familiar surroundings of the dinner table, the tropical Narcissus can contemplate his image without peril. But as soon as he goes out into the world and tries to translate his self-esteem into public authority, *choteo* steps in his path and cuts him down to size" (*Indagación,* p. 67). The other mention occurs in a passage on monstrosity to which I have already referred; at times, says Mañach, "our mockery aims at a more or less real weakness, distorting it, magnifying it, caricaturing it until even Narcissus has become a monster" (*Indagación,* p. 70). The myth of Narcissus offers an exemplary instance of what I earlier called sculptural mimesis, that is, the symmetrical correspondence of original and reflection. *Choteo* muddles this correspondence by transforming the subject into its polar opposite: the picture of beauty into the paradigm of deformity. *Choteo* is thus more closely allied with festive mimesis, which shatters mirror images and puts in their place copies characterized by a monstrous doubling of the originals. Texts of *choteo* relate to their models as the grotesque banquet in *Don Juan* relates to the dinner scene. (Question: since the concept of festive mimesis was first elaborated apropos of *Las galas del difunto,* does it follow that this *esperpento* is an "American" work—as American in its way as, say, *Tirano Banderas?* In order to answer this question, one would need to keep in mind the following facts: (1) when the *esperpento* begins Juanito has just returned from Cuba; (2) La Daifa points out to him that his speech has become contaminated by American expressions, by what Zorrilla regarded as the devil's words: "You picked that line up in Havana. . . . You speak just like all of the soldiers who have come back" [*Las galas,* pp. 14–15]; and (3) one of these imported words is none other than *relajo* [*Las galas,* p. 59]. Given these facts, is it really so preposterous to posit the *americanidad,* and even the *cubanidad*, of Valle's play? If Fernando Ortiz can write a book entitled *Entre cubanos* and publish it in Paris, can Valle write a "Cuban" play in Madrid?)

But to return to the question of mimesis: that *choteo* imitates by deforming is clear not only from the references to Narcissus but also from one of the jokes that Mañach cites. When I stated in the last chapter that *Indagación* contains only two examples of *choteo*, I failed to mention a third illustration. Here it is now:

In the living room of a house, a young lady is singing by a piano. She sings a sentimental ballad [*una romanza sentimental*], but without overdoing it. Besides, she sings it well; so much so that, from the sidewalk, a group of young men listen to her, entranced [*embelesados*]. When the girl finishes, however, the young men take a few steps back from the window and, in a falsetto voice, make a cruel jest [*una mofa despiadada*] of the same ability that had just delighted them. (*Indagación*, pp. 45–46)

Mañach relates this incident, which he says he witnessed, in order to illustrate *choteo*'s arbitrary qualities. To him the jeer seems gratuitous and evinces the systematic, habitual character of this vice. The young men—mockingbirds to the girl's nightingale— make fun not because the singer deserves it but out of pernicious habit. To my mind, nonetheless, the mockery, which consists of a disfigured repetition of the performance (inverting the myth, the young men play Echo to the girl's Narcissus), seems less than gratuitous, given that the girl was singing a *romanza*. Put it this way: had she been singing a native melody the incident might not have occurred. Rephrasing a Cuban proverb, one could counsel the singer: *olvida la romanza y canta bolero*. The phonic assault stems from the perceived foreignness of the song; to a Cuban even the word *romanza* may sound alien. I mean to say, then, that the binary pair formed by the *romanza* and the *mofa* is homologous with the other oppositions we have encountered, oppositions that are all instances of the center-periphery relation: *cara–culo; Don Juan–Juan Criollo; Narciso–monstruo*. The hyphen that divides (and joins) each pair designates the *choteo* connection. This connection involves a festive or carnivalesque copying in which the first term is transformed to the point of disfiguration.

choteo = aculturación

If Mañach's anecdote is representative, we can also say that *choteo*'s animosity toward foreign imports serves the cause of intellectual autonomy. *Choteo* is a defense mechanism against Old World charm, an antidote to cultural hypnosis. (Thus, perhaps the other necessary condition for the young men's derision is the bewitching quality of the singer's performance, which has them *embelesados.*) Mañach is quite right to stress the *choteador*'s repugnance toward limitation, though what has to be added is that these limitations are not only those imposed by local authority; they include also the restrictions and imperatives attendant to the New World's epigonism.[19] The paradox of this fractiousness, of course, is that in its search for an autochthonous expression the New World has no choice but to reprise, however monstrously, foreign airs. Even the search itself is probably derivative.[20] If uniqueness there be, it will reside less in the composition of a new tune, be it a *danzón* or a *romanza,* than in the tone and timbre of the echoes of foreign melodies. A book like *Juan Criollo,* composed in the heyday of the *mundonovista* movement and hence much concerned with New World specificities, makes the point quite clearly. Although Loveira intends to paint a realistic portrait of Cuban society at the turn of the century, he has to borrow his colors from a peninsular palette. And Mañach himself, in an inquiry into the distinctive traits of the Cuban character, resorts to the model of the Ortegan meditation.

Juan Marinello, writing at about the same time as Loveira and Mañach, put the problem this way:

Language is the truest mark of our Spanishness, the most powerful obstacle to a vernacular idiom, for we are born into a language, as into the world, without the opportunity for election: as soon as we begin to think, as soon as we begin to live, Castilian is already our only language. We exist through a language that is our own while being foreign [*Somos a través de un idioma que es nuestro siendo extranjero*]. Language has a life of its own. We strain to inseminate our mother tongue with native expressions [*criollismos*], only to find that our innovations were already alive centuries ago in Andalusia or Extremadura. Or that they could have been. The cloistral blood of language binds parents and children, and unwittingly engenders grandchildren that resemble them.[21]

As we will see in the next chapter, Marinello's law of linguistic belatedness might apply even to such an "obvious" *criollismo* as *choteo*. It certainly applies, on the broader level of literary expression, to *Juan Criollo*. No matter how bizarre or outrageous, the American copy does not cease being traceable to its peninsular forebears. The only palliative is that *choteo* puts a bright face on Marinello's fatalism, for it shows that one need not submit somberly to genealogical subordination. As *Juan Criollo* demonstrates, children always find a way of turning against their parents. Even if unlikeness can be approached only as a limit, the exploration of that frontier is already an act of defamiliarization, a symptom of that "prurito de independencia" that Mañach finds in every Juan Criollo.

Let us return to the young girl's Old World siren song. This incident is reminiscent of Mañach's primal scene of instruction, that passage early in the book where the author sees himself as going down to the streets to investigate the meaning of *choteo*. Both scenes feature the same cast of characters: a female protagonist (the women in Mañach's audience; the girl who sings); the representative Cuban (the *cubano de la calle;* the young men on the street) and Mañach. The difference is that in the later episode Mañach is only a passive bystander, while in the earlier one he had acted as the guardian of woman's virtue. In the singing scene the obstructing figure of the censor has been replaced by an open window through which the street's contagion penetrates into the room. Having no father, or cop, or priest, or lecturer to protect her, the singer remains directly exposed to pernicious *choteo*. We might say that she is portrayed as an orphan, and that this scene is an "orphan" version of the earlier one. The pertinence of this duplication for *Juan Criollo* should be clear. *Juan Criollo* is an orphan novel about orphanhood. Even though it is rooted in the same cultural milieu as Mañach's essay, the essay reflects the fatherly propriety of the scene of instruction, while the novel embraces the openness of the singing scene. The young men's catcalls—among which I cannot help hearing a *trompetilla* or two—thus take us back to the novel's point of departure, a street like the one Juan grew up in, teeming with dungheaps and mud puddles. Loveira's achievement is not letting us forget the role of such fetid surroundings in the germination of *choteo*.

6

The Devil's Dictionary

We can explore a bit further the link between the Cuban vernacular and *choteo* by looking briefly at another work contemporaneous with *Indagación del choteo* and *Juan Criollo,* but one whose very subject is that devilish jargon condemned by Zorrilla. I refer to Fernando Ortiz's thesaurus of Cuban words and expressions, *Un catauro de cubanismos,* published in book form in 1923.[1] What is a *catauro?* The entry in another dictionary of *cubanismos* says: "A kind of portable, rustic box or basket, made from palm bark, and used to keep or carry fruits, eggs, etc., and even to get water from wells."[2] If my discussion of *Juan Criollo* probed a trunk full of *papelitos,* the argument of this chapter will investigate a box full of *papeletas.* The transition from one text to the other is as easy as the exchange of a trunk for a box, a *papelito* for a *papeleta,* a *tesoro* for a *tesauro.* Even if they differ widely in form, both novel and dictionary emerge from the same cultural matrix and address similar issues. Like *tesoro* and *tesauro,* the two works are paronyms, diverse linguistic flowerings of a common root.

Leaving aside Ortiz's lexicographical contributions, which will not concern me here, the principal issue raised by the *Catauro,* as by *Juan Criollo,* has to do with the modes of connection between New World and Old World culture.[3] In Loveira's novel these connections are articulated on the plane of literary conventions and themes; in the *Catauro* the connections materialize on a more fundamental level, that of words considered singly. I find it revealing that Loveira's protagonist, in the course of reflecting upon his hidden treasure, rebaptizes it a *guaca,* exactly the sort of word one encounters in Ortiz's compendium. By renaming the letters with an autochthonous word, by relettering them as it were, Juan creolizes one of the elements in the novel that most readily bares its peninsular origins. The incident itself recalls (re-calls) the other onomastic rebirth in the book, Juan's own. Since the shedding of his patronymic also severs peninsular ties, the conversion of a *tesoro* into a *guaca* mirrors the protagonist's metamorphosis from Cabrera to Criollo. These twin acts of onomastic recall condense *Juan Criollo's* attempt to distance itself from its transatlantic models; beyond this, they point to the linguistic bedrock on which the battle for cultural or literary autonomy must be waged. Since language sediments human culture, a nation's most radical autonomy and its most degrading dependence are linguistic. Marinello's melancholy meditations, quoted at the end of the last chapter, underscore the fact that what is at stake in this war of words is nothing less than the New World's intellectual integrity. If Marinello's dictum is true—"Somos a través de un idioma que es nuestro siendo extranjero"—Spain's old colonies suffer from a peculiar schizophrenia for which there is no treatment. As Roberto González Echevarría has pointed out, Marinello's statement is a version of the Rimbaldian declaration of otherness, *je est une autre,*[4] for to be constituted as/through another's language amounts to experiencing one's Self as one's Other—and vice versa: not only *je est une autre* but also, *l'autre, c'est moi.* Grammatically what is rendered problematic is the first person and the singular number: one is at least two; behind the first person there is always a second. Culturally what is denied is the possibility of a native tongue or an autochthonous literature.

To be sure, Marinello is probably right. Language is alienating, and not just for those born in "Spanish" America. The ideal of a purely American sociolect or culture, a notion that achieved some currency in the early decades of this century, seems sheer delusion. To the present-day reader a tract like José Vasconcelos's *La raza cósmica,* with its millenary promise of a radical beginning, reads less like social science than like science fiction. Even Vasconcelos's title sounds like something out of *Star Wars.*[5] The point is that one cannot escape what Marinello, in the same essay from which I have quoted, labelled "Europe's learned fetters" [*los grillos sabios*

de Europa]. In the New World, Europe has the constraining role
of the fathers in *Don Juan* or the cop in "Los payasos," since it inscribes the center of gravity that retains the American continent
inside Europe's sphere of influence.

Even so, Ortiz's *Catauro,* while not making any of the extravagant claims of a work like Vasconcelos's, represents an attempt to
escape the Old World's gravitational pull by securing a partial
autonomy for the Spanish spoken in Cuba. In this respect the
Catauro is less a work of "objective" scholarship than a com-
mitted, polemical demonstration of Cuba's cultural autonomy, a
demonstration built on this culture's linguistic foundations. Ortiz's
recursive title, which creolizes the *vocabulario* or *diccionario* of
similar collections, already anticipates the book's encompassing
aim. It is no exaggeration to say that the *Catauro* is a profoundly
political treatise, a declaration of cultural independence addressed,
as we shall see, to those peninsular arbiters of linguistic propriety
whose task is to "establish, purify, and polish" the mother tongue.
The *Catauro* does just the opposite: it deranges, defiles, and pol-
lutes the mother tongue by seeding it with barbarisms, with what
Lista would have regarded as "harsh sounds" and "improper
words." As such the book voices one of those typically American
(North *and* South) barbaric yawps with which the New World
responds to Old World polish—a yawp that one might compare
to the *trompetilla* that greeted the performance of the *romanza*
in Mañach's anecdote.

In order better to understand Ortiz's polemical stance, let us
look first at another compilation of American expressions, Miguel
de Toro y Gisbert's "Reivindicación de americanismos," published
in the *Boletín de la Real Academia*—where else?—a couple of
years before the appearance of the *Catauro.*[6] Toro's title is every
bit as revealing as Ortiz's; how does one "revindicate" Americanisms? Simple: one shows that they descend from fine Castilian
stock. The article consists of a long list of items that, according
to its author, have been wrongly entered as Americanisms in various reference works—words like *calimba, manjúa, guagua, jabado,
bullarengue, mamalón,* and many more. Interestingly enough, one
of the revindicated words is none other than *choteo.* A look at this
entry will show us how the revindication is accomplished. The
entry begins:

Chotear: According to the Academy, a Cuban word. "To ridicule, to make fun of someone." It has been an addition of the last edition of the *Dictionary.*

It's also Mexican, according to Ramos.

The word is Spanish. In Besses we find, as a *caló* word, *Chotiar,* in the sense of to spit. In Pío Baroja (*Busca,* 102), we find a derived word: "That was some *choteo* that we had with the ladies."[7]

Toro goes on to relate *choteo* to *chota* and gives *choto,* small calf, as the root. He thus employs two complementary techniques of revindication. One is to trace an *americanismo* to its Spanish root-words. In the world of lexicography, etymological determinism takes the place of genealogical determinism. When Loveira's protagonist sheds Cabrera and adopts Criollo, he is subverting genealogy; when Toro y Gisbert, following the Academy, traces *choteo* back to *choto,* he is subverting Juan's act of subversion. The lexical antidote to creolization is excavating the Spanish roots of American words. (Coincidentally, Cabrera goes back to *cabra* and *choto* is a synonym of *cabrito.*) Toro's other ploy is to cite peninsular precedents for each of his entries. He seems to assume that the use of a word by Baroja or Pardo Bazán or Pereda (all three favorite sources) furnishes sufficient proof of its Spanish origins, even though, of course, by the nineteenth century Castilian Spanish had incorporated a good number of American borrowings. Interestingly, Ortiz evinces an antithetical blindness, for he assumes that no date of entry is too *early* to preclude contamination. His *Catauro* regularly cites Spanish authorities from the sixteenth century with the claim that the currency of the word in Spain is owed to the residence in Andalusia of black slaves.

More important than the accuracy of Toro's rerootings is the purpose they serve. This purpose is made clear in the introduction to the catalogue, where Toro—a Spanish bull—charges American lexicographers with ignorance of Castilian Spanish:

The Spanish reader who leafs through some Dictionaries of Spanish-American provincialisms is more than a little surprised by the incredible number of purely Spanish words that appear in these books, words that each author attributes to his own country.

One is astonished by the incredible shabbiness of our Dictionaries as well as by the ignorance of some Spanish-American writers with respect to the Castilian language.[8]

This ignorance, he says, is dangerous because it creates the impression that a wide gap exists between Castilian and American Spanish, and this impression may make American readers, who are "poco advertidos," give up the struggle to speak with Castilian correctness, *castizamente*. The political undercurrent of the diatribe comes to the surface a few sentences later: "Some Spanish-American writers, misguided by a faulty sense of national pride, and having no knowledge of our modern literature, figure that their political emancipation has endowed them with such linguistic vitality that they have been able to create a new language. I have already spoken several times in my books against such an absurd theory." From Toro's perspective, the collection of Americanisms serves illegitimate political ends. Toro is warning his American colleagues, in effect: do not think that political independence entitles you to linguistic autonomy. Etymology is destiny. Even though Spanish America may no longer be a complex of colonies, culturally it remains under the Spanish flag. A bit later, in an aside on the pains and pleasures of lexicography, he adds:

This tracking down of sources is long and tedious. But what a pleasure it is to stumble across the filiation of one or another word, expressive, elegant, correct [*castiza*], words which in Spain today are gathering dust in libraries or are disdained for their provincialism, while they lead youthful and vigorous lives in some Spanish-American territory [*comarca*]! And how it cheers me up to see how, day by day, the indissoluble bond of language [*el lazo indisoluble del idioma*] tightens more and more, reuniting us with our brothers from across the ocean![9]

I'm not sure why, but I find something unsettling in that gradual tightening of the "lazo indisoluble del idioma," perhaps because it reminds me of Marinello's somewhat different metaphor for the same idea, that of "Europe's learned fetters." One man's lasso is another man's noose. In any case, Toro's elation has a definite imperial quality. His implied comparison of the American nations to the Spanish provinces suggests that the New World is to the Old as the provinces are to the metropolis; moreover, the fledgling republics are identified only as *comarcas;* territories, and not as autonomous political entities. For Toro the American continent remains on the margins, geographically as well as culturally, and the fraternal kinship mentioned at the end is somewhat jeopardized by the filial image he had earlier employed ("to stumble across the filiation of one or another word"). Toro's is the delight of the colonizer who realizes that, political dispossession notwithstanding, in a deeper sense than the political these lands remain under his sway. He is an embattled Prospero, a magus of philological savvy who makes up for his deficit in political power by what he regards as a surplus of knowledge.[10] Note his superior atttiude vis-à-vis his transatlantic brothers. A "lector español" like himself immediately perceives the flaws of Spanish-American lexicography; but the "lector americano," being less knowledgeable or alert ("poco advertido"), is easily duped. The whole catalogue is nothing more than an exercise in linguistic recolonization, the repossession for Spain of what, in Toro's bull's-eye view, rightly belongs to her. Hence the title.

"Reivindicación de americanismos" reveals strikingly the ideological substratum of seemingly impartial scholarship. Toro y Gisbert's erudition, which is considerable, is nourished by a centrist bias in favor of Spanish cultural hegemony. In the *Catauro* a similarly impressive scholarly apparatus will be put to the service of a decentralizing impetus or centrifugal force. Although Ortiz employs many of the same ploys as Toro, particularly etymologies, they are used to sever, not cement, Cuba's peninsular connections.

One can identify three different stratagems or devices that work toward this end. The first consists in deracinating a word from peninsular soil by proposing a non-Spanish (usually Amerindian or African) etymology. Again our maligned and malignant *choteo* can serve to illustrate. Even though Ortiz concedes that *chotear* may well be related to its homonyms in *caló,* he argues that the derivation from *choto* is "arbitrary" and argues instead for a different derivation from the word *achote,* a red substance used by some Indians for body decoration. Since *choteo* embarrasses, makes its victims blush, it could be a metaphorical extension of the Indian word for the red dye. *Chotear* would then evolve from *achote* through the hypothetical middle step, *achotear:* "And this being the case, we would thus have another verisimilar etymology for *choteo*, through a common apherisis of the initial *a*" (p. 211).

In the *Glosario de afronegrismos* he goes a step further, suggesting, in addition to the Indian one, several African etyma for *choteo*. Again he discards the Academy's etymology: "The Academy supposes that the word comes from *choto* or 'baby goat.' This etymology is entirely unverisimilar. If the most learned Spanish corporation did not deserve our highest respects, we would say that this etymology was a joke [*una etimología de choteo*]." Ortiz's quip is itself, of course, an act of *choteo*. By incorporating the term under discussion into the rhetoric of the debate he is not so much begging the question as mocking the answer; he is subverting, making a *choteo*, out of the convention of scholarly disputation. He performs this gesture many times. The same joke had already been used in the *Catauro;* after mentioning that *chotiar* in *caló* means "to spit," Ortiz asks: "Isn't *chotear* to spit morally on someone, a suggestion I make without *choteíto*, or with only the indispensable amount of it?" (p. 36). In effect, Ortiz himself is spitting on lexicography, turning an erudite disquisition on *choteo* into a *choteo*.

The disparagement of the Academy's etymology is followed, in the *Glosario*, by a new theory, that *choteo* did not evolve from *choto*, nor even from *achote*, but from a *lucumí* or *yoruba* word meaning "to speak."

In spite of the foregoing, the Africanist thesis is more verisimilar, founded as it is on the *lucumí* or *yoruba* term *soh* or *chot*, which means "to speak," "to say," and, besides, "to throw," "to tear," "to cast out," all of which harmonizes with the despective sense of our *choteo*. From that root *cho* or *soh* are derived *sohroh* "to converse," *sohrohjehjeh* "to murmur," *sohrohlehin* "to speak of someone behind his back," *sohwerewere* "to speak without rhyme or reason."

Likewise, in *pongüé chota* is "act of spying," "to pry," and in *lucumí cho* is, also, "to keep watch," "to spy," which avoids the gypsy etymology of *chota*, as well as that of *choteo*.

Taken together, the entries in the *Catauro* and the *Glosario* propose no less than three different etyma for *choteo:* one *caló*, another Indian, and another African. The "Africanist thesis" itself has two variants, for Ortiz suggests roots not only in *yoruba* or *lucumí* but also in *pongüé*—all with a view to avoiding, as he says at the end, the "gypsy etymology." But the upshot of these multiple derivations is that *choteo* itself becomes a gypsy word, a lexical exile, wandering from place to place much as Juan in Loveira's novel or the clowns in Alvarez Guedes's joke.

Typically, Ortiz's defense of the non-Spanishness of the word is multifaceted. Not satisfied with one alternative etymon, he goes in for philological overkill. And all of this, it must be mentioned, comes from someone who had no firsthand knowledge of the African languages he so insistently exploited. Ortiz's procedure was to ransack dictionaries and grammars of African tongues (most of these works written in English or French; hence the peculiar-looking—to Spanish eyes—transcriptions of the African roots) in search of homonyms or paronyms of words used in Cuba. Having found them, he then tried to confect a semantic link between the African word and the Spanish one. Once this connection was established, the rerooting (and rerouting) was complete. Needless to say, etymologies thus elaborated are far from reliable, especially in view of Ortiz's fanciful interpretive leaps (*choteo* as a form of "throwing," for instance), and the excesses of his method are apparent even to the nonspecialist.[11]

But for my argument Ortiz's eccentricity is beside the point. Or rather, it is precisely the point, since I regard the *Catauro* as a work of philological fabulation, a "logofiction" that obeys a logic and incarnates a consistency different from those of scientific inquiry. I approach the *Catauro* as one would approach a novel— and perhaps as one should approach works of criticism as well: with an eye for the motif rather than for the syllogism, for texture rather than for truth. The accuracy of Ortiz's etymologies interests me less than the role they play in the book's plot; and I use the term "plot" advisedly, for in its mixture of the political and the literary the word traces the contours of the book.[12] The *Catauro* is a philological fiction with a political theme. One important motif in this theme is the excision of Cuban Spanish from its peninsular matrix, what Ortiz terms the "avoidance" of peninsular etymologies. The questions that need to be asked of the book are: Why should one feel compelled to avoid such etymologies? What is to be avoided by such avoidance? What danger or harm in a gypsy etymon? The answer to these questions will not come from the field of philology; it will come from a discipline sensitive to the play and display of forces even in "dry" works of scholarship, works seemingly barren of the layering and emplotment that enable interpretation.

The irony of Ortiz's avoidances, of course, is that Cuban Spanish is not Castilian only to the extent that it is African or Amerindian. Ortiz can only replant roots, not remove them altogether. One can imagine, nonetheless, that the discovery or invention of his African etyma must have caused him a pleasure similar to that felt by Toro. For both men the pleasure arises from recognition, from finding the familiar in unfamiliar surroundings. But while for the Spaniard the familiarity of the American lexicon reassures him about the filial or fraternal ties between Spain and her former colonies, for the Cuban the pleasure of recognition attaches to the cause of cultural autonomy. Toro imaginarily travels to the colonies in order to retrieve the mother tongue; Ortiz imaginarily travels to Africa or to pre-Columbian America to show that we are bastard sons of the devil, as Zorrilla would have it, or of "el diablillo del choteo," as in Mañach's phrase.

The *Catauro*'s second device cuts deeper than the first, for Ortiz will now bring his erudition to bear on words that, besides being used in Cuba, are also current in Spain. As a corollary to the same ploy, he will recommend acceptance by the Royal Academy of a number of words that, for one reason or another, have no good equivalent in peninsular Spanish. One example of a *cubanismo* used on both sides of the Atlantic is *garapiña* (*Catauro,* pp. 34–35); another is *mojiganga,* which Ortiz discusses at length in the *Glosario,* arguing that the word derives from the Congo language and its diffusion in Spain stems from the participation of Congo slaves in Spanish carnival festivities.[13] Examples of words whose acceptance he urges are: *pucha, financiar, enseriarse, vuelto, turismo, control, entresemana,* and *culear,* all of them entered in the *Catauro.* The effect, if not the purpose, of this dual device is to reverse the cultural flow between the peninsula and the continent. Ortiz inverts the center-periphery relation with the result that America becomes the cultural center that exports its verbal riches to Spain. The colonies threaten to colonize their colonizers. Since these entries demonstrate not the presence of Spain in America but of America in Spain, they constitute the exact opposite of those in "Reivindicación de americanismos." One might venture, indeed, that what motivates Ortiz here is a kind of peninsular envy, a vindictive wish to play the part of the usurper. By pointing out the Afro-Cuban provenance of a word like *mojiganga* or the need for other words like *pucha* and *culear,* Ortiz shows that the American nations have not limited themselves to absorbing Spanish culture; rather, their absorbent capacity has been complemented by procreative power.

Thus, if the first device implements a desire for *autonomy,* the second implements a desire for *influence.* The *Catauro's* third device, in turn, implements a desire for *legitimacy.* Strictly speaking, this last desire may not be consistent with the other two, for now we observe Ortiz arguing for the Spanishness, the *casticidad,* of a number of Cuban words. He will say that *cubanismos* like *calimba, fajatiña, moringa,* and *sabina* are in fact of peninsular origin, even though by so doing he is actually rehearsing Toro's argument, trying to outbully the Spanish bull. All this, strictly speaking. But if one insisted on strict speaking, one would never venture beyond the pages of the Royal Academy Dictionary. A text like the *Catauro,* from its title onward, is the work of a loose tongue, one that aims, precisely, to unloosen, to *relax* (*relajar*) the strictures of strict speaking. Strictly speaking, Ortiz would not.

Two things need to be said loosely in explanation of the third device. The first is simply that Ortiz's wish to legitimate the Cuban sociolect manifests the characteristic ambivalence that the colonized feel toward their colonizers. The American predicament inheres not only in the New World's fateful obligation to emulate Europe; part of the problem is that the New World persists in selecting Europe as the model to emulate. Those "learned fetters" that Marinello talks about are, to some extent, self-imposed. In his classic study of the North American ethos, *The American Adam,* R. W. B. Lewis organizes the nineteenth-century debate about the United States' separation from Europe by placing the participants in one of three camps: the party of Hope, the party of Memory, and the party of Irony.[14] The party of Hope was made up of those, like Whitman or Thoreau, who advocated a clean break from Europe. Ortiz's first two devices, and particularly the Africanist thesis, are stratagems of the hopeful. Lewis's party of Memory comprised those who, like the long line of Calvinist

preachers, insisted on shouldering the burden of the past. The
Catauro's third device can be situated in this camp. The third
party, made up of Ironists like Melville, mediated between Hope
and Memory by showing their intrication. This party argued that
one could escape the past no more than one could avert the future.
In its blending of hopeful and mnemonic motifs, the *Catauro* may
be labelled an ironic text. As much might be said also about *Juan
Criollo* and even about *Indagación del choteo*. Their contradic-
tions, their Janus-character—backward- and forward-looking, sub-
servient and rebellious—faithfully reflect the American cultural
predicament.

The second thing that should be said about Ortiz's third device
is that, on occasion, the memory exercise can be turned into a
weapon. Consider the entry for *torcaza*. After pointing out that
the Academy accepts *torcaz*, the adjective, but not *torcaza*, the
noun, Ortiz adds: "But we have to agree, against what Pichardo
thought, that *torcaza* is not a corrupt word, but a healthy and pure
one, one which—like several others—was kept alive in Cuba even
after falling into disuse and being *corrupted* in Castile" (p. 181;
italics in the original). Thereupon follow two verses from the
Libro de buen amor in which the word appears:

Vino el cabrón montes con corcas y torcaças . . .
A las torcaças matan las sabogas valyentes.

(The mountain goat came with deer and doves . . . The brave shads
are killing the doves.)

Since "archaisms" like this one are for Ortiz vital signs of health
and purity, Cuban Spanish in his eyes maintains a less corrupt,
more pristine state of the language than its Castilian counterpart.
This device thus involves another metaleptic reversal, for what is
being claimed is that certain items in the Cuban lexicon are actually "older" than their supposed ancestors. *Torcaza* is presumably a corruption of *torcaz;* and yet one finds it already in the
Arcipreste. In this sense Cuban Spanish antecedes that being
spoken at the same time in the peninsula. The fatherland is temporally posterior to its offspring and perhaps less hospitable to the
mother tongue.

The devices I have now mentioned circumscribe the three principal motifs in the plot of Ortiz's book: autonomy, influence, and

legitimacy. Something remains to be said, however, about the book's form and style. I have so far discussed the *Catauro* as if it constituted a response of sorts to Toro y Gisbert's "Reivindicación de americanismos." Conceptually this is true enough; but historically Ortiz's compendium needs to be situated with respect to two other works. One is the fourteenth edition of the Royal Academy Dictionary, to which Ortiz constantly refers. The other is Constantino Suárez's *Vocabulario de voces cubanas,* which spurred Ortiz to publish his *papeletas.* This is how Ortiz describes his text's relation to the other two: "If Suárez's *Vocabulario cubano* is an appendix to the fourteenth edition of the *Diccionario de la Lengua Castellana por la Real Academia Española,* this small notebook that follows will be, in turn, a kind of appendix to Suárez's *Vocabulario* and also, by extension, to the well-known academic catalogue" (p. 17). The *Catauro* is an appendix to an appendix, a supplementarity evident already in the title, since *catauro* is one *cubanismo* one will not find in *Un catauro de cubanismos.* If one is not familiar with the word, one has to resort to Suárez's vocabulary for a definition. For the non-Cuban reader, that is, for the reader who would perhaps find such a compendium most useful, the intelligibility of the title presupposes acquaintance with Suárez's work. And on a more abstract level, of course, this intelligibility rests on the reader's memory of the titular labels that Ortiz has displaced and replaced.

The *Catauro*'s supplementarity manifests itself in another way. Since its materials are actually a by-product of Ortiz's research into Afro-Cuban folklore, this collection derives from some of Ortiz's other works: "This year we hope to finish the *Glosario de afronegrismos,* which I have been working on for some time; and the entries [*papeletas*] that make up the *Catauro* are like the shavings [*virutas*] left behind as I chisel away to uncover the ebony heart that is the object of my unceasing labor" (p. viii). The *Catauro* is a chip off the old block, a box constructed from shavings left over from the author's work on things Afro-Cuban. These "cubicherías lexicográficas," then, consist only of "the notes gathered as a result of other projects on Cuban lore, like poor shavings [*virutas*] produced by the chisel or the plane during our long-standing work on the culture of the Afro-Cuban underworld"

(p. 255). It is somehow appropriate that a work so concerned with etymologies should so clearly uncover its duplex origins. Like some of the words Ortiz studies, his dictionary has both Spanish and African roots. Its derivativeness or secondariness with respect to these two sources seems a fitting emblem for the Cuban vernacular generally.

The residual, supplemental composition of the *Catauro* helps to explain its stylistic and structural quirks. As my reader will surely have noticed, Ortiz's tone is unlike what one would expect in a work of this nature. One can describe it as festive, or carnivalesque. His entries are full of puns, of outrageous suggestions (*marconigrama* for telegram; *autorista* for chauffeur), of amusing asides, of jibes at the Royal Academy:

Guayabo—El árbol que produce la *guayaba*, dice el Diccionario de la Academia. ¿Pero por qué añade: "En francés: *goyavier"? ¿Quiere decir con esto que es un galicismo? ¿Sí? ¿Pues qué, acaso en cada otra papeleta del Diccionario se trae a colación la traducción francesa de cada vocablo? ¡Fuera, pues, el *goyavier!* Esa etimología, si se propone como tal, *no vale una guayaba*, para decirlo en criollo. Recuérdese en cambio alguna de las 22 acepciones y derivados de *guayaba*, traídas por Suárez, que, como *guayabal, guayabera, guayabito*, harían mejor papel en el diccionario castellano que esa inexplicable etimología gabacha. ¡Qué no nos venga la Academia con *guayabas!*, y consignemos así, de paso, otro cubanismo. (p. 43)

(*Guayabo*—The tree that produces the *guayaba*, according to the Dictionary of the Academy. Why does it add: "In French: *goyavier"?* Does it mean to suggest that it is a gallicism? Really? Well, does the Dictionary by any chance provide the French translation of every word? No? Then out with the *goyavier!* The etymology, if that is what is being proposed, is not worth a *guayaba*, as we say. Let's recall, instead, some of the 22 acceptations and derivatives of *guayaba*, cited by Suárez, that, like *guayabal, guayabera, guayabito*, would look better in the Castilian dictionary than that inexplicable Frenchified etymology. This *guayaba* is just too hard to swallow!, and let us thus note, in passing, still another Cuban idiom.)

On occasion, Ortiz even parodies the style of academic dictionaries:

Cuajo—La Academia da en su 4a acepción el sentido siguiente: *Cuajar,* 1er. artículo. Este dice: Unir y trabar las partes de un líquido, convirtiéndose en sólido. Nos parece poco atinada esta definición en lo que debiera ser de química, como en lo de lógica; pero no ocupándonos de ella, digamos que en Cuba, *cuajo* tiene otro sentido, que académicamente pudiera ser expresado así: *Cuajar,* 3er. artículo. Y leyendo entonces la referencia tendríamos: Lograrse, tener efecto una cosa. (Pp. 39–40; see also *meter,* p. 42)

(*Cuajo*—The Academy gives in its 4th acceptation the following meaning: *Cuajar,* 1st entry, which says: To unite and thicken the parts of a liquid, turning it into a solid. This definition seems to us off the mark, as regards both chemistry and logic; but leaving this matter aside, let me say that in Cuba *cuajo* has another sense, which could be expressed academically in the following way: *Cuajar,* 3rd entry. And reading the reference we would have: To accomplish, to take effect.)

These passages embed a reflexive dimension that sets the *Catauro* apart from the academic dictionaries it supplements. Entries like these not only complete or correct the information in the Royal Academy Dictionary but also expose, indeed toy with and undermine, the conventions of the dictionary form. Nowhere is this more evident than in the disconcerting fact that the *Catauro* is a dictionary whose entries are not arranged in alphabetical order—nor in any other kind.[15] Since the work also lacks an index, the reader who wants to locate a particular *cubanismo* has to skim the whole compendium. He has, in effect, to read the *Catauro,* to treat it as one would an essay or a novel and not as one normally uses a dictionary, by "looking up" the item in question. One cannot look anything up in Ortiz's wordbook, for one would not know where to look—a situation complicated further by Ortiz's habit of discussing some words in more than one place (without cross-referencing) and of proposing a different theory each time.

The curious thing, however, is that occasionally one detects in the *Catauro* traces of alphabetical order. That is to say, one encounters clusters of entries that begin with the same letter or with consecutive letters; for example, *Pilotaje—Pintorretear—Pintorreteo—Revirarse—Revirado—Ribeteado—Saltaperico—Sanjuanero* (p. 56). This sequence is ordered to the extent that *p* is followed by *r* and *s* and that words that begin with the same letter are grouped. The semblance of order is momentary, nonetheless, since the words that immediately precede this sequence are *manguera, lucernario,* and *control;* and those that follow it are *novenario, tumbadero,* and *bocabajo.* But the *Catauro* contains many such discrete interludes, which cumulatively create the impression that at some stage in the book's prehistory the entries were indeed arranged alphabetically. Whatever the stages in the book's actual elaboration, the finished product gives the impression, not of randomness, not of haphazard disarray, but of deliberate deconstruction. It is as if, at some hypothetical time before publication, Ortiz's *papeletas* were indeed alphabetized; something then intervened—some devil or *diablillo*—to dishevel the list. Or perhaps the box *fell.* The obvious analogy is with a deck of cards that, even after shuffling, retains scattered vestiges of its former numerical ordering. Ortiz seems to have submitted his index cards to a similar shuffling.

Consider also the book's heterogeneous contents. Its author acknowledges that he has filled his box with "lexicographical notes, a sampling of words overlooked by earlier studies of the vernacular language, casual comments on uncertain etymologies, clarifications of the meaning of words, and evocations of forgotten Cuban folklore" (p. 256). This aggregation of diverse ingredients only increases the book's untidiness; one is reminded of the multiple uses of a *catauro:* "to keep or carry fruits, eggs, etc., and even to get water from wells." And then there is the *Catauro's* external form: it begins with a preface, "Al lector," followed by Ortiz's review of Suárez's *Vocabulario de voces cubanas,* followed by another preface, and then by the list itself. The list is in turn succeeded by a brief section of Cuban idioms, "Locuciones cubanas" (p. 248), and a conclusion, "Cerrando el *Catauro*" (pp. 248–53). The box does not stay shut for long, however, since "Una ambuesta de cubanismos," an addendum to the main list, comes after the conclusion. In its contents and external appearance, the book is as much a hodgepodge, as much an *ajiaco criollo,* as the list itself.[16]

Because of its festive tone, dishevelled structure, and miscellaneous materials, the *Catauro* is a barbaric dictionary of barbarisms, a carnivalization or *choteo* of the dictionary form, a "contradictionary." Its generative nucleus is either the carnival principle of motley—we have not strayed very far from the patchwork of Va-

lle's *esperpento*—or the *choteo* principle of excremental disarray.
Robert Adams has pointed out that some of the greatest literary
works of this century have an unequivocal tumular or dungheap
quality, since they have been confected from scraps, bits and
pieces, literary and cultural debris.[17] If this is so, Ortiz's dictionary
is one of our most typical and finest modern texts, a philological
fiction comparable to *Ulysses* or *The Waste Land,* of which it is
almost the exact contemporary. *Un catauro de cubanismos* is *The
Waste Land* of modern dictionaries.

I want to leave the *Catauro,* however, not in the wide spaces of
modernist culture but in the bounded textual universe of my corpus. This book offers an example of the operation of creolization
on linguistic material. The result is a dictionary that in its lack of
order, its heterogeneity, its derivativeness, resembles a trash pile or
garbage bin—a box that, like Juan's trunk, contains excrementi-
tious matter.[18] It is an odd thing indeed to see the Royal Academy
Dictionary and *Don Juan Tenorio* lumped together and turned
into shit, and it is even odder to see it done in the name of cultural
autonomy. America is what happens when the shit hits the fan.
Nothing succeeds like excess. There is a poetry in refuse. The
road to the New World is paved with "dark treasures."

Zorrilla was right; this must all be the devil's work.

Part Three

TUMORS AND TWINS

Soy prolijo y repetidor. Tengo que pedir
desde ahora absolución. Una absolución que
sólo podría llegarme desde alguna incierta
rama literaria y para la que no puedo ofrecer
mi arrepentimiento.

(I am long-winded and repetitive. I must
already ask for absolution. An absolution
that could only reach me from some uncertain
literary sect and for which I cannot offer
my repentance.)

LUIS MARTÍN-SANTOS, *Apólogos*

7

※

Magma

Tiempo de silencio, as the title makes clear enough, is a period piece. Set in Madrid in the autumn of 1949, the novel draws a vivid and detailed portrait of urban Spanish society during "los años del hambre" ("the years of hunger"). Because Martín-Santos intends, as the jacket blurb puts it, "to show with an ironic eye the complete panorama of the social strata of the city," he weaves into the action personages from every social sphere, from the top (Matías and his mother) to the utter bottom (Cartucho and his mother). It is no accident that Matías's mansion and Cartucho's hovel are described in contiguous scenes (pp. 117–27), for one of the points the novel makes is that these spheres or strata are more intimately connected than would appear at first glance.[1] The principal nexus, of course, is Pedro, who constitutes the topic of conversation in both places, and who moves easily (and sometimes not so easily) among the different social classes. In this sense he functions less as a character than as a copula; his task is to make possible such unlikely juxtapositions as that of Matías and Cartucho or Muecas and Ortega y Gasset.[2] This role is best exemplified by the sequence in which several of the important characters pursue each other through Madrid in search of Pedro (pp. 157–63). The narrator compares them to a species of worm, "the processionary pine-moth caterpillar," that secretes a fibrous substance: thus Matías, Amador, Cartucho, and Similiano are guided through the labyrinthine city by the "thread" that leads to Pedro.

But there is one character—the German-Jewish neoexpressionist painter who appears briefly early in the book—who does not form part of the fabric of Spanish society. Pedro and Matías run into him at the coffee house; there they get drunk together and at the German's urging go to his studio for a private showing of his work. Soon after, the German disappears, "swallowed" by a taxi-cab (p. 76). This episode occurs at an important juncture: Mar-tín-Santos places it in the middle of the "Sabbatical night," during which Pedro will rape Dorita and become embroiled in the abor-tion and death of Florita. Unlike the other episodes in the section, which advance the plot, this one appears as a hiatus in the narra-tion, a retardatory interlude that distends the link between Pedro's inebriation and its consequences. Appropriately, the studio is fig-ured as a ship about to capsize. This incident will also sink, disap-pear, and play no further part in the narrative flow of events. And, as we have just seen, if the studio sinks the German is swallowed. Effacement seems to be their common fate.

To fix on the painter and his surroundings is thus to attempt to graft onto the novel what is essentially a "foreign" substance, from the standpoints of both ethnic origin and plot. Even the style of his work—neoexpressionist—suggests that he has arrived late, that he does not fit, that he belongs to another "tiempo." Because he con-stitutes a historical anachronism in a historical novel, he is sig-nally alien to much of what transpires in the text. But then again, other, equally foreign substances figure prominently in the novel. The mice with which Pedro conducts his experiments have been imported from Illinois; Pedro himself hails from the provinces; and *Tiempo de silencio* as a whole revolves around what is, in our century, the foreign substance *par excellence*—cancer. A peculiar homology thus obtains: the German "fits" in the novel as a can-cerous growth "fits" in the body; in other words, he is a tumor nestled in the body of the text. To examine his role, to attempt to motivate his presence, is an endeavor that curiously mirrors, or re-peats, the work's enabling pretext: Pedro's search for the etiology of a certain strain of cancer. One senses that Pedro and Matías's inarticulate friend is more than a marginal figure; or rather that his marginality, like that of a malignancy, is continually on the verge of becoming central.

One can begin to form some idea of the expansive impetus of such marginality by extending the four-term homology to an additional pair of terms: not only cancer and the body, and the painter and the novel, but also—more generally—painting and writing, the image and the word. The cohabitation—and the conflict—between the two media become manifest in the scene describing the conference of the Philosopher (a thinly veiled Ortega y Gasset), which Martín-Santos renders by superposing Goya's *Le Grand Bouc* on the proceedings. Ortega turns into a male goat and the women who attend the conference become the hags that surround it. In addition to exploiting to the fullest the visual resources of words, to coming as close to a picture as a text can come, this scene illustrates the threat posed by such exploitation. The superposition of the painting arrests the progress of the narration and freezes the characters into a fixed gesture. A temporal medium is contorted into a spatial pose; succession surrenders to simultaneity. Were this procedure to spread, to metastasize, the novel would decompose into a tableau. Moreover, since the conceit has the effect of demolishing Ortega's posturings as philosopher, one can extract from the scene an implied confrontation between two modes of representation—one abstract and nonvisual, the other concrete and evocative. Let me say, to simplify, a confrontation between "scientific" and "artistic" rendering. In this scene the latter (Martín-Santos's transposition of the painting) overwhelms the former (Ortega's lecture). This vanquishment, in turn, can be taken as one of the ways in which the novel signifies the inevitable defeat of any scientific project. In *Tiempo de silencio* tumors (of various sorts) prevail.

But let me return to the concrete circumstances of the German's intervention in the novel. When Pedro and Matías see his painting, their first impression is markedly unfavorable. In order to convey his disapproval Matías resorts to a strange value term. His criterion of artistic excellence is "magma." A good painting "has magma"; a poor one "doesn't have magma." Now what, exactly, is magma? Or as the German puts it, "Pero, qué ser magma?" To which Matías replies:

Magma be all. Magma the pregnant reality of adhering matter. Magma the protoform of nascent vitality. Magma the fuliginous stickiness of sperm. Magma the molten rock before it petrifies. Magma the Jews in their ghetto reproducing among themselves indefinitely. (p. 75)

Were it not for the fact that the German interrupts him, the enu-meration, like the Jews themselves, might proliferate endlessly. If the notion is as capacious as Matías asserts, if magma is all, one is hard-pressed to find a suitable stopping place. One is equally hard-pressed to contrive a rigorous definition. Matías, who does not offer one, limits himself to explaining the concept by denotation; all we are given is a series of verbal snapshots: magma as adhesive growth, magma as sperm, magma as molten rock, magma as population ex-plosion. Nevertheless, from the catalogue one can gather that this substance is a discharge different from those of the body mainly in the hyperbolic intensity of its activity. As a kind of super-semen or bionic dung, it can only be described by recourse to such words as "pregnant," "protoform," "vitality." A glance at the neoexpression-ist painting confirms this impression:

On a dark brown background, in a lighter brown and with touches of a hellish red, the counterfeit ruins of a bombed city had been painted. Stones were piled too high along both sides of an urban canyon not totally blocked by the rubble. The argument of the picture showed a large throng of beings, apparently human but antlike and much smaller than normal. Forming a kind of vast river, these beings gushed down to the foreground of the painting. (p. 73)

The painting, says Pedro, embodies the "essential magma." Its author, one could add, is a wizard of ooze. And when I say that the painting "embodies" magma, I intend the verb in its literal sense, for the neoexpressionist cityscape can be construed as an anatomi-cal allegory or biofiction. On the topography of the city, on its can-yons and canals, the figure of the (lower) body must be super-imposed. In this respect one of the novel's best-known passages furnishes the appropriate gloss: "a man is the image of a city, and a city a man's viscera turned inside out" (p. 16). This vision is precisely what the painting portrays: innards turned inside out and placed on display. And it so happens that the exhibition occurs at a moment when the city-body is undergoing a total evacuation of its contents. Hence the narrator's reference to "the fecal character of the painting and the verminous appearance of its protagonists" (p. 73), descriptions in which the excremental and the seminal in-termingle. Evacuation of the body / evacuation of the city—as we will verify later, the comparison that underlies this analogy recurs several times in the novel. Like the wager between Juan and Luis, the neoexpressionist painting constitutes a *mise en abîme,* a framed spectacle that embeds the novel's nuclear motifs. And again like the wager, the painting is not self-contained, since its magmatic substance will spill over the frame and suffuse the entire text.[3] Spilling over, in fact, is precisely what the scene enacts. Magma leaks; it does. What is the "essence" of magma? Fecal matter and semen, confounded, gushing out of the same orifice.

In its proliferating, excessive abundance, magma resembles feces and semen. For this very reason, it is also like cancer. (Magma: cancer-cum-dung.) To speak of "Jews . . . reproducing among themselves indefinitely," as Matías does, and of a "tumultuous uncontrollable reproduction," as Pedro does in the passage quoted below, is to name, with an almost identical vocabulary, the same phenomenon:

Among the genes of these mice there was a particular one that catalyzed the production of an enzyme that stimulated the commencement of the tumultuous uncontrollable reproduction that, escaping the laws of harmony by moving to a relatively anaerobic metabolism, ends up destroying its host. Although it could well be a virus and not a gene, a virus lodged in the same cellular nucleus, in intimate contact with the chromosomes, so much so that it could hardly be distinguished from a gene, since it could only reproduce itself within the reproductive apparatus of the living cell and since, like the gene, it would act from a distance, by means of catalytic substances that deform the metabolic rate of the deoxyribonucleic acids creating those monstrous proliferations we know as multipolar mitoses, asymmetric mitoses, explosive mitoses, without—and in spite of so gigantic a disruption and departure from the norm—without—and here is the amazing thing—making life impossible for the individual cell (thus solving the problem) but instead letting the surrounding protoplasm, painfully though luxuriantly, continue developing, assimilating, dividing, growing, consuming blood from that being that was itself, and even becoming necrotic in vivo, when the reactive growth of the blood vessels becomes insufficient to allow it to continue its riotous career. (pp. 196–97)

The repetitive, *tumorous* intensity of some of this writing, reminiscent of Matías's anaphoric catalogue, leaves little doubt that malignancies behave like magma. This connection is strengthened by the fact that Pedro's cancer-bearing mice must also inbreed, and that in Muecas's hovel they do so uncontrollably—"paren sin parar," as Amador puts it (p. 12). But the equivalence works both ways, for if magma proliferates like cancer, cancer "flows" like magma. In the digression on Cervantes Pedro thinks of writers as "men who spilled their own cancers on white papers" (p. 65). Since he seems to be paraphrasing the Biblical account of onanism (Gen. 38), the assimilation of cancer into the body's fluids is difficult to overlook. In an appropriately magmatic way, his metaphor confounds substances: writing consists of the ejaculation of a tumor. A similar fusion (or confusion) of substances occurs elsewhere: Muecas describes tumors as being like testicles ("That's why they got those lumps like testicles, if you'll pardon the expression, and when they died you'd be up all night studying why, when it was nothing but the cold" [p. 52]), and Pedro mentions some women's mistaking of menstruation for tumor-induced hemorrhages (p. 8). Sexual function and cancer have of course been linked many times before, but here the equation, like the mitosis of rebellious cells, is multipolar and asymmetrical, as it comprises not only cancer and semen but also excrement, magma, and writing.[4]

This confluence of fluids leads to the formulation of what might be termed the "cloacal complex" of *Tiempo de silencio*.[5] The body's discharges coalesce and become analogized to magma, the discharge of the bowels of the earth. Because the novel makes the body's and the earth's discharges interchangeable, one can posit for them the fantasy of a common source, an *ur*-ifice—perhaps a "celeste anus immense" (Lautréamont), perhaps a cosmic version of the equivocal "canyon" in the neoexpressionist painting—from which all would issue.[6] What needs to be emphasized, however, is the vicious circularity of the magmatic chain. In saying that these substances are interchangeable, that they can stand for each other, one is performing the kind of agglutination that the substances themselves denote. Magma and cancer are not simply metaphors for each other; they are also, and perhaps primarily, metaphors for metaphoricity itself, for the *stickiness* ("the fuliginous stickiness of sperm"; "the pregnant reality of adhering matter") that binds vehicle and tenor. Inscribed in each of the parts of the system are the properties of the system as a whole. Magma thus signifies every individual member of the chain (semen, cancer, dung, and writing—so far), as well as the process by means of which such chains are constructed. (Magma: even the word is sticky; it doubles back on itself, reiterating letters, creating its own echo.)

This stickiness or circularity has two important consequences. First, the novel tends to constitute objects and scenes that invite naturalization as emblems of the entire text. In other words, *Tiempo de silencio* is full of metaphors of *Tiempo de silencio*. (In the neoexpressionist painting we have already come upon one of them.) For this reason—and using a language consistent with the novel's own—one might say that studying the self-referentiality of *Tiempo de silencio* is tantamount to giving an onanist a hand. Second, one cannot interpret magma, one cannot make connections and draw out parallels, without immersing oneself in the substance. Connections and parallels are the very stuff, the "essence" of magma. Critical distance and disinterested contemplation become impossibilities. The reader, like the German, is "swallowed" by the novel. In this respect, if the painting is one of the metaphors of *Tiempo de silencio,* the reader can find himself represented in the semino-fecal creatures that flood the scene: what the narrator labels "that insectlike and filthy world" where "there seemed to be expressed a collective despair in which the pain of infinite suffering combined with an awareness of the strict justice with which it had been deserved" (p. 73).

But let me leave the reader to his or her own devices and continue tying together the sections of the magmatic chain, whose missing links can be located by a closer inspection of the place and function of the body in the novel. One such "place" is the cemetery where Florita is interred, and which the narrator describes with a mock-scientific jargon that draws attention to the efficiency of its operation. For one thing, by means of a well-planned division of labor, no time is wasted. For another, space is used economically. In this cemetery, it turns out, bodies are not only placed alongside each other; they are also superposed, stacked vertically one on top of the next. Thus Florita shares her grave with several other corpses, separated only by a thin sheet of dirt between caskets. Now this superposition of bodies works in the novel in two ways. First, the recumbent position of the corpses, one on another, connotes the sexual act. Florita herself sleeps with three others ("three companions of diverse gender had lain down on top of Florita's youthful body" [p. 146]), and the narrator does not forgo the opportunity to remark on the "vertical promiscuity" of such an arrangement (p. 193). Since Florita has wound up in the cemetery as a result of (her father's) sexual promiscuity, it is deeply ironic that she should spend eternity in motionless and silent intercourse, an irony underscored by the fact that at the *chabola* she also slept with three other companions of diverse gender, her parents and her sister, all of whom shared one mattress. In this novel the grave is neither a private place nor one that prevents embracing. Her burial repeats, and in some sense memorializes, the rape.

Second, the vertical burials also alert us more generally to the importance of the metaphorical superposition of the body in the novel. As we will see presently, Martín-Santos resorts repeatedly to extended anatomical comparisons, to the extent that the topography of Madrid, like the German's painting, acquires a distinct anatomical configuration. When Pedro pictures himself as "hanging in a little pouch from the warm neck of the city" (p. 99), he is asserting a correspondence that is insinuated diffusely in several descriptive passages. Interestingly, here too one is remanded to the cemetery and to Florita, for it is her body that Pedro evokes, and to which Madrid is compared. Moreover, since he has landed in jail as a result of his participation in the abortion, his fate does actually hang on the body of the girl. And since his fate is primarily what the novel is about, one might say that the body of the text, the body that is the text, is Florita's body. The image with which Pedro concludes his final monologue, an image which evokes also a superposed body, captures neatly this relationship: St. Lawrence fastened to the grill, the body "fastened" to the novel, and Pedro fastened to the body (Florita's).[7]

The metaphor of Pedro in the pouch, "pendiente de una bolsita en el cuello recalentador de la ciudad," also points to his marginality. He sees himself as an appendage, an ornament even, but not as an integral part of the organism. This marginality is usually converted into philosophical or psychological terms. Pedro himself adopts such an attitude when he remarks, "I will never learn how to live; I will always remain marginal [*al margen*]" (p. 92). For the moment, however, I would prefer to retain the visual primacy of the image: enclosed in the pouch, hanging from the neck of the city, he inhabits margins that are physical, geographical as it were. In this respect his eccentricity resembles that of the organic components of the magmatic chain. Like cancer, semen, and feces, Pedro exists at the margins of the body, and shares with these substances an ambiguous territorial status—it is not clear to whom or to what he and they belong. One might think, indeed, that they "belong" nowhere and only serve to designate the points of intersection of self and world, body and nonbody. In addition, as a kind of swelling on the breast of Florita, the pouch recovers both the shape and the place of a malignancy. And tumors, in turn, are analogized by Muecas to a different variety of pouch or sac that also hangs from the body—"those lumps like testicles . . ."

Undoubtedly, Pedro's geographical estrangement from the world is most pronounced when he is incarcerated. In one of those scenes organized around a sustained anatomical metaphor, Martín-Santos portrays the prison as a gigantic body nourished by the incoming convicts. Descending to one's cell is tantamount to passing through the intestines of the organism and being digested. "The next mouth opens on a scaled tortuous throat, along which, without any choking, ingestion is aided by the peristaltic movement of the granite, thus leading—through more grilles—to the ample gastric plaza where the digestion of the well-chewed remnants begins. There all personal belongings are stripped away" (pp. 170–71). By the time the prisoner reaches his destination (the cell, terminus of the digestive tract) he has become excrement. All that remains is remains, matter that the body has not assimilated, human waste. Might one not even intuit a certain scatological coloring in the description of the prisoners as "certain slight creatures of a greenish hue and unshaven beard, members of a race not yet classified anthropologically" (p. 168)? And cannot one relate the generic indeterminacy of these creatures to that of the "apparently human" beings of the neoexpressionist painting, whose fecal composition I have already remarked? Like the metaphor of the pouch, Pedro's imprisonment denotes a confinement that consists primarily in a separation (the literal sense of excretion) from the body. The difference between the pouch and the cell lies in their approximate location in the magmatic chain. The pouch circulates in the vicinity of semen and cancer, in the region of the groin ("cancer inguinal") and the genitalia. The jail cell has closer ties with excrement and thus with the backside of the body.

Pedro's journey through the prison can be superimposed on his earlier descent into the *chabolas*. In the later journey the destination is a jail cell; in the earlier one, the interior room of Muecas's hut. The resemblances between the two incidents are manifold and significant. At the level of plot, they relate as cause and effect. The first descent, which leads directly to Pedro's intervention in the abortion, produces the second. One witnesses here a conflation similar to that of Florita's vertical burial: just as her entombment repeats the rape, Pedro's imprisonment (also an entombment of sorts) reenacts his trip to the *chabolas*. And what is more, Muecas's abode also serves as a prison—for mice: Pedro in his jail/*jaula,* the mice in theirs. And this takes us back, once again, to the nuclear metaphor of the pouch with its implicit depiction of Pedro as mouse. What I should like to stress, however, is the anatomical correlate woven into the portrayal of the *chabolas,* for Muecas's hovel shares with Pedro's cell the distinction of also being a mansion pitched in the place of excrement.

Let us look, first, at the sequence in which the Philosopher's conference is described. The gathering takes place at a movie house with three levels. The basement serves as a dance hall for the lower classes; in the middle level the Madrid literary set congregates; and the upper level, actually the stage of the theater, is reserved for the Philosopher. This arrangement gives the building the appearance of an orderly universe: "Like any well-ordered cosmos, the place in which the event was unfolding was divided into superposed spheres. There was then a lower sphere, a middle sphere, and an upper sphere, peak and flying buttress of the whole edifice" (p. 130). Yet the structural model here clearly oscillates between the cosmic and the human, for the three spheres can also be referred to the traditional division of the body into an upper, middle, and lower region. If in cosmic terms the lower region represents the underworld, biologically it is the realm of "the genesically reproductive, the prior-to-being-punished voluptuously pleasurable" (p. 130), and it functions to assure "primary biological continuity" (p. 132). The Philosopher, in contrast, resembles nothing so much as a head, as a talking and thinking machine:

"oracle, journalist, essayist, orator, he-who-said-it-before-Heideg-ger"; "endowed with a great head" (p. 133).

The entire scene bears more than a passing resemblance to the following excerpt from Benjamín Jarnés's *Viviana y Merlín:*

> King Arthur's castle is built like a human organism. It is divided into three parts—with its three corresponding souls—, each one as different from the rest as the different organs that exist under the same skin.
>
> The bottom floor—kitchens, stables, cellars—bustles with small, talkative people who work, struggle, and murmur. It's the area of the belly and of the lower extremities, which do their job without understanding anything.
>
> . . . . .
>
> Above that one finds the principal floor of the castle, the great meeting room of the Council, the chapel, the big hall for parties, where the conversation centers on love, hunting, and war.
>
> . . . . .
>
> And then there is the third sector. Inside it is the motor that drives and propels this dynamic group of pursuers of golden horns and red female hearts. On top of everything, between the castle and the stars, is Merlin's tower, the brain of the palace. Because this palace—I repeat—is built like a robust male body. At the top, Merlin thinks and oversees, while in the great hall torches of love burn and in the basement the vile appetites stir.[8]

Martín-Santos's attack on Ortega may well include a parody of a work by the best-known practitioner of Ortega's aesthetic theories. Instead of a palace, *Tiempo de silencio* portrays a "cheap movie house"; instead of courtiers, "poets of various genders"; and instead of Merlin, the Goyesque caricature of a philosopher. The purpose seems to be to reveal the underside—or the human side—of Jarnés's conceit by supplying degraded doubles for the fairy-tale setting and personages in *Viviana y Merlín.* But the superposition strikes also in the opposite direction, since it is as detrimental to Ortega as to Jarnés. As *el gran buco,* Ortega appears as the epitome of baseness; as Merlin the magician, as the epitome of fluff. The net effect is to lock Philosopher and Novelist, Master and Disciple, in a sticky, mutually destructive embrace. In any case, for my purposes the excerpt from *Viviana y Merlín* is valuable because it helps us see more vividly the anatomical subtext in the scene from *Tiempo de silencio.* By making use of the ancient topic of the *corpus politicum,* Martín-Santos transforms the movie house into an embodiment of the social strata of the city.

But if Madrid is the body, where are the *chabolas?* One can answer that the hovels hover at the *edge* of the body, at that point of intersection between self and world that also marks the location of other magmatic substances, as well as of Pedro himself.[9] Socially as well as geographically, the *chabolas* lie at the limen—like cancer, like semen, like dung. But especially like dung. They have been built out of the city's refuse, with which Muecas and his wife have concerted "a mutually beneficial economic pact" (p. 48). Their exact location is a "small valley hidden away between two lofty mountains" (p. 42)—an anatomical positioning reprised in other passages:

"Are those the hovels?" Don Pedro asked, pointing to a group of small lime-washed constructions with one or two black orifices, from one of which a thin column of grayish smoke was issuing. (p. 32)

There, in some hidden orifice, inferior to man and by him dominated, the mice of the cancerous strain kept on eating the diet invented by Muecas. (p. 45)

These marginal and filthy hovels, unlike the other ones, did not even pretend to resemble houses but resigned themselves to being foul-smelling holes without any claim to dignity. (p. 117)

In light of the foregoing, one can hardly overlook the scathing scatological humor of the following apostrophe:

What wonderful powers of improvisation and originality Iberian man displayed in these constructions! What a clear demonstration of the spiritual values for which other people envy us in the way in which a life-giving breath [*soplo vivificador*] had erected a harmonious city out of waste and nothingness! What a moving spectacle, source of pride to their compatriots, this valley completely covered with proliferating and garrulous living matter! (pp. 43–44)

It is a little surprising that one commentator of the novel, even while conceding the sarcasm of this passage, hears in it a "romantic resonance."[10] Contained in that "soplo vivificador," the resonances here are of another sort and have more to do with the *trompetilla* than with romanticism. Quevedo will name them for us in untranslatable terms: "la voz del ojo, que llamamos pedo, / ruiseñor de los putos." As for the "proliferating and garrulous living matter," one might do best to defer to another authority in such matter, Jonathan Swift, who in a poem entitled "The Lady's Dressing-Room" entreats us to admire "Such Order from Confusion sprung, / Such gaudy Tulips rais'd from Dung."[11]

Thus the anatomically rendered hovels also form part of the magmatic chain. One might say that they constitute the architectural correlate of magma, its "monumentalization" (they are called at one point "splendid bastions of misery" [p. 427]). For this reason, one would expect them to be multivalent and symbolic, and indeed one is not disappointed. Martín-Santos does not limit himself to asserting an organic connection between the hovels and Madrid; to this metaphor he adds others. Foremost among these is the specular correspondence that links the city and its suburbs. Like Madrid, the hovels contain a society that is organized hierarchically. At the top one finds Muecas and the other "notables of the Republic" (p. 59); in the middle, the (bogus) professional classes—doctors, lawyers, entrepreneurs (pp. 56–57); and at the bottom, the newly arrived *coreanos,* whom Muecas regards with contempt (p. 58). Modelled on that of the "nearby city," the legal code of this society makes possible "second-degree speculations, sales, leases, evictions, barters" (p. 57). The "subchabolas"—an even more poverty-stricken section—make this correspondence exact, for their existence shows that within the region occupied by the hovels there is a section in respect to which Muecas's neighborhood is central. The *subchabolas,* "marginal and filthy hovels," make the relation of eccentricity intrinsic to the *chabolas* themselves—just as if the mirror, in addition to whatever else it might reflect, also mirrored itself mirroring. In brief, the hovels function as a *mueca,* as a contorted semblance of the visage of Madrid. And Muecas himself, head of this sub-urban society, might be regarded as a disfigured Ortega y Gasset.[12]

But the specular correspondence does not exhaust the metaphorical charge of the hovels. To the specular metaphor one can add economic, temporal, and oneiric ones. The hovels feed on Madrid like parasites (p. 58). They represent a throwback to a more primitive stage in the evolutionary process (p. 44) as well as a prefiguration of the future (p. 58). They are "phantasms that appear in our dreams" (p. 45) and "oneiric constructions" (p. 42). As these images proliferate, the hovels begin to take on the stickiness of magma—the stickiness *and* the mobility, for no sooner is one metaphor articulated than it gives way to the next. The collapse of diverse figurative relationships, some of them incompatible, is succinctly illustrated in a recapitulatory passage that likens the hovels to "the shifting earth [*la tierra movediza*] that surrounds the city, that protects, creates, nourishes, and destroys it" (p. 202). The hovels exist as the movement of metaphoricity itself within an intricate network of correspondences. If one wanted to give their filiation with magma a geological basis, one might say that the *chabolas* are the *crevices* ("la tierra movediza") through which magma escapes. And if one wanted to underscore their connection with cancer, one would need only to mention Martín-Santos's description of metastasis as "the ultimate movement" [*el sumo movimiento*] (p. 7).

These different layers of meaning create a hermeneutical impasse. Because the *chabolas* have so ample a capacity for signification, for metaphorical layering, they transcend any one attempt at interpretation, no matter how encompassing or well motivated. This is why univocal readings of the novel, whether undertaken from a psychoanalytic, mythical, or existentialist perspective,[13] seem particularly unconvincing. There is something about *Tiempo de silencio*—something I have labeled "magmatic"—that, even as it enables these readings, makes them fall short of the mark. In his description of the *chabolas* the narrator turns critic and offers a series of "readings" of the relationship between the city and the suburbs. His results I take to be emblematic: precisely because the *chabolas* are multivalent, they signify nothing other than the process of signification itself, the stickiness that glues a metaphor to its referent—and a reader to a page. As "proliferating and garrulous living matter," they link up with those other proliferating and garrulous substances I have already discussed.

In *Tiempo de silencio* attention is repeatedly called to those parts of the body that lie at its outer and inner limits. This emphasis evokes what Bakhtin has called the "grotesque body": "Contrary to modern canons, the grotesque body is not separated

from the rest of the world. It is not a closed, completed unit; it is
unfinished, outgrows itself, transgresses its own limits. The stress
is laid on those parts through which the body itself goes out to
meet the world."[14] If one asks why the grotesque body should
figure so prominently in *Tiempo de silencio,* the quotation from
Bakhtin supplies the answer: the grotesque body, constantly growing, constantly transgressing its own limits, exhibits all of the
characteristics of a malignancy. It is a "foreign" body, a "magmatic" body, a body of fluids and orifices, one that behaves very
much like a tumor. My consideration of the presence of the body
in the novel therefore leads back to my earlier remarks on the
circularity of the magmatic chain. Not only do bodies proliferate
in the text, but each body individually exemplifies such proliferation. And here also one thinks of Florita, this time on the make-
shift operating table, hemorrhaging with "unusual and alarming
abundance" (p. 101). Is it excessive to suggest that, in its openness, in the generosity with which it escapes itself and goes out to
meet the world, her body can also serve as an emblem for the
novel?

It is clear, at least, that the sadistic fantasy of the mutilated, immobilized body recurs several times in *Tiempo de silencio.* In
addition to Florita bleeding to death, one can mention St. Lawrence on the grill, the eunuchs buried in the sand (of which more
in chap. 8) and, above all, the mice under the microscope. This
fantasy is important because it points to the existence of a counter-
plot in the novel whose intent would be to arrest the expansive
urges of the grotesque body. This is especially so once we realize
that the mutilation is generally aimed at the locus of growth—the
embryo (Florita), the testicles (the eunuchs), the tumors (the
mice). This pattern is consistent with the findings of earlier chapters. In almost all of the texts I have discussed, the expansive
liminal force clashes with an arresting impulse, be it the fathers in
Don Juan Tenorio and *Las galas del difunto,* Mañach in *Indagación del choteo,* the cop in "Los payasos," or the Royal Academy
Dictionary in *Un catauro de cubanismos. Tiempo de silencio* rein-
carnates this impulse in its most violent, extreme form; here the
cop's exemplary injunction of immobility—"No se me levante
nadie"—is given a sadistic anatomical rendering.

The problematic of doubleness, of the specular relation between a center and its periphery, thus persists throughout *Tiempo de silencio* in the relationship between the slums and the city, or—what amounts to the same thing—between a tumor and its host.[15] Martín-Santos's novel also depicts a mimetic conflict, but not between two rivals, an author's younger and older selves, or a text and its models. The site of strife here is the body itself and the warring factions the body's own cells. Susan Sontag has catalogued (with dismay) the military terms that pervade our thinking about cancer: cancer is our "enemy," a "killer" against which medical science mounts a "campaign" or "crusade"; the patient, in turn, is a "casualty" in whose body the healthy cells "fight off" an "invasion" by the diseased ones, and so on.[16] The one trope I would add to the arsenal of cancer rhetoric is the notion that the hostile cells are not only the body's enemy but its *double*—in the same way in which the *chabolas* constitute a double of Madrid. Just as we think of a malignancy as an invading army, we also tend to think of it as a monstrous alter-ego, a sort of antibody or fetal mass that is both a part of and apart from our organism, that gestates in our bodies and yet possesses a life and will of its own. As Sontag mentions, the connection between cancer and pregnancy is an old one, and even today theories about their effects on each other abound.

For this reason filial or familial metaphors of the kind that describe the relationship between the slums and the city are just as appropriate as military ones. I find a striking real-life illustration of the familial idea in the case of a young man named (somewhat aptly) Nick Hill. Ever since birth Nick Hill had carried inside him, inside his skull, two fist-sized masses. When they were finally removed in his twenty-first year, his doctors discovered that one was a tumor and the other, consisting of hair, bone, and skin, an "undeveloped sibling."[17] The hermeneutical conundrum posed by Nick's hills is this: a sibling in relation to whom? One way to "read" the incident is by looking upon the mass of hair as Nick's twin or even, Minerva-like, as the offspring sprung from his head. But one can also regard the mass of hair and the tumor as twins, since both grew to the same size and were indistinguishable until the moment of surgical delivery.[18] The tumor would then be Nick's twin's twin, and hence the double both of Nick himself and of his undeveloped sibling. Although the newspaper story does not say whether the tumor was malignant or benign, Nick's case serves me as an allegory of the link between doubling and cancer, a link given architectural form in the hovels. Every tumor aspires to the condition of wholeness; every tumor is a *mise en abîme,* a "mass" *en abîme,* that both reflects and threatens to overwhelm the framing body. The texts in *my* body, my corpus, embody a type of liminality that combines the properties of tumors and twins—expansiveness and specularity. Carnival, the letter, the belated poet, the derivative text, the festive copy, *choteo*—they all aspire to usurp the place of that in respect to which they are marginal or secondary. Like a tumor, these entities occupy a periphery ever on the verge of centrality.

Magma is the new name, the neo-expression, with which Martín-Santos baptizes this expansive and converging marginality. My conclusion, then, is that magma is "central," that it lies at the "core" of the novel. I could say that it constitutes, in Spitzer's phrase, the spiritual etymon of the book, except that, as we have seen, in *Tiempo de silencio* etymology and etiology coalesce and writing is imaged as the spilling of a cancer. Let me try a different image. As Matías is about to leave the painter's studio, he indulges in a bit of typical bombast (what used to be called *tumor*): "Quick! Let's descend from this temple of art! Let's abandon this vessel that has run aground in the rooftops of the night! The tempest is going to disperse its worm-eaten boards [*tablas*]! To the boats! Everybody to the boats!" (p. 75). The episode in which magma surfaces ends with this figurative disintegration of the studio; it ends also, thus, with a magma-leak. My examination of the novel, in this and the next chapter, attempts to trace the pattern of dispersal of the liquid and of the boards—where have we met *tablas* before?—into that Sabbatical night. Magma leaks; it does. Oh, my *yiddische* magma.

8

✣

Phonic Rape

The young girl's blood—once again—
made him dizzy for a moment.
(*Tiempo de silencio,* p. 109)

That woman! It seems as if it might
have been, for a moment—I'm obsessed.
Of course they're both in the same shape.
Why is it, how is it that I can no longer
distinguish between them, now that
they're dead, buried on top of each
other, in the same hole: an autopsy for
this one also.
(*Tiempo de silencio,* p. 234)

Pedro's obsession with the parallel lives of Dorita and Florita may
strike the reader as inappropriate. The two incidents that underlie
the parallelism seem, at first glance, incommensurable. One is a
rape; the other an abortion. As if there were no distance between
the acts, as if the womb and the tomb were really the "same hole,"
Pedro equates the inception of life with its termination, and insists
on the equation until it acquires the intensity of an obsession. The
comparison is inevitable, nevertheless, because of the many coincidences between episodes. Both events occur during the space of a
few hours during the "Sabbatical night." In both, as Pedro remarks, there is a spilling of blood. Pedro's participation is in each
case initiatory and will result, moreover, in a curtailment of his
freedom. Beyond these similarities, one can perceive a kind of fan-
tasy-logic in the chronology of events: first the rape and then the
abortion—as if the violation of one woman precipitated the preg-

nancy of the other (just as, in the actual course of events, Florita's abortion will bring about Dorita's murder). The suggestion, enforced by the near-homonymy, is that Dorita/Florita, like the masses in Nick Hill's brain, are practically indistinguishable—not two names but one name, not two characters but one character. Their fates duplicate each other: violation (of Florita by her father, of Dorita by Pedro), death (causally linked to the violations), and autopsy. The only worthy conclusion to this sequence of repetitions would be interment in a common grave. And unless Pedro is hallucinating in the second of the epigraphs above, the two women are indeed buried in the "same hole."

The sequence of repetitions, however, does not end here, for Pedro's obsession cannot be restricted to a pendular oscillation between two terms. Rather than as a pendulum, it should be conceived as a ramifying network of replications; searching for an apt image, one thinks of the multipolar mitosis of cancerous cells. The second epigraph hints at something of this proliferating quality: the obsession consists not only in identifying the two women but also—perhaps primarily—in seeing every woman as a reincarnation of the nuclear pair. In the German's studio the text furnishes an exact pictorial correlate of this phenomenon. When Pedro and Matías enter, they discover that the studio's walls are covered with "almost innumerable" nude portraits of the same woman, painted by the German's roommate. By means of the "combinatory art" of their author, the pictures manage to convey "an approximate idea of infinity" (pp. 71–72). Pedro's obsession materializes as the exercise of a similar combinatory art that involves, also, the replication of a body. This connection is important, for by giving his obsession a pictorial basis, the novel insinuates that it too circulates in the magmatic chain. As the "artist" of his obsession, Pedro sets in motion a series of repetitions that will far surpass the coincidental resemblances in the lives of the two women.

The association of art and obsession is made more evident by the fact that Pedro is *also* a drawer of nudes:

Sketch the siren using the stain on the wall. The wall looks like a siren. Her hair falls over her shoulders. With the tip [*hierrito*] of the shoelace that somebody dropped one can scratch the wall and draw the picture suggested by the stain. I've always been a lousy draftsman. She has a tail like a little fish. She's not your run-of-the-mill siren. If I lie here the siren can look at me. (p. 176)

Pedro's urge to trace on the wall of his cell the outlines of a siren is synoptic and symptomatic. As he perhaps realizes, the siren conflates attributes of Dorita and Florita. Florita is present both in the accusatory look and in the reference, a few sentences later, to mutilation: "The tail is made up of two thighs, tightly closed. The girl of the tail is not willing to split her tail with a knife because she is not in love. Thus she keeps her thighs together, like a fish's tail" (p. 177). The flowing hair of the siren, on the contrary, reminds one of Dorita, swaying in the rocking chair, during the nightly *tertulias:* "The girl leaned back in the rocking chair, rested her head on the low, curved back of the chair, and her hair—more abundant than the other two women's had ever been—cascaded down" (p. 38). And on the night of the rape the lure of her body is likened to the call of a siren: "Like a silent siren the call of this body resounds behind the always erotic literature of the world" (p. 95). But these reminiscences, which rest on substantive analogies between the two women and the siren, are less significant than other, more general and disturbing parallelisms prompted by Pedro's activity. Compare, to give a first example, the scratching of the cell wall with the actions described in the following passage:

One has to climb the stairs holding on to the worm-eaten balustrade. One has to feel along the wall for the button that, when pressed, lights the room. Having found it one has to reflect, so as to make certain that it is not the doorbell instead. Not being sure, one has to leave it alone and go up blindly, counting the steps in the darkness while one's hand becomes impregnated with the broken plaster on the wall, always so rough, so scribbled, so full of enigmatic inscriptions and deformed drawings. Finally one has to enter, resorting to a miraculous ability that allows one to open the door at the first try. (p. 93)

Pedro's entrance into the *pensión* the night of the violation also seems to involve a hand running along a wall. But let me adduce a further example:

So Don Pedro continued with deliberately skillful, almost tactile, movements to feel, as though with a finger, whether the velvety and bloody mucus still held any fragment through which the life of the patient might escape—if life there was. Time passed long and slow. He continued going over the dark internal surface, imagining the shape of the already clean cavity, listening and at the same time feeling in his hand the crackling of broken tissue, rigidly transmitted by the instrument. The dead girl no longer suffered and tamely submitted to maneuvers that had nothing to do with her. (p. 110)

This excerpt belongs to the narration of Pedro's intervention in the abortion, and here also a finger runs along a surface, along another sort of wall. One is thus confronted with an activity—surface-scratching—that, like the girls' bodies, recurs obsessively. By way of scratching the surface of surface-scratching, let me make three observations.

1. The passages that I have quoted equate three different types of interior cavities: the prison cell, the boardinghouse, and Florita's womb. All are spaces that entrap or confine Pedro. The boardinghouse, moreover, is also a womb: the door must be opened with "a large key" (p. 93); once inside, Pedro "submerges" himself in the "great body" that exudes "a visceral warmth" (p. 94). His entrance into the house thus anticipates the violation and foreshadows the "entrance" into Florita's womb, which then becomes a sexual act. One might even associate the rhythmical movement of copulation with the methodical scraping of the uterine wall: in both instances, the old in-and-out. One can also equate the obvious phallic symbols that figure in each scene: the *hierrito* of the shoelace, the hand, and the spoonlike instrument with which the cleaning is performed. Pedro's obsession consists, in part, of the repetitive *simulation* of sexual intercourse. As we saw in the discussion of the vertical burials, simulacra of the sort tend to recur in the novel. And Pedro's recognition of his obsession, quoted at the beginning of this chapter, occurs alongside a reference to the superposition of bodies in Florita's grave.

2. If surface-scratching is an erotic activity, it is also an art. For Pedro each situation appears as a technical or creative problem to be solved. The delineation of the siren must be undertaken slowly and deliberately, "little by little" (p. 177); the penetration into the house demands "miraculous ability"; and the cleaning also requires deftness ("deliberately skillful movements") in addition

to a strict obedience to the "norms of the art" (p. 110). Hence in each episode one witnesses the play of memory and imagination, of retrospective and prospective visualization. Just as Pedro visualizes the siren on the wall, he also remembers the drawings and inscriptions on the stairwell of the boardinghouse. Inside, the *image* of Dorita comes to him: "An image appears clearly in his mind's eye. Dorita is sleeping in her room, with her supple body extended on the best mattress of the house" (p. 94). During the *raspado,* even as he recalls the textbook explanation of the procedure, he attempts to "see" Florita's insides ("imagining the shape of the already clean cavity"). One is struck by the pronounced "fantastic" element in surface-scratching. By touching each wall, Pedro accedes to the realm of fantasy—the realm of sirens and of simulacra. It is no accident that different forms of the word *imagination* occur in the excerpts just cited, for surface-scratching is preeminently an image-producing activity.

3. One thus encounters in all three scenes references to painting: the drawing of the siren, the "enigmatic inscriptions and deformed drawings" in the boardinghouse, and even the passing allusion to the "norms of the art" (of abortion). Four times one is taken back, not surprisingly, to the studio: first, because an affinity exists between the siren and the nudes; second, because the "deformed drawings" can be linked to the neoexpressionist painting; third, because of the color coordination between this painting and the shoelace: "On a dark brown background, in a lighter brown and with touches of a hellish red, the counterfeit ruins of a bombed city had been painted" (p. 73); "the brown shoelace from the brown shoe" (p. 177); and fourth, because one enters the study, like the boardinghouse, by ascending darkened stairs, at the end of which awaits the *image* of the naked body of a woman:

After going up the darkened stairs, clinging to each other so as not to stumble, the painter opened the door after several futile maneuvers, in which several keys were tried and discarded. Finally inside, in the darkness, they were met by the smell of fresh paint. Again after several tries, the light was turned on and before their eyes there appeared an almost innumerable collection of canvases that covered the walls of the ample studio, all nude portraits of plump, rosy women. (p. 71)

More unexpectedly, this isotopy of pictorial references leads back to the *chabolas,* apparently the locus of all things base and unaesthetic. Early in the description of the interior room of Muecas's hovel, one reads: "The cages were hung artistically in a pattern that produced a harmonious distribution of space, of light and shade, as in a picture gallery whose owner—excessively rich—has bought more paintings than the walls will accommodate" (p. 54). This passage connects both with the "almost innumerable" canvases of the studio and with the plaster on the wall of the *pensión,* "so rough, so scribbled, so full of enigmatic inscriptions and deformed drawings." In all three locations one finds walls full of pictures, *excessively* full, and the word itself surfaces to describe the wealth of the collector ("excessively rich").[1] In *Tiempo de silencio* painting possesses an odd, proliferating abundance—like magma. We see it confirmed here once again. And part of its magmatic quality is a vicious circularity that operates in two ways: first, because finding excess inscribed in the nodes of the network of repetitions reveals the distinctive feature of the whole embedded in its individual instances; second, because the last relay in the network leads back to the first—thus the cages of the mice in Muecas's "art gallery" take us back to the point of departure, Pedro's cell. The circuit of connections disclosed by Pedro's obsession can be summarized as follows: prison-rape-abortion-studio-*chabolas*-prison. With the last term the series begins anew. A bit later we will encounter another such circuit; for the present I want only to remark that it is in terms of such an overdetermination of connective links that the much-discussed "construction"[2] of *Tiempo de silencio* must be perceived.

> Let him speak to me about her,
> even if it wounds my ears.
> ZORRILLA, *El puñal del godo*

Since Pedro's surface-scratching is a form of penetration, the description of his entrance into the house contains some rather strange phrasing. He has to ascend the stairs while his hand "becomes impregnated with the broken plaster." The instrument of penetration, oddly, becomes the object of a reciprocal insemination.

This suggestion is carried over into the scene of the real penetration, for Pedro analyzes his predicament thus:

He lives in another world, where a girl cannot enter simply by being languid and luscious. He's chosen a more difficult path, at the end of which waits another kind of woman, for whom the important thing will not be this elemental and cyclical exuberance but a firm and free lucidity. He must not fall like a fly into the open flower and smear his tiny legs. (p. 95)

Here again the phallus is feminized, "smeared" by the pollen of the flower; the seducer is himself seduced. Furthermore, it is not Pedro who enters Dorita, but Dorita who "enters" Pedro (his intentions notwithstanding, she does "enter" his world). Since Pedro has indeed fallen into a trap, has been figuratively screwed, this language appropriately connotes passivity. One would expect a similar passivity to be signified in the abortion and prison scenes, for here also Pedro is being "screwed." I should like to argue that Pedro's passivity is signified in the acoustic component of each episode; in each of the three instances he is "possessed" by sound.

In a sense, the acoustic dimension has been present in my discussion all along, since the most obvious of all the repetitions I have mentioned lies in the *sound* of the girls' names. But the echo of the names is only one relay in an intricate phonic network that begins with the novel's initial words and reverberates throughout the whole text. *Tiempo de silencio* opens with a slight paradox. It opens with a burst of noise: "Sonaba el teléfono y he oído el timbre" ("The phone was sounding and I have heard the ring"). The first sentence can be commented in a number of directions. The novel, from its inception, offers an illustration of what Martín-Santos has termed "monólogo dialéctico," that is, the procedure of transcribing the mental states of characters by intertwining mental and material events.[3] The sentence consists, in effect, of a material fact along with its mental correlate: on the one hand, *sonar;* on the other, *oír.* And in the passage from the "sonaba" to the "he oído," from the past to the present, from the physical to the psychical, and from the third person to the first, the sentence intimates that the novel will be concerned with the canonical novelistic theme—the ways in which an individual shapes, and is shaped by, his or her surroundings. Martín-Santos reveals as much a few pages later when he states that "a man finds in his city not only his determination as a person and his reason to be, but also the multiple impediments and invincible obstacles that prevent him from being himself" (p. 16). As always, the subject is the inter-play of a *yo* and its *circunstancias*. What is worth noting is that Ortega's formula, adduced any number of times by different critics as a gloss of the novel, should find already in the initial sen-tence its first illustration.

The sentence also serves to introduce a counterpoint between lack and plenitude. As the book begins, the light in the laboratory goes out, the cells that Pedro is studying freeze, and the reader discovers that Pedro is out of mice and that no funds are available for the purchase of additional ones. If one posits at the origin of any narration a lack or a void, a desire to be satisfied or a goal to be fulfilled, *Tiempo de silencio* begins in exemplary fashion. The first sequence opens a void, and one can look upon the subsequent events in the novel as issuing from the inaugural "hole" in an unsuccessful attempt to replenish it. But if one stays with the first sequence, what covers the lack of material means is a plenitude of sound that because of its prominent placement acquires symbolic value. If, on the physical plane, the book commences with a call, once one moves to the motivation of the characters the starting point becomes a call of another order—Pedro's vocation as a scien-tist, which sets in motion the chain of events that will lead to his imprisonment and exile. Placed at the laboratory, at the precise moment when he discovers that his research cannot continue, the call becomes an emblem for the calling.

This inaugural call is not, however, the only one in the text. Near the end of the Sabbatical night, shortly after Dorita's viola-tion, Muecas comes to the *pensión* to enlist Pedro's aid:

The messenger who was to carry out this mission and who had man-aged to give it the urgency necessary to overcome the diverse barriers—distance, the unusual hour, closed doors and feminine prudence and modesty—and irrupt violently into the intimacy in which Pedro's fatigue took refuge was none other than Muecas, who, giving his voice a specific emphasis and mobilizing his facial muscles to produce the appropriate grimace, screamed out: "Don Pedro, for mercy, Don Pedro!" (pp. 100–101)

Again Pedro becomes the target of an acoustic assault, of a penetration by sound. I employ a vocabulary allusive to the sexual act because Muecas's arrival involves, in effect, phonic rape. After he surmounts the "barriers" posed by the *mundus muliebris* of the boardinghouse, his scream "irrupts violently" into the "intimacy" of Pedro's quarters. One cannot but see in this forced entrance a reenactment of Pedro's own violation, perpetrated only moments before, of the "great body" of the house, with the difference that, in the interim, Pedro's role has been reversed. No longer the aggressor, Pedro is now the victim of aggression. Muecas's part, however, remains unchanged: first he rapes his daughter, and then, in order to undo the consequences of the incest, he goes on to rape her potential rescuer.

If one moves from the beginning of this episode to its conclusion, one finds that it ends in a symmetrical manner. As Pedro is leaving the *chabolas* after Florita's death, Amador tries to detain him by shouting, "¡Don Pedro! ¡Don Pedro! The certificate!" (p. 114). The episode is thus framed by two calls directed at Pedro; an initial acoustic stimulus is succeeded by an auditory lapse. The narration of Dorita's murder falls into the same pattern. The first sign of the *verbena* is the "pleasant hum-hum" of the orchestra (p. 226). When Cartucho stabs her, Dorita screams, but Pedro does not hear her: "Dorita dio un grito, pero nadie se enteró" (p. 232). And with this phrase—"nadie se enteró"—the novel, almost at its conclusion, takes us back to its beginning: "Sonaba el teléfono y he oído el timbre. *No me he enterado bien.* He dejado el teléfono" (my italics). The same pattern of perception and deafness, with Pedro at its center, is repeated, uncannily, at three different important junctures in the novel. If visually one of the metaphors for *Tiempo de silencio* is the neoexpressionist painting, aurally the appropriate metaphor could well be the repetitive ringing of a telephone.

This admittedly speculative reading of Muecas's break-in gains credibility from the identification of voice and virility elsewhere in the novel. Of Amador it is said that "being a man of potent lips, he kept his wife satisfied" (p. 155). A similar relocation of the male organ can be observed in the eunuchs mentioned in Pedro's closing monologue:

There's something that explains why I am letting them castrate me and why I don't even scream. When the Turks castrated their slaves on the beaches of Anatolia in order to manufacture eunuchs for their seraglios, it is well known that they left them buried in the sand of the beach and that many miles away sailors out in the high seas could hear, night and day, screams of pain or perhaps screams of protest or of farewell to their virility. An effective system of asepsis, having them buried up to their waist in the sand, a clean, absorbent substance that does not let secretions putrify, that eliminates them and lacks pathogenic germs, impregnated as it is with iodine and other marine salts of carminative effect. But we have it better nowadays, when people not only don't shout but don't even feel pain and cannot therefore act as an acoustic lighthouse [*faro acústico*] for careless sailors. (p. 237)

Unlike Pedro, the eunuchs do not accept their emasculation passively. Buried waist-deep in the sand, screaming disconsolately, they seem to *become* the very organ from which they have been separated, a conversion suggested by the pun in the last sentence—"faro acústico" but also "falo acústico." In both examples I have cited the seat of virility is pushed upward to the mouth or the lips and incarnated in a voice. Pedro is then entirely consistent when he names the moment of orgasm with another acoustic conceit, "the brutal ringing of a bell" (p. 166). If Amador can satisfy his wife by virtue of the size of his lips, and if the eunuchs can compensate for their mutilation by metamorphosing into acoustic phalluses, it is not surprising that orgasm should consist of a brutal ringing.

We should remember, in addition, that episodes of acoustic aggression have appeared in almost every manifestation of the liminal structure: such episodes appear in *Don Juan Tenorio,* where Inés is inseminated by the reading of a poisonous letter; in "Los payasos," where the punch line is a scream that violates the women in the audience; in "El pecado," where the uttering of *culo* violates the sanctity of the confessional; in *Indagación del choteo,* one of whose illustrations portrays a group of men assaulting a young lady with jeers; and even in the *Cataura,* with its listing of barbaric *voces.*[4] Phonic rape keeps recurring in these texts, I believe, because it is a liminal resource, a weapon to be used by those who—like Don Juan, Muecas, or *el choteador*—inhabit the margins. In all of these episodes a force from the outside, from the periphery, impinges upon a (usually enclosed or protected) center, be it the boardinghouse in Martín-Santos, "the center of a cloister" (1.2.9) in *Don Juan Tenorio,* the confessional in "El pecado," or the drawing room in *Indagación. Tiempo de silencio* makes the connection between phonic rape and liminality quite clear, since the perpetrator of the violation is Muecas, the hovel dweller. When he emits his vocative shout, the *chabolas* speak through him. Muecas, who has come to the heart of Madrid, to what in Spanish would be called *el centro,* in order to take Pedro back with him, gives a voice to the hovels, to expansive margins, to all of those entities I have linked in the magmatic chain. Phonic rape is the call of the margins, the part yearning after the hole. By yelling "Don Pedro, for mercy, Don Pedro," Muecas makes magma music.

The three surface-scratching incidents provide further corroboration of this "musical" reading of the break-in. Note, first of all, that the acoustic element is literally written into the prison episode, for to *draw* a siren, as Pedro thinks of doing, is to render visually a being that is generally thought of as the quintessence of sound. Pedro's activity while in prison thus materializes as an attempt to inscribe a voice, to give sound a visual shape. Yet the siren cannot be silenced: "With the small metal tip of the shoelace that someone left behind one can draw on the wall by scratching the lime. One scratches little by little and the unpleasant rasping [*denteroso*] sound of the metal tip, of the small piece of tin folded by some machine around the brown shoelace from the brown shoe, slides along the wall making a drawing that gradually takes on a semihuman shape" (p. 177). Strangely enough, the scraping of the uterine wall produces the same sound: "When scraped by the instrument, this tissue makes a rasping [*dentero*], grating sound that seems to indicate that the matter being stripped away is not living but rubbery, wooden, stony" (p. 109). As one wall comes alive with the siren, the other turns dead, inorganic, like wood or stone. But in the process they emit identical noises—"denteroso" and "dentero"—a phonic and semantic equivalence that recovers and prolongs the echo of the girls' names.

This unpleasant, rasping sound, directed at the tympanic membrane, constitutes the acoustic analogue of a violation and is thus of one piece with Muecas's break-in. The "breaking" that lies at the etymological root of *irrumpir* ("irrupts violently") is implicit here also. And if we turn to the remaining incident of surface-scratching, Dorita's violation, the motif of phonic aggression becomes even more noticeable: "But the woman's conscience (ever on the watch, even at the moment of a violation, in the early dawn, at the hands of an irresolute drunkard) *wounds* him by demanding an answer to the preliminary and essential question: 'Do you love me?' " (p. 96; my italics). The "wound" inflicted by the question establishes a relation of reciprocal penetration. This same reciprocity had come into play in Florita's abortion ("listening and at the same time feeling"), in the drawing of the siren (he draws the siren even as he succumbs to her "music"), and earlier in the "impregnation" of Pedro's hand. In every instance surface-scratching appears as a phono-graphic event, as an intertwining of the acoustic and the visual that renders Pedro's active-passive position in the novel. Is there a metaphor for this aural-optical relation that also betokens sexual ambiguity? I have just been discussing it—the *faro acústico,* lighthouse and siren, and also emblem of the indeterminate sexuality of the eunuchs.

Hence: Eunuch, or The Ambiguities. Ambiguous first because of the pun on *faro;* and then again because of my play on *siren.* Screaming from the beaches of Anatolia, with only their torsos showing, these creatures are enchantresses as well as noisemakers, and therefore doubles of Florita-Dorita, both of whom Pedro has likened to sirens.[5] Their screams of consciousness, situated in the midst of Pedro's stream of consciousness, resonate with long echoes. One might say that the eunuchs do not so much scream as *ring,* for the other obvious parallel in the novel is with the phone mentioned in the opening sentence. And is not a telephone also a *faro acústico?*

Eunuch, or The Ambiguities. Ambiguous, a third time, in that such a person is both male and female. Castration makes a difference because it unmakes a difference; the eunuch is neither man nor woman—or both man and woman. The Turks, as Pedro mentions, used the eunuchs to guard the entrance to the seraglios. This assignment symbolizes their condition: the eunuchs stand at the door, on the threshold between the man's and the woman's worlds.

Occupying a "liminal" zone where sexual differences converge, they themselves incarnate such a blurring. Their unsexing follows a rigorous logic. Since only women cannot violate women, the guardians of the seraglios must be like women; but since only men can ward off other men, they must also resemble men. Solution: find or fabricate men who are also women; find or fabricate she-males, as in the song.

In the previous chapter I chose to broach my discussion by focusing on the neoexpressionist canvas. This painting, nevertheless, represents only one point of access into the text, only one of several ports from which the reader can sail into the novel's gummy sea. It would have been equally possible, for instance, to begin with the eunuchs, who, buried in the sand, constitute also a kind of *mise en abîme* (or perhaps, a "miss" *en abîme*). The striking thing about Martín-Santos's novel is that it contains many such points of departure. Any of the nodes in the magmatic chain, or in the phonic network, would serve the purpose. *Tiempo de silencio* invites interpretation. Like the eunuchs' screaming, the novel's call is loud and unceasing. Only the irremediably deaf or the irredeemably incurious could resist such an uproar.

9

Carnival and Cure

The subject of this chapter is not, as its title might indicate, the cathartic or therapeutic virtues of carnival. Although I do want to talk about carnival, my discussion, as in the first chapter, will be oriented toward the elucidation of one text, Luis Martín-Santos's *Libertad, temporalidad y transferencia en el psicoanálisis existencial* (henceforth *LTT*), a dense, sometimes murky psychoanalytical treatise by the author of *Tiempo de silencio.* I will not attempt, however, to apply Martín-Santos's psychoanalytical theories to this novel; I aim rather to bring *LTT* into my corpus by showing that this work contains yet another "conversion" of the liminal structure. Thus, *LTT* will figure here as a "primary" text, interpretable in its own right, and not as the hermeneutical key with which to unlock the secrets of Martín-Santos's other, more properly literary, works. In fact, since carnival motifs like the grotesque body play a prominent role in *Tiempo de silencio,* in broaching the subject of carnival again apropos of *LTT* I will be insinuating a kind of affinity between the two works that tends to put in doubt the distinction between precept and example or theory and illustration. From my perspective, the novel no longer appears as a fictional case history that exemplifies the ideas propounded in the theoretical work;[1] instead, novel and essay occupy proximate territories that share a jubilant border or festive fringe. Put another way, if a substratum of carnival allusions underlies both works, the precept-example relation becomes reversible and the texts become twins, for the novel can be used to gloss the essay in the same way that the essay has been used to gloss the novel. *LTT* loses its position of interpretive privilege with respect to the fictional text.

To be sure, literary commentaries on *LTT* have regularly used this work as a launching pad for an explication of *Tiempo de silencio.* In studies like those by José Schraibman and Robert Spires, for example, the novel is regarded as a fictional case history, as the empirical working out of *LTT*'s argument. These critics look upon Pedro as a patient undergoing treatment and upon the novel as the narration of this process. According to Schraibman, Pedro's final monologue, where he demonstrates a newly acquired awareness of his problems, marks the culmination of the "cure." But one stream-of-consciousness monologue does not psychotherapy make. The shortcomings of this approach to a work as complex as *Tiempo de silencio* are, I think, fairly obvious. Even if one grants that Pedro is neurotic (a dubious and unverifiable "diagnosis"), this hypothesis does little to account for the details of the novel's design and content. The superposition of theory and illustration is too imprecise, too sloppy, to allow for any real insights into the novel. What does it mean, anyway, to say that Pedro is undergoing a "cure"? Where is the give-and-take between analyst and analysand that Martín-Santos considers crucial to psychotherapy? If Pedro is the patient, who is the analyst? In order to construe the novel as a psychoanalytical cure, one has to ignore the fact that the basis for such a cure is the intricate interaction of two individuals within a highly rarefied setting. One has to ignore, that is, the *specificity* of this type of treatment.

Yet *LTT* is almost entirely dedicated to detailing this specificity. According to Martín-Santos, Freud's discovery of the analyst-analysand relationship is his most original contribution, since "the analytic relation has no precedent in the history of human relations and supposes a crucial milestone in the evolution of the objective spirit. It is a relation between men that is not reducible to any other."[2] For this reason the analytic encounter cannot be equated with other interpersonal encounters—like that between teacher and pupil or confessor and sinner—to which it bears a superficial resemblance (p. 193). Much less, I would add, can it be equated with the situation of a character in a novel. Besides failing to encompass *Tiempo de silencio,* this reduction does not do justice to Martín-Santos's perceptive, finely nuanced account of the dynamics of analysis.

LTT, whose subtitle is "Toward a phenomenology of the psychoanalytic cure," undertakes a description of the conditions—material and psychological—under which Freudian psychotherapy takes place. Although the book contains some metapsychological speculation, Martín-Santos is less interested in Freud's metapsychology than in the concrete circumstances of the interaction of analyst and analysand. He even makes the rather surprising observation that a cure depends less on the body of psychoanalytical theory than on the dialectics of the analyst-patient confrontation, since "this dialectical process is the true essence of psychoanalysis; the theoretical superstructure is much less important and can be substantially modified without thereby vitiating Freud's most authentic contributions" (p. 232). Thus *LTT* evolves not from Freud's theoretical writings but from his papers on technique, which touch upon many of the points that Martín-Santos develops in his book. For Martín-Santos the technique of the treatment, to which Freud gave relatively little attention, is more fundamental than the theory that explains the patient's symptoms. Technique relates to theory as base to superstructure; so long as the base remains intact, the theoretical superstructure can be modified almost at will without thereby endangering the therapeutic result. In what amounts to an inversion of the customary hierarchy, Martín-Santos makes Freudian metapsychology aleatory, incidental, while bringing to the foreground Freud's reticent observations regarding technique. If the Freud of ego psychology is the "Anglo-American" Freud and that of the castration complex the "French" Freud, *LTT* perhaps limns the portrait of a third Freud, a "Spanish" Freud, whose profile would be found in the *Papers on Technique.*

Martín-Santos's attention to the analytic relationship derives in part from his status as a practicing psychiatrist;[3] it may also owe something to the suspicion with which Freudian theory was regarded in Spain during the Francoist era. But since *LTT* as a whole represents a wary attempt to meld Sartrean anthropology and Freudian psychoanalysis, the subordination of theory to technique responds, conceptually, to Martín-Santos's adherence to existentialist thinking.[4] This attempt leads Martín-Santos to reject the determinism of Freudian theory and to argue instead that, even if instinctual drives and infantile complexes exert a powerful influence on behavior, there still exists a "margin of indetermination" (p. 44) that allows the individual to *elect* (a favorite word) a certain stance toward his or her biological and environmental determinants. The Freudian notion of a *complex* to which the individual passively submits is supplemented by the Sartrean notion of a *project* that he or she freely chooses. Thus, says Martín-Santos, in the case of someone suffering from feelings of inferiority, "the Oedipal constellation was real and unmodifiable, but it was assumed in a certain way. The subject is not inferior; he has *elected* inferiority. Instead of an inferiority complex that the subject suffers, there is an inferiority project that the subject realizes" (p. 51; italics in the original).

Since the patient's freedom manifests itself most palpably during treatment, it is not difficult to see why Martín-Santos elects to concentrate on the circumstances of the cure. The very decision to enter analysis, what Martín-Santos calls *el ponerse en cura*, already attests to a choice that cannot be construed deterministically. The subject's initiative, his willingness and persistence in seeking help, constitute the condition of possibility of the cure. Without this assertion of his freedom, the treatment would not even begin. Martín-Santos's emphasis on technique answers to the crucial importance of this decision taken in the face of the resistance to treatment built into the neurosis. Technique over theory is one plausible psychoanalytical rendering of the Sartrean view that existence precedes essence. Instead of being defined *a priori* by the sway of the instincts or by the insertion into a family structure, the individual retains the capacity for overcoming or dealing with these forces in a personal way. The responsibility for behavior, including that which will result in the restoration of mental health, does not shift away from the subject to his family history.

LTT will then describe phenomenologically what happens when a neurotic subject elects to overcome his illness by undergoing psychotherapy. Most of the book, consequently, addresses the distinctive features both of the analytic relationship and of the setting in which it unfolds. After discussing, in the first chapter, the general aims and preconditions of analysis, Martín-Santos devotes the three subsequent ones to various facets of the cure. Since he traces in chronological order the course of the treatment from its inception (described in the first chapter, "The presence of liberty in the psychoanalytical cure") to its termination (described in the last, "Psychotherapy considered as a dialectical process"), his account reads in some ways like a novel. (In this sense also, the connection between this work and *Tiempo de silencio* is more complicated—and more interesting—than that between precept and example.) In other words, *LTT* contains an implied narrative whose protagonist is the subject of analysis and whose four-part plot is summarized in Martín-Santos's outline of the stages in the treatment:

a neurotic man
by acquiring consciousness of the complex and its effects on the repressive-instinctual plexus
and by acquiring consciousness of the project and of his own responsibility
becomes a new man. (p. 56)[5]

What makes possible the regeneration or renewal of the neurotic is the unique relationship he establishes with the analyst. This relationship, in turn, depends on the peculiar spatial and temporal characteristics of each session. Spatially, the analytic session is defined on the one hand by the subject's seclusion in the analyst's office, and on the other by the disposition of bodies within this enclosed space. Martín-Santos goes along with classical psychoanalytic thought in recommending that the analysand lie or recline with his back to the analyst, for, in his view, by submitting to this position the patient signals that he will acquiesce in the analyst's prying. This asymmetrical disposition establishes from the outset the latter's visual (and hence cognitive) superiority. In exposing himself physically as he will psychically, the patient voluntarily confines himself in a kind of panoptikon, a wall-less chamber that assures his visibility while sheltering the analyst in obscurity. The other metaphor that suggests itself for the analysand's situation is that of an actor on a stage, for in a theater there exists also an imbalance between what the performers and the audience can see; even though an actor normally faces his audience, his vision is impaired by the darkness of the auditorium. Like the analysand, the actor places himself in the predicament of being seen and not seeing, of performing in the dark—but of this more later.

Since the analyst's office encloses an alien, somewhat mysterious space, analysis is unhomely. During each session the analyst "places himself in the uncontrolled space, in the dark space that the individual generally tries to keep empty, or better still, occupied by a solid mass" (p. 195). Even after the patient has been in treatment for a long time, the perceptual asymmetry prevents him from achieving a sense of security or intimacy: "The analyst remains in an irreducible 'behind' that prevents the environment of the cure from becoming part of the patient's intimate surroundings" (p. 196). The opposite of this uncontrollable, unfamiliar environment is, of course, the subject's home, which contains no dark spots, no hidden presences. When he is lying on the couch, the one thing the patient does not feel is at home. But this unhomely sensation is precisely the intended effect of the perceptual asymmetry. Since a neurotic's conduct never slips from the grooves of his illness, the neurotic is a slave to repetition. During analysis, however, he is forced out of his groove, for he discovers that his usual pattern of behavior cannot deal effectively with the new circumstances. His symptoms are foregrounded; his defense mechanisms become empty gestures; even his transferential projections find in the analyst an impassive, essentially unresponsive object. Being unlike his quotidian surroundings, the space of analysis gives the patient a forum, a medium, in which to evolve a new self. In proving unreceptive to the neurotic's regressive homing instincts, this unfamiliar and unfamilial space sets the stage for an eventual cure.

Temporally, the analytical setting is characterized by the imbrication of multiple chronologies. Here again the analysand is wrenched from his usual surroundings, for instead of inhabiting a world organized by the orderly progression of clock time, he is thrust into a confused, equivocal temporal milieu where past and present interpenetrate. No less than four chronologies, four distinct narrative lines, intertwine in the analysand's discourse:

1. the patient's story in the order in which it really happened;
2. the patient's story in the order in which it is recounted during analysis;

3. the story of the changes—disappearance of symptoms, modifications in the ego structure, etc.—that occur in the patient as the treatment advances; and
4. the story of the process of transference and counter-transference.[6]

We can better appreciate these four levels if we translate them into a more familiar vocabulary. Stories 1 and 2 correspond to the Russian formalists' concepts of *fable* and *sujet* ("story" and "plot" in Robert Scholes's rendering).[7] Story 1 comprehends the *fable,* the events in the subject's biography in their actual sequence. As Martín-Santos points out, this narrative, which possesses only a virtual existence, can be pieced together only with a good amount of guesswork and speculation (p. 132). More important to the treatment is Story 2, the *sujet* or plot, which contains the same material as Story 1 but emplotted according to the syntax of the patient's neurosis. Still following the Russian formalists' usage, one could say that Story 2 comprises Story 1 plus the "motivation," the motivation being in this instance the hidden associative connections that the analysis will disclose.[8] Stories 1 and 2 are alike, however, in that both belong to the realm of the *énoncé,* of the events narrated retrospectively by the analysand. Stories 3 and 4, by contrast, belong to the realm of *énonciation,* since they record events that appertain to the narrative situation itself: Story 3 registers the modifications undergone by the "narrator" in the act of narration, while Story 4 registers the evolving relationship between the "narrator" and his "audience," between analysand and analyst.[9]

Although this literary gloss begins to suggest the multilevelled temporality of the analytic encounter—the analysand's discourse is an autobiographical account that focuses, alternately, on the narrator's life history, his present condition, and his interaction with his interlocutor—it does not fully render the imbrication of the different levels. Martín-Santos's point is not only that several chronologies penetrate the analysand's discourse; equally important is the interference and reciprocity among the different stories. For example: since the transference narrative (Story 4) essentially involves the projection into the analytic situation of the patient's biography, Stories 1 and 2, on the one hand, and Story 4, on the other, repeat each other. Story 4 is nothing other than Story 1 encoded and displaced—the family romance *à clef*. However, since the exposure and exegesis of the transference mechanisms allow the patient to gain new insight into his past, Story 4 not only shapes the patient's ordering of his biography (Story 2), but throws light on the virtual raw materials (Story 1) from which this narration has been compounded. A similar thing happens with Story 3, which records the erosion of the patient's symptoms, the gradual obsolescence of his defense mechanisms, the overall modifications in his personality. These are precisely the factors that determine the shape of Story 2; presumably, after analysis the ex-neurotic would no longer reconstruct his past in the same way, since that particular reconstruction was motivated by the neurotic defenses that the treatment dissipated. Because Freudian psychotherapy assumes that the telling changes the teller (and vice versa), *énoncé* and *énonciation* interpenetrate to an extent that perhaps sets the analysand's discourse apart from other first-person accounts. Martín-Santos's own term for this interpenetration is "revivencia copulada" (p. 238), by which he means to evoke the intimate coupling of past and present, the reliving of the past in the present (Story 4) and of the present in the past (Stories 2 and 3), that defines the patient's performance.

Another element that further complicates the narrative situation of analysis is the analyst's own participation in these multiple plots. Like Cervantes in *Don Quijote,* the analyst functions as the "second author" of his patient's discourse. If this discourse, in one respect, oscillates between past and present, in another respect it oscillates between analyst and analysand. The patient's account comprehends, as it were, intersecting pendular movements: one in time from past to present, and another in space from speaker to listener. Since the analyst has to sort out and rearrange the different threads in the account, he is the one, in fact, who separates out the four different stories, which in the process of narration appear "inextricably entangled" [*enmarañadas*] (p. 127). This task will require, as Martín-Santos states, a kind of "stereoscopic vision" (p. 129) that enables the analyst to keep track of the multiple chronologies and their sources in heterogeneous psychic materials (dreams, memories, fantasies, etc.). He must accomplish this structuring even though he is himself implicated in the process that needs elucidation: "In psychoanalysis, the analyst finds himself inside the process he pretends to narrate: modifying and, to some extent, being modified by it" (p. 126). Resorting again to a literary analogy, one might compare the analytic situation to the sort of self-reflexive fiction that weaves the author and his audience into the fabric of the narration.

That all of this takes place within a succession of limited time periods, of brief *plazos,* only heightens the richness, the built-in tension and compactness, of the analysand's account. During each session patient and therapist inhabit a world no longer governed by clock time. For the patient the session opens a "hole" or a "parenthesis" in his daily schedule (p. 140), a hiatus rigidly circumscribed by time limits but within which temporal distinctions dissipate. This special temporality, "confused" (p. 127) and "equivocal" (p. 137), creates an "ambiguous disorder" (p. 142), a "fluid disorder" (p. 144), a "chaos" (p. 134). The patient perceives a clear demarcation between this disorder and the orderly flow of events beyond "the frontiers of the psychoanalyst's office" (p. 114). This contrast, in turn, engenders a therapeutic high, "a certain state of ecstasy," comparable to those induced by drunkenness, religious meditation, or intense work (p. 140). Sensing the possibility of a renewed existence, the patient goes into a sort of trance; like the mystic or the drunk, he loses his sense of time and place and lets his mind wander.[10]

What I have said so far should already suggest the parallel I am driving at. At least as it is construed in *LTT,* analysis bears some striking resemblances to carnival, and more concretely, to the wager scene in *Don Juan Tenorio.* Like carnival, analysis is a framed event whose protagonists perform in a state of intoxication; like carnival, psychoanalysis inflects the linear flow of events; like carnival, the analytic session ushers in an interval of disorder during which quotidian norms no longer hold.

These similarities obtain, more narrowly, between the psychoanalytic session and the wager. Discussing the function of the frame in the psychoanalytic setting, Marion Milner comments that "the frame marks off the different kind of reality that is within it from that which is outside it, but a temporal-spatial frame marks off the special kind of reality of a psychoanalytic session [and] makes possible the creative illusion called transference."[11] The drama of transference is a "creative illusion"; Don Juan's wager is "an illusory game" (1.1.16). Join these two phrases to Martín-Santos's description of psychotherapy as "the game of analysis" (p. 127), and one begins to form some idea of the similarities between the two events. Like the wager, analysis involves the narration of past events, a narration largely focused—in the analysand's discourse no less than in Juan's and Luis's accounts—on seduction and murder. More generally, both analysis and the wager are interpersonal encounters that unfold in a "liminal" zone between "art" and "life," "fiction" and "reality." The analyst's office is no less a stage than Buttarelli's tavern; the neurotic who acts out his infantile dramas is no less a performer than Juan and Luis. As a recessed or secondary play, the wager stands halfway between dramatic illusion and (fictional) reality; even though the rivals' confrontation is "real," their emphatic, self-conscious performances give the whole scene an unmistakable metatheatrical character that makes the wager border on pure illusion ("It seems an illusory game!"). The analysand's discourse, with its mixture of fact and fantasy, recollections and dreams, with its projection onto the analyst of the parental roles, also occupies a border between reality and illusion. In fact, one of the first distinctions that collapses when one enters analysis is that between fact and fiction. From the therapist's perspective, fantasies are just as significant, just as much a part of the therapeutic "game," as actual events.

By juxtaposing Buttarelli's tavern and the analyst's office, I do not intend, however, to reduce one to the other. The analytic relationship, as Martín-Santos observes, is irreducible; the same could be said of Zorrilla's play. Thus I prefer to speak of *conversion* rather than of *reduction:* as instances of the liminal structure, these two settings, these two texts, are mutually convertible. They (and the other works in my corpus) form not a hierarchy but a "heterarchy," that is, a configuration without gradations, without a "high" or a "low."[12] (Even the neurotic "high," as we will soon see, is a form of lowness.) Because they exist on the same level, the elements in a heterarchy cannot be reduced, but only converted, into one another. There is no bedrock level, no lowest common denominator. And even what I have called the "liminal structure," as nothing more than the geometrical instance within the heterarchy, is itself convertible to, on a par with, its own textual variations. Although the geometrical model served me as a convenient point of departure, any of its conversions could have fulfilled the same function: I could have begun alternatively with a meditation on magma, an excursus on exile, or a deliberation on belatedness. And my preliminary introduction could just as well have been a postliminar conclusion.

This multiplicity of entrances, one of the characteristics of the magmatic chain in *Tiempo de silencio,* also typifies the liminal structure. But this means that my investigation of the center-periphery connection—in *LTT* as well as in the other texts under discussion—is itself uncentered, since it lacks a privileged position around which the different elements would arrange themselves. Bearing out in its own way the primacy of technique over theory, my book has no point to prove, no "central" thesis to demonstrate. I wish I could say I had written it without "concentrating." Does the neurotic on the couch concentrate? Or does he wander from incident to incident, from association to association, like Juan Criollo from house to house, or better, like the clown from *cara* to *culo?* Perhaps I will be allowed a neoexpression: to eccentrate, defined as the generative activity of a discourse that goes text-hopping, that makes connections and reaches conclusions and proves or demonstrates exactly nothing. The best criticism is too good to be true. The best criticism, it seems to me, compels by the virtuosity of the performance rather than by the rigor of its truth claims. The phrase "critical fiction" is a paradox, a *point,* when it should be a pleonasm.

I do not want, of course, to push too far the resemblances between the wager and the "analytic game" (p. 127). For the most part these resemblances are obvious and it would be superfluous to insist on them. Let me just supplement what I have already said with a few additional observations. The temporal parallelism between the wager and an analytic session is clear; as we saw in the first chapter, the wager also unfolds in a fluid, dislocated temporal medium starkly at odds with clock time. Less clear, perhaps, is the relevance to the wager of the perceptual asymmetry of analysis, since Juan and Luis, the protagonists of the wager, actually *confront* each other. But Juan and Luis are not the only players in the game. What if the two rivals, who mirror each other with arithmetical precision, are both analysand figures; then the role, or rather the *position* of the analyst would fall to Diego and Gonzalo, the fathers, who sneak into the tavern masked and unnoticed. Seen in this way, the disposition of bodies during the wager reproduces almost exactly the "special disequilibrium" of analysis (p. 197). Like the analyst, Diego and Gonzalo position themselves so that they will see but not be seen. While Juan and Luis occupy center stage, the station of utmost visibility, Diego and Gonzalo opt to remain in the wings, to maintain their distance (Martín-Santos: "The relation of a psychoanalytic cure is, above all, the maintaining of a distance" [p. 197]). As Gonzalo tells Buttarelli,

Quisiera yo ocultamente
verlos, y sin que la gente
me reconociera. (1.1.5)

(I would like to see them covertly, without having people recognize me.)

Note also how this scene concludes: with Diego's unmasking and murder. Symbolic parricides and unmaskings are obviously the stuff of which not only dreams but transference dramas are made.

One can notice, furthermore, that both Buttarelli's tavern and the analyst's office are liminal sites that recursively embed the liminal structure. Secluded in the therapist's office the analysand occupies a marginal location that itself breaks down into a center (the couch) and a periphery (the "dark" area behind the couch). Similarly, the stage of the tavern comprehends both a center (the table where Juan and Luis sit) and a periphery (the table where Diego and Gonzalo sit). The spatial relation of Juan and Diego, on the one hand, and of analysand and analyst on the other, matches or mimes that of the stage and the wings, on the one hand, and that of the analyst's office and the outside world on the other. This same embedding appeared in the marginal hovels, which contained a section in respect to which Muecas's shack became central; and also in "Los payasos," whose structural similarity to the wager I have already discussed. Blending Martín-Santos's vocabulary with my own devilish jargon, one might label this recurring arrangement "the primal scene of the limen," for in every case there is a double dramatization, a recursive rendering in theatrical or scenic rather than in geometrical terms, of the liminal structure. These scenes show eccentricity eccentrating, doubling back and containing itself. Because of Martín-Santos's emphasis on the exceptionality of analysis, *LTT* allows one to see with particular clarity the recursive dimension of this containment.

Again, I do not want to stretch my luck by prolonging these comparisons between a romantic play and a psychoanalytic treatise; but consider now Martín-Santos's description of the end result of psychotherapy, the neurotic's change of project:

> The change in project constitutes an irrational leap, an effective actualization of the freedom inherent in man's "for itself." It is a phenomenon that can be called *conversion*. By means of the conversion the individual changes his fundamental project and, with it, his most essential and persistent truth. We affirm that this change arises from an act of freedom: that is to say, it is not logically comprehensible or compulsively explainable. In conversion there is an irreducible *novum*. In the true conversion a new life begins, a new man emerges. There is no continuous line of sense between the former subject and the convert. A leap has taken place. (pp. 53–54; italics in the original)

Given the widespread use of "conversion" in psychoanalytic literature, it is strange that Martín-Santos would employ this term to designate a phenomenon that transcends psychoanalytic categories. In fact, he uses the word in a sense almost antithetical to the psychoanalytic meaning. In the Freudian sense "conversion" names the transposition of a psychological conflict into a somatic symptom.[13] For Martín-Santos, however, conversion names a process not of somatization but, in effect, of spiritualization, since it designates the moment in the treatment when the individual overcomes his instinctual and biological determinants. As Martín-Santos himself realizes, his usage harks back to the older, religious meaning of the word:

> The terms *conversion* and *new man* have been employed in religious language. For us they are especially apt because they point to existential and psychological facts that are similar to religious ones. Religious conversion can also be considered the realization of a radical *cure*. Although of course the assumptions and intent of psychotherapy and of the apostolate are very different. (p. 54; italics in the original)

The issue is the connection between *la cura* and *el cura*. Is the priest a soul-therapist? Might the therapist be looked upon as an analytic converter? For Martín-Santos, at least, priest and analyst are similar in that both lead their faithful to a conversion. Phenomenologically, psychoanalytic treatment consists of a period of intoxication that climaxes in a conversion-cure.

But is this not also a description of what happens in *Don Juan Tenorio*—carnival followed by conversion? Don Juan's regeneration at the end furnishes a textbook illustration of the phenomenon described in *LTT*, since his conversion does indeed involve a radical break with the past, an irrational leap that generates a new man. Anticipating his final turn-around, Don Juan says about Inés:

Su amor me torna en otro hombre,
regenerando mi ser,
y ella puede hacer un ángel
de quien un demonio fue. (1.4.9)

(Regenerating my being, her love turns me into another man, and she can make an angel out of a demon.)

As the curtain falls, Juan's and Inés's souls leave their mortal bodies and ascend toward heaven. This separation marks not only the moment of death but also the discontinuity between Juan's old and new selves, his carnal and spiritual identities. The shedding of the body symbolizes Juan's reunification with God and Man, Church and Society. Up to that moment his career had been nothing more than a string of falls and falling-outs; with that final ascent his life changes direction and the outcast is accepted back into the Mystical Body as well as into the body politic. As we saw in an earlier chapter, moving down is synonymous with moving out, with decentering. Complementarily, moving up is synonymous with moving in, with recentering. Don Juan's apotheosis thus indicates that he is no longer a displaced person; he has transcended or risen above his marginality.

The secular conversion promoted by analysis also involves a cancelling out of the convert's marginality. The terms Martín-Santos likes to use are *integration* and *religature:* "The total cure of the neurotic, that is, the full maturity of a human being, is only accomplished through his voluntary and consciously ethical integration into universal historical process" (p. 241; see also pp. 244–45); "This commitment to mankind, this wanting to accept what, in a certain sense, is inevitable, is accomplished through a visible and comprehensible *religature* [*religación*] with the totality of the universe" (p. 245; italics in the original). Even though History here takes the place that in Zorrilla belongs to God, the process remains the same. Just as Don Juan exchanges his fallen body for the Mystical Body, the recovered neurotic substitutes collective History for his own subjective, fragmented biography. In both cases there occurs a recentering of the displaced, an assumption of the fallen.

Like religious conversion, psychotherapy is thus a liminal experience, a rite of passage, in van Gennep's processual sense. The neurotic, says Martín-Santos, is a child; analysis provides the means whereby this child matures into an adult (pp. 90, 215). This is a transition, furthermore, that everyone—neurotic or not— must effect: "The difficulty inherent in being human is based in part on the fact that, in order to reach a complete and healthy maturity, a man must, at a given puberal or post-puberal moment, change his originary election. A *conversion* of some sort is inevitable" (p. 76; italics in the original). Psychotherapy's liminal aspect is evident also in that this conversion essentially consists of an overcoming of one's separation anxieties, which Martín-Santos discusses under the rubric of "the primitive terrors" (pp. 242–47). A successful treatment culminates in the patient's losing his cosmic fear, which originates in the individual's separation from his mother, his fear of the other, which originates in the threat of separation from his phallus, and his tragic fear, which originates in the threat of separation from life. Once cured, the patient will be able again to form part of the world of things and of society. As in van Gennep's tripartite scheme (separation-limen-reaggregation), the end result is, once more, integration or religature.

In this book I have elected (to use Martín-Santos's favorite verb) to stop short of that final conversion. The opposite of *religación* is *relajación, relajo*. Etymologically, *ligare* vs. *laxare*. My own analysis has been laxative, not ligative, since I have elected to address and prolong the laxative interim that precedes the reestablishment of cosmic, societal, or somatic regularity. Thus the three parts of this book have attended respectively to cosmic *relajo* (carnival), social *relajo* (*choteo*), and somatic *relajo* (disease, physical and mental). And the protagonists of my book—from Don Juan to the neurotic, and including Juanito Ventolera, the *choteador,* Juan Criollo, Muecas, and the neoexpressionist—are all "foreign" bodies or marginal men. Expressed in Martín-Santos's developmental terms, they are children of all ages, individuals who never matured into full adulthood. For this reason my discussion of *Don Juan Tenorio* has focused, almost entirely, on the first part of the play. The Don Juan that interests me is the adolescent or preadolescent rogue who incarnates the carnival spirit of the letter. He is the figure who will resurface in the other works: recall, for instance, the diminutive suffix in Juanito, Mañach's comments on the immaturity of *choteo,* or Pedro's definition of neoexpressionism as a "putative masturbatory Dachau" (*Tiempo de silencio,* p. 72). *Literature and Liminality* is an exercise in adolescent criticism. I have attended to the pubescent moment, to the pimple phase, in my corpus of works; and though I know that pimples—like roses—fade, and that masturbation finally loses out to copulation, my effort has been to treat this festive, festering phase as if it held a permanent condition, as if acne were forever.

But what has adolescent criticism to do with serious, adult literature? According to Martín-Santos, neurosis relates to mental health as "low" literature relates to serious literature:

After analysis, the break with the objectal pattern—that imprisoned him like a deforming mold—allows the other to exhibit before the neurotic the enormous range of his possibilities. The same real man begins to be seen and grasped without recourse to oversimplifying categories: good, bad, desirable, undesirable. It is a phenomenon comparable to literature. The transition from inferior literature [*subliteratura*] to authentic literature is accompanied also by an abandonment of the categories of good and bad in the creation of characters. A literature that portrays lifelike men no longer discovers good and bad guys, but men in the true sense of the word. (p. 214)

A bit later, in a parallel passage, he discriminates between "authentic" and "egoistic" creation:

Sublimation, that is, authentic creation. To create is to contribute something to the shared work of history. Only through a commitment to totality does sublimation reach all of its creative potential. And in creative sublimation lies the highest spiritual pleasure to which a man can aspire and the source of his serenity.

The potential creator who encloses himself in pure egotistical individualism, without any sort of commitment, is really comparable—as the orthodox Freudian would say—to the child who plays with his own excrement. (p. 246)

An interesting pair of opposed associative chains thus obtains. On one side: authentic literature, mental health, adulthood, sublimation, history. On the other side: low literature, neurosis, infantilism, anality, solipsism. All of these polar terms, I think, convert into the center-periphery dichotomy. The sequence headed by true literature links "central" entities, while that headed by *subliteratura* links "marginal" ones. In this book I have tried to counter Martín-Santos's representatively centrist view by arguing for a "liminalist" perspective on a few "central" texts, including a couple by Martín-Santos himself. Utilizing a kind of sub-reading or lumpen-commentary, I have endeavored to produce a deliberately "low" version of these texts, one that wrenches them from their canonical placement. Even if unflattering, the image of the child playing with his feces is not a bad summary of my emphases. But I could just as well invoke the picture of Don Juan, Juanito, or Juan Criollo playing with their *papelitos,* or of Ortiz playing with his *papeletas,* or of the German playing with his pigments, or of Muecas playing with his daughters and his mice.

This liminalizing effort is implicit in the disposition of my book in two ways. The first emerges from the analysis of *choteo* in part 2. Even though this section, which deals with three Cuban texts, occupies the middle of the book, the center to the periphery of parts 1 and 3, my argument here swerves, geographically as well as contentually, to the margins. At the center of the book lies liminal *choteo,* a tropical tropism that travels from navel to anus, that turns the other cheek. Even at the center of my center, in chapter 5, one finds a novel, *Juan Criollo,* that recounts a seemingly unending series of displacements. (*Literature and Liminality* is an exercise in adolescent Cuban-American criticism.)

The liminalizing effort appears, secondly, in the arrangement of parts. In its swing away from and back to the peninsula, the main land (parts 1 and 3), the book seems to incorporate the archetypal pattern of exile and return, or separation and religature. But the return, as *Tiempo de silencio* made evident, takes us into a metropolis besieged by images of cancerous growth, of malignant margins. And in this chapter, the return trip ends in the analyst's couch, another liminal site. The margins, as someone has said, are everywhere.

Let me simply conclude by noting that the analyst's couch is one last element in *LTT* that circles back to *Don Juan,* to that famous *sofá* where Inés is wooed and where she confesses, "loca estoy" ("I am crazy"; 1.4.1.). In light of this confession one can imagine a contemporary version of this scene with Inés as the neurotic narrator of a novel set in a psychiatrist's office, and perhaps entitled, *Inés's Complaint.* (*Literature and Liminality* is an exercise in adolescent Cuban-American-Jewish criticism.) Such a crazed, eccentric imagining summarizes the "project" of this book. Liminal literary analysis consists in finding the couch inside the sofa.

Conclusion: Of Limits

I should like to conclude by reflecting, briefly, on one more liminal text, a fragment from the introduction to a well-known work of literary theory, Claudio Guillén's *Literature as System:*

It has seemed to me that a cultural whole or a literary system could be visualized, metaphorically speaking, as the verbal and imaginary equivalent of an ancient yet living, persistent yet profoundly changing *city.* The great cities we have all admired, merging stone with flowing water, monuments with gardens, humble streets with spacious plazas, Gothic churches with Baroque palaces, accomplish time and again the integration of a plurality of styles in an existing, growing environment. Who has not paused to feel and recognize this unity—the immediacy of an old building, the manner in which small things are granted a role or mediocre places vindicated, the peculiar atmosphere of the great city? As I remember those I myself have loved best—Seville, Paris, Cologne, Lisbon, and a few more—I venture to think that their "atmosphere" is like a silent sign of the presentness of the past. The freedom and vitality of the great city are such that they succeed in assembling not only a variety of styles and ways of life but a series of historical moments, layers of historical time.

Civitas verbi: artistic wholes and literary systems are, like great cities, complex environments and areas of integration.[1]

Perhaps one word describes best the content and tone of this passage: urbanity. Guillén's elegant metaphor summarizes for me the best and most characteristic moments of a certain kind of critical discourse and of its attendant theory of literature, a discourse and a theory that my reader—like Don Diego with Don Juan—will not have recognized in the preceding chapters. Guillén is interested in evolution and unity, in religature, to use once again Martín-Santos's term. His organicist language emphasizes two attributes of the city: its wholeness and its harmonic growth. He speaks of the city's "merging" of stone and water, of its "assembling" of different styles, of its "integration" of a "growing environment."

As any city-dweller knows, however, cities are not just stone and water. Guillén idealizes the city as he idealizes literature. His city is a succession of monuments—plazas, palaces, cathedrals, fountains. His city of words is, likewise, monumental—a succession of literary sights, of verbal icons. But cities, material and verbal, have another side, an underside. My discussion has drawn attention to the underside of the city, to the hovels of Havana, where Juan Criollo grows up, or to the *chabolas* of Madrid, where a certain gentleman-farmer breeds malignant mice and sleeps with his daughters. I have been more interested in disintegration than in integration, more attentive to monstrous growths than to harmonic development: the city as cancer and the city as slum. I have also been interested, therefore, in the outer and inner fringes, in the backstreets and *barrios* of the *civitas verbi*. Because the works I have discussed are themselves monstrous or slummy, they imply a conception of literature less tidy, less monumental and reverential, less systematic than Guillén's. Perhaps it is as useful to insist on the disruptive elements in literary works as it is to insist on their concinnity. As Morse Peckham has said, "[There is] something seriously wrong with the current and dominant conception of art. I believe that that serious wrongness lies in the ancient effort to find order in a situation that offers the opportunity to experience disorder. After so many centuries of praising order, I think it is time to praise disorder a little."[2]

Guillén's city, besides, is strangely quiet; it has none of the hustle and bustle, none of the moiling uproar of a modern metropolis. My city is nothing if not deafening, with its piercing screams and its "garrulous matter" (*Tiempo de silencio,* p. 44). If Guillén's cityscape is a rosary of "silent signs" (and let us not forget his "stylistics of silence"), mine is a riotous conflagration: not a monument but a spectacle. In an essay entitled "Ecrivains et écrivants," Roland Barthes has written that someone like Balzac—

a consummate cityscapist—turns explanations into spectacles: "il convertit . . . toute explication en spectacle."[3] Like Barthes, I hold to a spectacular conception of both the literary and the critical performance: carnival is a spectacle, the circus is a spectacle, *choteo* is a spectacle, the *chabolas* are a spectacle, even metastasis is a spectacle. My own book, I would like to think, is also a spectacle. I have tried to present explanations, explications, in a spectacular way.

One of the significant features of a spectacle is its hyperbolism: it cannot be taken in, comprehended, all at once. If we return to Guillén's ideal city, we notice that he gives us a bird's-eye view of the urban landscape; it is as if he were surveying the city from a distance, positioned at a point from which the city's multifariousness has coalesced into an "artistic whole" (not coincidentally, one of the longest and most enlightening essays in his collection is dedicated to the metaphor of perspective). The eyewitness to a spectacle has no such holistic, integrative vantage-point, for a spectacle, as Bakhtin mentions, engulfs its spectators, converting every passive bystander into an active participant.[4] The observer of a spectacle is too much a part of what he sees to evolve a sense of the whole. My readings, therefore, have not achieved (or aimed at) that breadth of vision implicit in Guillén's metaphor (and amply evident in Guillén's book). I have been concerned more with parts than with wholes. For me, literary criticism is a partial art: its truths—its fictions—inhere in details, in minutiae, in "entirely local surprises."[5] A criticism that gets stuck on its texts, as mine often does, cannot achieve enough autonomy to generate general principles or encompassing theories. When the spectacle is textual, the convergence of actors and spectators translates into an inmixing, a "liming," of commentary and its objects.

Literary criticism is a partial art; it can also, on occasion, become a martial art. Let me proffer one last illustration. In *Tiempo de silencio,* the bellicose proliferation of diseased cells is labelled a "gigantesco estropicio" (a "gigantic havoc"; p. 197). In *Don Juan Tenorio,* the impact of carnival—and of Don Juan—on Seville (one of Guillén's favorite cities) is described thus:

¡Válgame Dios! ¡Qué bullicio!
¡Cómo se le arremolina

chusma . . . ! ¡Y cómo la acoquina
él solo . . . ! ¡Qué estropicio! (1.1.3)

(God help me! What an uproar! How people swirl about him . . . !
And how he scares them away all by himself! What havoc!)

What's in a word? A depiction of cancer as a carnival site, of
metastasis as a conga line or festival procession? What's in a
word? *Estropicio* descends from the Latin *deturpare,* to disfigure,
which in turn goes back to *turpis,* ugly or deformed. But who is
the breeder of cancerous mice, the avatar of *estropicio,* if not
Muecas, whose very name *is* disfigurement?

Are these connections far-fetched? Are they themselves an
estropicio or disfigurement of the critic's task, of his desire for
intelligibility? Perhaps. In the end, the issue comes back to urbanity: I would like to think that there is room—in our literature,
yes, but especially in our criticism—for a discourse that is *not* ur-
bane. Urbanity implies civility, polish, detachment, understate-
ment, good breeding. I want to make a plea for critical rudeness,
for critical crudeness, for overstatement, for *relajo,* for what I
would call sub-urbanity, were it not for the hygienic connotations
of the word in contemporary society. When this book was in
manuscript, one of its early readers commented that it dealt with
"some of the most repugnant bodily acts."[6] But criticism, I would
maintain, is itself a bodily act, and even a repugnant one, in the
literal sense of the word. I want to make a plea for repugnant
bodily acts: the house of fiction could use an outhouse of criticism
(an in-house outhouse, however—an in-and-out house—for criticism *is* a fictional kind). I want to make a plea, finally, for a discourse of limits that is also, unabashedly, a discourse off-limits.

Notes

Preliminaries

Unless otherwise indicated, all translations from the Spanish are my own.

1   Victor Turner, *The Ritual Process: Structure and Anti-Structure* (Chicago: Aldine, 1969), 95.

2   Arnold van Gennep, *Les Rites de passage* (Paris: Emile Nourry, 1909), 14.

3   Turner, *The Ritual Process,* 99–100. I have also profited from several of Turner's other works, particularly *The Forest of Symbols* (Ithaca: Cornell University Press, 1967) and *Dramas, Fields, and Metaphors* (Ithaca: Cornell University Press, 1974). For an interesting discussion and application of Turner's ideas see Barbara Babcock-Abrahams, " 'A Tolerated Margin of Mess': The Trickster and His Tales Reconsidered," *Journal of the Folklore Institute* 11 (1975): 147–86.

4   Jacques Derrida, "Structure, Sign, and Play in the Discourse of the Human Sciences," in Richard Macksey and Eugenio Donato, eds., *The Structuralist Controversy* (Baltimore: Johns Hopkins University Press, 1972), 247. Derrida's work, of course, is much concerned with margins; his most sustained meditation on the subject is perhaps "Living On: Border Lines," in Geoffrey Hartman, ed., *Deconstruction and Criticism* (New York: The Seabury Press, 1979), 75–176. On the importance of marginality in post-structuralist thought generally, see Jonathan Culler, *On Deconstruction* (Ithaca: Cornell University Press, 1982), 139–40, 215–16.

5   Turner, *The Forest of Symbols,* 103.

6   For those readers as yet unfamiliar with *choteo,* suffice it at this point to quote Jorge Mañach's definition, which will be discussed at length in chap. 4: "*Choteo* is a desire for independence that is externalized in a mockery of every non-imperative form of authority."

7   One example of the "centrist" view of literature will be examined in the last chapter. A useful introductory discussion of the question of

marginality as it applies to Western and non-Western theories of literature may be found in Michel Benamou, "Postface: In Praise of Marginality," in Michel Benamou and Jerome Rothenberg, eds., *Ethnopoetics*
(Boston: Alcheringa, 1976), 133–41.

8 I take this useful phrase from Geoffrey Hartman, *Criticism in the
Wilderness* (New Haven: Yale University Press, 1980). Let this reference to Hartman also serve as another preliminary indication of the
"text-milieu" of my own work.

9 Contemporary critical theory has begun to question the self-evidence
and validity of some of these notions. See, for example, Michel Foucault,
"What Is an Author?" in *Language, Counter-Memory, Practice* (Ithaca:
Cornell University Press, 1977), 113–38.

10 David Hirsch, "Deep Metaphors and Shallow Structures," *Sewanee
Review* 85 (1977): 163.

Chapter 1

1 In "Cuatro palabras sobre mi *Don Juan Tenorio*," Zorrilla admits as
much; commenting on the opening lines, he states: "Let the truth be said
in peace and with God's grace; but when this quartet was written, it was
my statement more than Don Juan's; because I didn't yet know what to
do with him, nor what nor to whom I was writing." In José Zorrilla,
Obras Completas, ed. Narciso Alonso Cortés (Valladolid: Librería Santarén, 1943), 2: 1800. I will be quoting from the text of the play contained in José Luis Varela's edition for Clásicos Castellanos (Madrid:
Espasa-Calpe, 1975). Passages will be identified by part, act, and scene
numbers.

2 Pérez de Ayala, *Obras Completas* (Madrid: Renacimiento, 1924),
11: 256.

3 See, for example, Gerald Wade's edition of *El burlador de Sevilla*
(New York: Charles Scribner's Sons, 1969), 51–53; also Orrin Klapp,
"The Clever Hero," *Journal of American Folklore* 67 (1954): 21–34.

4 Paul Radin, *The Trickster* (New York: Schocken Books, 1972),
18–20. On the detachable phallus in Trickster stories see Karl Kerényi,
"The Trickster in Relation to Greek Mythology," in *The Trickster,*
173–91.

5 Zorrilla, *Obras Completas,* 2: 1802.

6 For a discussion of the death of Don Juan see Guido Mazzeo, *"Don
Juan Tenorio:* Salvation or Damnation," *Romance Notes* 5 (1964):
151–55; and Fred Abrams, "The Death of Zorrilla's *Don Juan* and the
Problem of Catholic Orthodoxy," *Romance Notes* 6 (1964): 42–46.

7 "The first act begins at eight; everything happens: Don Juan and Don
Luis are arrested, and they tell how they have managed to escape prison:
Don Juan and Ciutti prepare the trap for Don Luis, and the second act
concludes with Don Juan saying:

> At nine in the convent,
> at ten on this street.

Going by the clock, and there was one in the entrance of the theater in which the play premiered, it's nine forty-five—and that's not counting what happened between acts. These two-hundred-minute hours are property of the clock of my Don Juan. . . . The unity of time is *marvelously* observed in the four acts of the first part of my *Don Juan*, and it has two very special traits: the first is miraculous: that the action transpires in much less time than it materially and absolutely requires; the second, that neither the characters nor the public ever know what time it is" (Zorrilla, *Obras Completas*, 2: 1802–03).

8 Edmund Leach, *Rethinking Anthropology* (London: The Athone Press, 1961), 124–36; and Roger Caillois, *L'Homme et le sacré* (Paris: Gallimard, 1950), 130–40. See also Le Roy Ladurie, *Carnival in Romans*, trans. Mary Feeney (New York: G. Braziller, 1979), 305–07.

9 It seems evident, moreover, that Zorrilla generally regarded literary performance as a race against time, a deed to be accomplished within a *plazo* of some sort. In the dedication to *El puñal del godo* he avers that this work was undertaken "by a bet in a certain number of hours" (Zorrilla, *Obras Completas*, 2: 1115); of the writing of *Don Juan Tenorio* he says that it was done in a self-imposed deadline of twenty days (*Obras Completas*, 2: 1799); and of the composition of the *zarzuela* based on the play he makes a similar confession (*Obras Completas*, 2: 1721). These references help to confirm the autobiographical quality of the opening scene of *Don Juan*.

10 Mikhail Bakhtin, *Rabelais and His World*, trans. Hélène Iswolski (Cambridge, Mass.: M.I.T. Press, 1965), 7.

11 Carlos Feal, "Conflicting Names, Conflicting Laws: Zorrilla's *Don Juan Tenorio*," *PMLA* 96 (1981): 375.

12 Bakhtin, *Rabelais and His World*, 7. Compare also Julia Kristeva, "Le mot, le dialogue, le roman," in *Semiotiké: Recherches pour une semanalyse* (Paris: Seuil, 1969), 160–61: "Celui qui participe au carnaval est à la fois acteur et spectateur; il perd sa conscience de personne pour passer par le zéro de la activité carnavalesque et se dédoubler en sujet du spectacle et object du jeu. . . . Ainsi la scène du carnaval, où la rampe et la 'salle' n'existent pas, est scene et vie, jeu et rêve, discours et spectacle."

13 This merging of roles is already evident in the letter-writing episode, which presents a schematic portrayal of the dramatic situation with its twin components of actors and spectators. Juan is the actor; Ciutti and Buttarelli observe (and interpret). But Ciutti becomes one of the actors as soon as Juan asks him to deliver the letter. Like the wager, this scene ends when the actor-spectator distinction collapses.

14 The rivalry between the two protagonists will be discussed in the next chapter, where the part-whole confrontation recurs in the conflict be-

tween fathers and sons. Offspring are usually thought of in partial terms, as in the saying, "a chip off the old block." *Don Juan Tenorio* demonstrates that sometimes the chip is larger than the block.

15   There also exists an important connection between monstrosity and metalepsis: monsters are metaleptic freaks, as is indicated by the word's etymological kinship with "omen." An omen is a nesting of the future in the present, and monsters were originally thought to be portents, ominous in the strict sense.

Chapter 2

1   Zorrilla, *Obras Completas,* 2: 1721.

2   René Girard, *Violence and the Sacred* (Baltimore: Johns Hopkins University Press, 1972).

3   Ibid., 119–26.

4   See Ladurie, *Carnival in Romans,* 313–14; and Bakhtin, *Rabelais and His World,* 434.

5   Some of these parallelisms have been mentioned by several commentators of the play. See, most recently, Feal, "Conflicting Names, Conflicting Laws"; Varela, *Don Juan Tenorio,* xliii–xliv; and Robert ter Horst, "Ritual Time Regained in Zorrilla's *Don Juan Tenorio,*" *Romanic Review* 70 (1979): 80–93.

6   This statement occurs in Zorrilla's correspondence with his publisher, Delgado, to whom Zorrilla wanted to sell a "corrección, refundición o repetición" of the *Tenorio;* it is quoted in Narciso Alonso Cortés, *Zorrilla. Su vida y sus obras,* 2nd ed. (Valladolid: Librería Santarén, 1943), 1124.

7   Varela, *Don Juan Tenorio,* 67.

8   I take this term from Wilhelm Stekel, *Compulsion and Doubt,* trans. Emil A. Gutheil (New York: Washington Square Press, 1967), 449. Stekel's ideas can be compared profitably to Harold Bloom's better-known notion of the "anxiety of influence," for which see note 11 below.

9   Zorrilla, *Obras Completas,* 1: 2209.

10   Ibid., 574.

11   See Harold Bloom, *A Map of Misreading* (New York: Oxford University Press, 1975), especially 101–05. The most succinct exposition of Bloom's ideas remains *The Anxiety of Influence* (New York: Oxford University Press, 1973). On metalepsis in *The Anxiety of Influence,* see 139–47.

12   John Dowling has recently mentioned that this scene may well reflect Zorrilla's antagonism toward his biological father; see "Traditional Spain in the Works of José Zorrilla: The Poet and His Father," *Crítica Hispánica* 2 (1980): 97–108.

13 Quoted in Cortés, *Zorrilla*, 1148. Zorrilla is here again referring to his projected revision of the play, which I will discuss shortly.

14 Zorrilla described the new *Don Juan* thus to his publisher, Delgado: "Everybody knows that my Tenorio is the recasting [*refundición*] of the *burlador* of Seville and the guest of stone. Well then, my new Don Juan is The guest of stone, and he retains from my old Don Juan the sayings, which have become famous, and the *décimas* of the fourth act. The buffoon is back, because today's public wants to laugh, and the first part is a very complicated plot, full of rendezvous, knifings, mistakes and movement and abduction of women, etc., all of which almost assures its success" (quoted in Cortés, *Zorrilla*, 1122).

15 Zorrilla, *Obras Completas*, 2: 1801.

16 Metalepsis seemed to haunt Zorrilla even after his death. A miscellany of his correspondence was published in 1934 with the title: *Zorrilla, comentador póstumo de sus biógrafos*, ed. Francisco Rodríguez Marín (Madrid: C. Bermejo, 1934).

17 Quoted in Cortés, *Zorrilla*, 339.

18 Varela, *Don Juan Tenorio*, xliii.

19 The *zarzuela* is discussed in Cortés, *Zorrilla*, 770–80. Other attempts by Zorrilla to rewrite the *Tenorio* in a different genre are *Un tenorio bordalés* (fiction) and *La leyenda de los Tenorio*, both incomplete. Zorrilla referred to the latter as "the introduction and preparation of my new Don Juan" (Cortés, *Zorrilla*, 1154).

20 Zorrilla, *Obras Completas*, 2: 1682.

21 Ibid., 1721.

22 Ibid., 1686.

23 Compare the stage directions of the two works: "out on the stage come the Students, dressed with colored capes, swords and shields, and two of them with harps and guitars and with them Pispireta, with a shawl and a feather cap" (*No hay plazo que no se cumpla ni deuda que no se pague, y Convidado de piedra*, in Ramón de Mesonero Romanos, ed., *Dramáticos posteriores a Lope de Vega* [Madrid: Rivadeneyra, 1859; *Biblioteca de Autores Españoles*, vol. 49, part 2], 412); "the Comendadores, Gentlemen, etc., through the left; the Students, Soldiers, etc., through the right, bringing in front of them and pushing Jacarilla" (Zorrilla, *Obras Completas*, 2: 1683).

24 This same impulse led Zorrilla to title his projected revision *El convidado de piedra* (see the passage cited in note 14).

25 Zorrilla, *Obras Completas*, 2: 1687.

Chapter 3

1 These changes may owe something to *El burlador de Sevilla*, since here Ana de Ulloa writes a letter to her suitor that is intercepted by Don

Juan. I have not found in versions earlier than Zorrilla's a similar importance attached to Don Juan's writings. In Zamora, for instance, even though Juan composes a love letter, this document hardly figures in the play. Zorrilla seems to have been the first to exploit fully the ruse of the letter.

2 Page references are taken from Ramón del Valle-Inclán, *Martes de carnaval* (Madrid: Espasa-Calpe, 1964).

3 The most thorough studies of *Las galas*'s kinship with *Don Juan Tenorio* are: Juan Bautista Avalle-Arce, "La esperpentización de Don Juan Tenorio," *Hispanófila* 7 (1959): 29–40; María Eugenia March, *Forma e idea de los esperpentos de Valle-Inclán* (Chapel Hill, N.C.: Estudios de Hispanófila, 1969), 147–59; and Dru Dougherty, "The Tragicomic Don Juan: Valle-Inclán's *Esperpento de las galas del difunto,*" *Modern Drama* 23 (1980): 44–57.

4 Maluenda's metaphor finds unexpected confirmation in José Lezama Lima, who says in "El coche musical," "Bailar es encontrar la unidad que forman los vivientes y los muertos" ("To dance is to find the unity formed by the living and the dead").

5 Rodolfo Cardona and Anthony Zahareas, *Visión del esperpento* (Madrid: Castalia, 1970), 189–90.

6 Joaquín Casalduero, "Sentido y forma de *Martes de carnaval,*" in Anthony N. Zahareas, ed., *Ramón del Valle-Inclán: An Appraisal of His Life and Works* (New York: Las Américas Publishing Co., 1968), 687. See also John Lyon, *The Theatre of Valle-Inclán* (Cambridge: Cambridge University Press, 1983), 134–36.

7 Antonio de Zamora, *No hay plazo que no se cumpla ni deuda que no se pague,* in Ramón de Mesonero Romanos, ed., *Dramáticos posteriores a Lope de Vega,* 412.

8 Thus *Las galas* contains not "la pharmacie de Platon" but rather "la botica de Sócrates." If one wanted to pursue the Derridean connection one more step, one could read Sócrates Galindo's rejection of his daughter's epistle as a latter-day manifestation of the Socratic contempt for "poisonous" writing, for which see Jacques Derrida, *La Dissémination* (Paris: Editions du Seuil, 1972).

9 Valle-Inclán, *Luces de bohemia* (Madrid: Espasa-Calpe, 1974), 106.

10 Another important feature of the mirror is that it is self-effacing, and thus unsuited to convey the self-conscious dimension of *Las galas*.

11 It is also a transfiguration in the generic sense, since when *Las galas* was first published in "La Novela Mundial" under the title *El terno del difunto,* it carried the subtitle "novela."

12 Valle-Inclán, *Luces de bohemia,* 106.

13 Cordona and Zahareas, *Visión del esperpento,* 37.

14 Avalle-Arce, "La esperpentización de Don Juan Tenorio," 34.

15 On the relation between banquet imagery and carnival, see Bakhtin,

Rabelais and His World, 278–302. The collective title of the *esperpentos, Martes de carnaval,* points to the determining function of carnival in these works; and if *Las galas del difunto* is the first work in the collection, it is perhaps because, since the model is *Don Juan,* this particular *esperpento* most palpably evidences the carnival connection.

16 Valle-Inclán, *Luces de bohemia,* 133.

Chapter 4

1 Page references in my text are taken from the second edition of *Indagación del choteo* (1940; reprint, Miami, Fla.: Mnemosyne Publishing Co., 1969). The essay was originally published in 1928.

2 Two recent examples: Reynaldo L. Jiménez, *Guillermo Cabrera Infante y "Tres tristes tigres"* (Miami, Fla.: Ediciones Universal, 1977), especially chaps. 4 and 5; and William Luis, "Myth and Reality in César Leante's *Muerte de caballería,"* *Latin American Literary Review* 8 (1980): 256–65. Mañach's is not, to be sure, the only study of *choteo,* but it is the best and the best known. Other discussions may be found in: Mario Guiral Moreno, "Aspectos censurables del carácter cubano," *Cuba Contemporánea* 4 (1914): 121–33; Calixto Masó, *El carácter cubano* (Havana: n.p., 1941; written in 1922); Fernando Ortiz, *Entre cubanos* (Paris: P. Ollendorf, 1914); and José Antonio Ramos, *Manual del perfecto fulanista* (Havana: Biblioteca "Studium," 1916). Some of the ideas in these works are incorporated in *Indagación del choteo.* Mañach himself anticipated the gist of the essay in his pamphlet, *La crisis de la alta cultura en Cuba* (Havana: Imprenta y Papelería "La Universal," 1925).

3 In *La crisis de la alta cultura en Cuba,* Mañach regards *choteo* as invariably pernicious. Referring to the early days of the Cuban republic, he says: " 'Choteo' was, in effect, one of the pernicious elements that entered Cuban life at that time" (p. 18).

4 Compare Mario Guiral Moreno, "Aspectos censurables del carácter cubano," p. 125: "This propensity to make fun [*chotearse*] of everything has relaxed the bonds of mutual respect among citizens and erased the lines of separation that exist in every country between social classes. As a general rule, in Cuba there is no distinction between the boss and the servant."

5 Guillermo Alvarez Guedes, *Malas palabras, buenas palabras y otras palabras* (Caracas: n.p., 1980), 111–12.

6 I say this because I am aware of the circularity that results from this or any choice of illustrations: I need concrete instances from which to elicit a definition; but my choice of this and not other examples presupposes a prior, tacit definition. The same objection can be levelled at Mañach's own examples. The only way of achieving an "inductive" definition, thus, is by analyzing examples that a "competent" (in the linguistic

sense) audience would class as instances of *choteo*. I believe that my examples meet this criterion; that is, they would be recognized as instances of *choteo* by those so lucky as to have "*choteo*-competence."

7   Cf. Mañach: "All mockery supposes an authority, or at least, a competition" (p. 26).

8   One such "functionalist" argument is developed by Max Gluckman in *Custom and Conflict in Tribal Africa* (New York: Free Press, 1965).

9   Fernando Ortiz, *Glosario de afronegrismos* (Havana: Imprenta "El Siglo XX," 1924), 185–86. Ortiz defines *choteo* as "burla de palabra."

10   On the "spectacular" nature of carnival, see Laurent Jenny, "Le discours du carnaval," *Littérature* 16 (1974): 19–36.

11   Severo Sarduy, "Tu dulce nombre halagará mi oído," in Gladys Zaldívar and Rosa Martínez de Cabrera, eds., *Homenaje a Gertrudis Gómez de Avellaneda* (Miami, Fla.: Ediciones Universal, 1979), 20. On the importance of orality in Cuban culture, see also Octavio Armand, *Superficies* (Caracas: Monte Avila, 1980), 132–33.

12   See Norman O. Brown's classic study of the subject, *Life Against Death* (Middletown, Conn.: Wesleyan University Press, 1959).

13   Bakhtin, *Rabelais and His World*, 370.

14   Mary Douglas, *Purity and Danger: An Analysis of the Concepts of Pollution and Taboo* (London: Routledge and Kegan Paul, 1966), 40 and 35 respectively.

15   Ibid., 97.

16   Alvarez Guedes, *Malas palabras, buenas palabras y otras palabras,* 113.

17   See, for example, Octavio Paz's discussion of this topos in *Conjunciones y disyunciones* (Mexico City: Joaquín Mortiz, 1969), 12–17.

18   As in the doggerel verse:

Voy a un lugar sagrado
donde acude mucha gente;
hace fuerza el más cobarde
y se caga el más valiente.

19   The signal exception to the law of the liminality of latrines is the so-called "guest bathroom," which, to insure accessibility, is usually located in the center of a house. But a guest bathroom, like a mobile home, is almost a contradiction in terms: one should not go to the bathroom anywhere but at home; and home is what does not move.

20   On wit as sublimation, see Brown, *Life Against Death*, 188. For Mañach's non-Freudian distinction between wit and *choteo*, see *Indagación*, 42–49. Interestingly, one of the early reviewers of *Indagación del choteo* reproached Mañach for not taking account of Freud's insights into humor (Raoul Maestri Arredondo, "Balance literario 1928," *Revista de Avance,* 15 December 1928, 345).

21 Guillermo Alvarez Guedes, "Cada vez que pienso en ti," transcribed from the record, *Alvarez Guedes 6,* GEMA, 5055, 1977.

22 Geoffrey Hartman, *Criticism in the Wilderness* (New Haven: Yale University Press, 1980), 143.

23 Quoted in Varela, *Don Juan Tenorio,* xli.

Chapter 5

1 Although the first edition of the novel bears the year 1927 on the title page, most critics give 1928 as the date of publication. In any event, upon publication the novel was regarded as "the novelistic hit of 1928" by Raoul Maestri Arredondo ("Balance literario 1928," *Revista de Avance,* 15 December 1928, 346). Page numbers in my text will refer to Carlos Loveira, *Juan Criollo,* ed. Carlos Ripoll (New York: Las Américas, 1964).

2 Loveira profiles his protagonist thus: "sensual, noblote, imprevisor, escéptico instintivo, dignidad siempre en guardia, rica mina cerebral gastada en salvas, incoherencia de ideas, de acción y de propósitos, y alguna vez en la vida, jugador, burócrata y político" (434).

3 For Mañach's remarks on the relationship between *choteo* and *parejería,* see *Indagación,* 56–57.

4 Zorrilla, *Obras Completas,* 2: 1687.

5 A term used by Marcelo Pogolotti, *La República de Cuba al través de sus escritores* (La Habana: Lex, 1958), 26–28.

6 There is, however, at least one interesting echo of *Las galas del difunto* in Loveira's novel: when Juan goes to visit Nena dressed in his best, if ill-fitting, clothes, a passer-by remarks: "Hey! I think the dead man was bigger than you" (p. 241).

7 See Sigmund Freud, "On the Transformation of the Instincts with Special Reference to Anal Erotism," in *Collected Papers* (London: Hogarth Press, 1933), 2: 162–71.

8 In the dedication Mañach labels his text a "meditation." Ortega y Gasset's influence on the writers who collaborated in the *Revista de Avance,* Mañach among them, has been discussed by Roberto González Echevarría, *Alejo Carpentier: The Pilgrim at Home* (Ithaca: Cornell University Press, 1977), 52–54.

9 The second act of part 2 begins:

Tal es mi historia, señores:
pagado de mi valor,
quiso el mismo emperador
dispensarme sus favores.
Y aunque oyó mi historia entera,
dijo: "Hombre de tanto brío
merece el amparo mío;
vuelva a España cuando quiera."

(Such is my story, gentlemen: served by my courage, the emperor himself wanted to favor me. And although he heard my entire story, he said: "A man with so much vigor deserves my protection; let him return to Spain whenever he wants.")

10   The last words in the novel, which are spoken by Juan, are: "¡Que vengan regeneraciones! Ahí nos las den todas." They echo Tirso's "¡Que largo me lo fiáis!" and Zorrilla's "Largo el plazo me ponéis" (1.1.12), except that the creole Don Juan never comes to regret his foolhardiness.

11   Norman Friedman, "Point of View in Fiction: The Development of a Critical Concept," *PMLA* 70 (1955): 1177.

12   *Lazarillo de Tormes,* Everett W. Hesse and Harry F. Williams, eds. (Madison: University of Wisconsin Press, 1969), 57.

13   Juan Marinello, *"Juan Criollo.* Novela," *Revista de Avance,* 15 May 1928, 130; Manuel Pedro González, "La literatura de hoy: Carlos Loveira," *Revista de Estudios Hispánicos* 2 (1929): 188–89; J. Riis Owre, *"Juan Criollo* After Forty Years," *Journal of Inter-American Studies* 9 (1967): 396–412.

14   For a summary of this debate see Francisco Rico's introduction to *La novela picaresca española* (Barcelona: Planeta, 1967), vol. 1: xliv–xlix.

15   An up-to-date discussion of this split may be found in George A. Shipley, "The Critic as Witness for the Prosecution: Making the Case Against Lázaro de Tormes," *PMLA* 97 (1982): 179–94. For a more extended discussion of narrative perspective in the picaresque, see Francisco Rico, *La novela picaresca y el punto de vista* (Barcelona: Seix Barral, 1969).

16   Juan's role as narrator is anticipated by the many references to his writing talent. Moreover, the journal that he keeps while in a Mexican prison may well be considered a preliminary sketch for some parts of the novel. This aptitude, by the way, is another link between Loveira's protagonist and Don Juan, who is also a "great writer" (1.1.1).

17   Because it both names and explains its bearer, "Juan Criollo" is what Geoffrey Hartman has called a "specular name," one that—unlike the arbitrary "given" name—defines or confines one's identity. Not incidentally, *criollo* etymologically goes back to *crear.* On the specular name, see Hartman, *Saving the Text* (Baltimore: The Johns Hopkins University Press, 1981), 100 ff.

18   Zorrilla, *Obras Completas,* 2: 1806. The quotation that follows occurs on the same page.

19   Compare also the following passage from *Indagación:* "A lot of newcomers arrive in Cuba wanting to regain lost prestige, or simply wanting to fulfill their professional illusions. They arrive like conquerors, puffed-up with foreign self-sufficiency. A *trompetilla* soon deflates them" (p. 66).

20   For a provocative discussion of this dilemma, see Roberto González Echevarría, "José Arrom, autor de la *Relación acerca de la antigüedades*

de los indios (picaresca e historia)," in *Relecturas* (Caracas: Monte
Avila Editores, 1976), 17–35.
21   Juan Marinello, "Americanismo y cubanismo literarios" (1932), in
Ensayos (Havana: Editorial Arte y Literatura, 1977), 48–49.

Chapter 6

1   This work was originally published in several parts in the *Revista
Bimestre Cubana* during 1921 and 1922. A revised edition appeared post-
humously under the title *Nuevo catauro de cubanismos* (Havana: Editorial de Ciencias Sociales, 1975). I will be quoting from the first edition
(Havana: n.p., 1923). For reasons which will become apparent later on,
page numbers are needed in order to locate the entries in the *Catauro*. I
will also be discussing, though less extensively, Ortiz's *Glosario de
afronegrismos* (Havana: Imprenta 'El Siglo XX,' 1924).
2   Constantino Suárez, *Vocabulario de voces cubanas* (Havana: Librería
Cervantes, 1921).
3   For a general overview of Ortiz's life and works, see Salvador Bueno's
two essays: "Don Fernando Ortiz: al servicio de la Ciencia y de Cuba,"
in *Temas y personajes de la literatura cubana* (Havana: Ediciones Unión,
1964), 209–18; and "Aproximaciones a la vida y obra de Fernando Ortiz," *Casa de las Américas* 113 (March–April 1979): 119–28.
4   Roberto González Echevarría, *Alejo Carpentier: The Pilgrim at
Home*, 29. González Echevarría adds: "Marinello subverts the notion
that the Latin American identity can be found on an ideal level, where
the stock answers will supply satisfactory solutions, and makes the language in which they are cast part of the problem itself."
5   In a lucid discussion of New World Utopianism, Peter G. Earle
rightly labels Vasconcelos's essay an "aesthetic fantasy." Peter G. Earle,
"Utopía, Universópolis, Macondo," *Hispanic Review* 50 (1982): 148.
6   Toro's article appeared in several installments: vol. 7 (1920): 290–
317, 443–71, 603–27; vol. 8 (1921): 409–41, 481–514.
7   Miguel de Toro y Gisbert, "Reivindicación de americanismos," *Boletín de la Real Academia* 7 (1920): 459.
8   Ibid., 290. The quotations that follow are taken from the same page.
9   Ibid., 298.
10   The "American" reading of *The Tempest* to which I allude here has
been developed by Roberto Fernández Retamar in *Calibán: Apuntes sobre
la cultura en nuestra América* (Mexico City: Editorial Diógenes, 1972).
11   Ortiz's Africanist view of *choteo* apparently has not found favor
with professional philologists. It is not mentioned by J. Corominas in his
Diccionario crítico etimológico de la lengua castellana (Madrid: Gredos,
1954).
12   I should underscore that my discussion makes no claims about what
Ortiz "intended" to accomplish in the *Catauro*. Though I do not doubt

that some of the notions I impute to his text were also harbored by its author, my argument addresses only what exists in the text. If I sometimes say "Ortiz" where, strictly speaking, I should say *"Catauro,"* it is only because of stylistic convenience.

13 Corominas, who thinks that the word derives from *vejiga,* does not accept the African etymology. He states in the *Diccionario crítico etimológico:* "Don Fernando Ortiz writes me that he is not convinced by my etymology and continues to believe in the one he has proposed. I record here, with due deference, the opinion of the master of Afro-Cuban research, while I wait for the proofs that he promises, but I must say now that the origins of the documentation indicate a Spanish etymology, rather than an African or Caribbean one, and that the fact that blacks took over the word later is not evidence of its black origin; as regards the *bantú* etymology suggested by Ortiz in his glossary, it is too far-fetched to appear probable."

14 R. W. B. Lewis, *The American Adam* (Chicago: University of Chicago Press, 1955), 7. There exist enlightening parallelisms between the cultural situation in the United States at the beginning of the nineteenth century and that in Cuba a hundred years later. Leafing through the pages of reviews like *Cuba Contemporánea* or *Revista Bimestre Cubana* is sufficient to ascertain the resemblances between the "dialogue" (Lewis's term) that took place in Cuba during the early years of the Republic and that which unfolded in this country a century before. The biggest obvious difference, however, is that in the "Cuban myth" the Adamic figure has been replaced by its antitype, the *pícaro* (as in *Juan Criollo*).

15 In the second, posthumous (and, as we shall see, post-humus) edition, the entries have been put in alphabetical order.

16 It is worth remarking that Ortiz has proposed the *ajiaco* as the culinary emblem of Cuban society. In "Los factores humanos de la cubanidad," in *Orbita de Fernando Ortiz,* ed. Julio Le Riverend (Havana: U.N.E.A.C., 1973), 149–57.

17 Robert M. Adams, *Bad Mouth* (Berkeley and Los Angeles: University of California Press, 1977), 122 ff.

18 I could make something, but I won't, of Ortiz's statement that his box contains overripe and even rotten fruit (p. 255).

Chapter 7

1 Luis Martín-Santos, *Tiempo de silencio,* 8th ed. (Barcelona: Seix Barral, 1971). Page numbers refer to this edition.

2 The connection between Muecas and Ortega y Gasset is treated below and in note 14. See also Gonzalo Sobejano's remarks on the "pensión-chabola clash" in *Novela española de nuestro tiempo* (Madrid: Editorial Prensa Española, 1970), 360.

3 There is at least one direct reference to the Don Juan legend in

Tiempo de silencio; after Dorita's murder Pedro realizes "that the vengeance had been carried out, that there is no deadline that does not expire, and no debt that is not paid" [*no hay plazo que no se cumpla ni deuda que no se pague*] (p. 232). For some remarks on this passage see Carlos Feal Deibe, "En torno al casticismo de Pedro: El principio y el fin de *Tiempo de silencio,*" *Revista Iberoamericana* 116–17 (July–December 1981): 207–08.

4 My discussion can thus be considered an oblique gloss of the following statement from Susan Sontag's *Illness as Metaphor* (New York: Farrar, Straus and Giroux, 1977): "Nobody conceives of cancer the way TB was thought of—as a decorative, often lyrical death. Cancer is a rare and still scandalous subject for poetry; and it seems unimaginable to aestheticize the disease." In the identification of cancer and writing one can perceive the beginning of such aesthetization, an incipient onco-poetics. One is tempted to affirm that Martín-Santos's style, with its intricate, proliferating periods, constitutes a scriptural analogue of cancer. A passage like the one just quoted *in extenso,* with its elaborate process of qualification, of conceptual and syntactical division and subdivision, might be regarded as a sort of textual mitosis. Or, moving in the opposite direction, one might say that a tumor is a biological "amplification," a cellular hypotaxis. On disease in literature, see also Gian-Paolo Biasin, "From Anatomy to Criticism," *MLN* 86 (1971): 873–90; and Enid Rhodes Peschel, ed., *Medicine and Literature* (New York: Neal Watson Academic Publications, 1980).

5 The cloacal complex can be defined as "A sexual theory of children which ignores the distinction between vagina and anus. The woman is pictured as having only one orifice, which is confused with the anus. This orifice is thought to serve for both parturition and coition." From J. Laplanche and J.-B. Pontalis, *The Language of Psychoanalysis,* Donald Nicholson-Smith, trans. (London: Hogarth Press, 1973), 69. For Freud's discussion of the concept, see "On the Sexual Theories of Children," in Sigmund Freud, *Collected Papers* 2: 68–69.

6 The issue of semen through an *ur*-ifice would of course be called an *ur*-gasm.

7 "There he is, flattened out, stunted, imitating the grill where it is said that St. Lawrence was vivisected, Lawrence who died for our sins, the one you've heard about, the one I've become, that one, Lawrence who said turn me over because I'm already done on this side," etc. (*Tiempo de silencio,* p. 240).

8 Benjamín Jarnés, *Viviana y Merlín* (Madrid: Espasa-Calpe, 1936), 15, 16, and 19 respectively.

9 One might also connect the image of Madrid-as-body with the superposition of bodies in the vertical burials. In Florita's grave three bodies lie on top of her; in the city, three (layers of) bodies rise above the *chabolas.*

10   Gemma Roberts, *Temas existenciales en la novela española de postguerra* (Madrid: Gredos, 1973), 191.

11   *Collected Poems of Jonathan Swift,* ed. Joseph Horrell (London: Routledge and Kegan Paul, 1958), 1: 247. This is Swift's advice to his interlocutor, Strephon, who is somewhat put off by the discovery that his lady, Caelia, "sh——." The fragment from Quevedo is quoted by Octavio Paz in *Conjunciones y disyunciones,* 34.

12   Muecas is clearly something of a philosopher. On hearing his theories about the breeding of mice, one of his daughters remarks: " 'Where are you going to stop, father?' Once he starts into his explanations there's no stopping him. That's why my father should have been a preacher or a dentist. And still people say he's stupid. He might do stupid things but he's smart" (p. 52).

13   See, respectively: Carlos Feal Deibe, "Consideraciones psicoanalíticas sobre *Tiempo de silencio,*" *Revista Hispánica Moderna* 36 (1970–71): 117–27; Julian Palley, "The Periplus of Don Pedro," *Bulletin of Hispanic Studies* 48 (1971): 239–54; Gemma Roberts, *Temas existenciales,* 129–203.

14   Bakhtin, *Rabelais and His World,* 26.

15   It persists also, as we will see in the next chapter, in the Dorita-Florita coupling.

16   Sontag, *Illness as Metaphor,* 64–65 and throughout.

17   I take my information from a newspaper story that appeared under the heading "Undeveloped Twin in Man's Skull?" in *The Miami News,* 12 December 1980, 1:

> Until recent surgery, Nick Hill carried inside his skull what doctors think was part of an undeveloped sibling.
> The 21-year-old Bonners Ferry resident survived complicated brain surgery this year in Spokane, Wash. The case has drawn the attention of the "That's Incredible" television show.
> A surgical team removed two fist-size masses from Hill's brain last January and March. One mass was a tumor.
> But the other—consisting of bone, skin, and hair—may have been a twin that never developed, doctors said.
> Before the operations, Hill said he suffered constant headaches. They have stopped.

It might be relevant to mention that there is a type of tumor, called a teratoma, that regularly has hair, teeth, sometimes partially developed limbs, even eyes. These tumors usually appear in connection with ovarian cancers.

18   It is surely a coincidence that the delivery occurred when Nick was twenty-one, that is, when he was on the threshold of adulthood, perhaps old enough to "bear" children. It is also coincidental that he even suf-

fered "labor pains" (the headaches) which stopped when the masses were excised. But of such coincidences interpretations are wrought.

Chapter 8

1   The novel contains one other picture that, like the mice's cages, hangs from a wall—Ramón y Cajal's likeness, which Pedro keeps in his laboratory: "the painting of the man with the beard, in front of me, the man who saw everything and who freed the Iberian people of their native inferiority toward science" (p. 7). What sort of criticism is this that likens Ramón y Cajal to a cancerous mouse?

2   One example: Alfonso Rey, *Construcción y sentido de "Tiempo de silencio"* (Madrid: Porrúa, 1977).

3   Janet Winecoff Díaz, "Luis Martín-Santos and the Contemporary Spanish Novel," *Hispania* 51 (1968): 234–35. For a different interpretation of the opening of the novel, see Feal Deibe, "En torno al casticismo de Pedro."

4   The sound parallelism between *Don Juan Tenorio* and *Tiempo de silencio* goes a step further, since the play, like the novel, also begins with an episode of acoustic aggression:

¡Cuál gritan esos malditos!
Pero, ¡mal rayo me parta
si en concluyendo la carta
no pagan caros sus gritos! (1.1.1)

(Damn them, how they scream! But may lightning strike me if, as soon as I finish the letter, they don't pay dearly for their screams!)

5   The eunuchs' screaming is anticipated early in the novel by the howling of the laboratory dogs, which have also been mutilated and immobilized.

Chapter 9

1   This approach has been taken by José Schraibman, "Notas sobre la novela española contemporánea," *Revista Hispánica Moderna* 35 (1969): 113–21; and Schraibman, "*Tiempo de silencio* y la cura psiquiátrica de un pueblo: España," *Insula* 365 (April 1977): 3; Robert Spires, "Otro, tú, yo: La creación y la destrucción del ser auténtico en *Tiempo de silencio*," *Kentucky Romance Quarterly* 22 (1975): 91–110; and Walter Holzinger, "*Tiempo de silencio*: An Analysis," *Revista Hispánica Moderna* 37 (1972–73): 73–90.

2   Luis Martín-Santos, *LTT* (Barcelona: Seix Barral, 1975), 193. Other page references are given in the text. This work was first published in 1964.

3   From 1951 until his death in 1964 Martín-Santos was on the staff of the psychiatric hospital in San Sebastián.

4 In the preface to *LTT* Martín-Santos acknowledges his debt to Sartre, a debt abundantly borne out in the Introduction that follows, which consists of a close paraphrase of the section on existential psychoanalysis in *L'Etre et le Néant*. Sartre's influence on *Tiempo de silencio* has been studied by Gemma Roberts in *Temas existenciales en la novela española de postguerra*, 164–74.

5 It will have become obvious by now that for Martín-Santos psychoanalysis is a therapy for males by males. In his choice of examples, he almost invariably uses male patients.

6 I am here paraphrasing the outline which appears on p. 127. Martín-Santos's word for "story" is *historia*, which might also, of course, be rendered "history."

7 Robert Scholes, *Structuralism in Literature* (New Haven: Yale University Press, 1974), 80.

8 On "motivation," see Boris Tomachevski, "Thématique," in *Theorie de la littérature*, ed. Tzvetan Todorov (Paris: Seuil, 1965), 263–307.

9 On *énoncé* and *énonciation*, see Emile Benveniste, "L'Appareil formel de l'énonciation," *Langages* 5, no. 17 (March 1970): 12–18.

10 Even though Martín-Santos repeatedly disclaims the "thaumaturgic power" (p. 150) of the analyst, his remarks on the ecstasy of analysis show that psychotherapy retains something of the old cures by hypnosis or suggestion.

11 Marion Milner, "The Role of Illusion in Symbol Formation," in Melanie Klein, ed., *New Directions in Psychoanalysis* (London: Tavistock Publications, 1955), 86.

12 I take the term "heterarchy," which is used in information theory, from Douglas R. Hofstadter, *Gödel, Escher, Bach: An Eternal Golden Braid* (New York: Vintage Books, 1980), 134.

13 I am following the definition given in Laplanche and Pontalis, *The Language of Psychoanalysis*, 90.

Conclusion

1 Claudio Guillén, *Literature as System* (Princeton: Princeton University Press, 1971), 12–13.

2 Morse Peckham, *Man's Rage for Chaos* (New York: Schocken Books, 1967), 40.

3 Roland Barthes, *Essais critiques* (Paris: Editions du Seuil, 1964), 149.

4 Bakhtin, *Rabelais and His World*, 7–8.

5 I am quoting Jeffrey Mehlman, *Revolution and Repetition* (Berkeley: University of California Press, 1977), 69. "We would suggest that a reading of a text be valued above all in terms of its capacity to 'read' other texts, to liberate energies otherwise *contained* elsewhere. Moreover, to the extent that a reading would be radical, the quality of that energy

should be determinable as a multiplicity of entirely *local* surprises. For there is a micropolitics of interpretation calculable in terms of effects that more teleologically oriented efforts—the very category 'Marxist-theory-of-literature' is exemplary here—invariably miss." Mehlman's position might be summarized with the dictum that emerged from the discussion of *LTT:* technique over theory.

6   Is there some connection between this repugnance to the body and David Hirsch's "repugnance" to criticism as a primary activity (in the passage quoted in the "Preliminaries")? Perhaps so, since Hirsch's repugnance is essentially an aversion to criticism's materiality, to its corporealness. What Hirsch can't stomach is that the critic should not efface himself, that he should be/have some-body.

Index of Names